a handbook
for
headteachers

a handbook
for
headteachers

Marilyn Nathan

**KOGAN
PAGE**

First published in 1996 as *The Headteacher's Survival Guide*
This edition 2000

Apart from any fair dealing for the purposes of research or private study, or criticism or review, as permitted under the Copyright, Designs and Patents Act 1988, this publication may only be reproduced, stored or transmitted, in any form or by any means, with the prior permission in writing of the publishers, or in the case of reprographic reproduction in accordance with the terms of licences issued by the Copyright Licensing Agency. Enquiries concerning reproduction outside those terms should be sent to the publishers at the undermentioned address:

Kogan Page Limited
120 Pentonville Road
London N1 9JN
UK

Stylus Publishing Inc.
22883 Quicksilver Drive
Sterling
VA 20166–2012
USA

© Marilyn Nathan, 1996, 2000

The right of Marilyn Nathan to be identified as the author of this work has been asserted by her in accordance with the Copyright, Designs and Patents Act 1988.

British Library Cataloguing in Publication Data

A CIP record for this book is available from the British Library.

ISBN 0 7494 3179 2

Typeset by Saxon Graphics Ltd, Derby
Printed and bound in Great Britain by Clays Ltd, St Ives plc

CONTENTS

INTRODUCTION

I am delighted to have the opportunity to produce a new edition of *A Handbook for Headteachers* (formerly *The Headteacher's Survival Guide*). A person who handles the first stages of headship well can usually look forward to ongoing success. The demands on headteachers have grown rather than lessened since the first edition appeared in 1996, and although new headteachers have an entitlement to mentoring and training under the Headlamps system, making your mark as an effective new headteacher requires a lot of thought and hard work. This book is all about how you manage your first headship. It is a practical and, I hope, easily readable handbook. Although it is aimed particularly at new headteachers and deals with the kinds of problems and situations you might have to face when you take up your first appointment, it could also be useful for more experienced headteachers, who want to reflect on their practice. It remains true that the most successful schools are learning organizations. The third group for whom this book is intended is aspiring heads. Whilst not telling you how to fill in your application form or what interview questions you will be asked, reading this book could help you formulate answers, particularly to the 'What would you do about?' questions, and clarify your approach to management issues.

A Handbook for Headteachers focuses on people rather than on systems and organizations, hence there are chapters on the senior management team, delegation, motivation, managing staff performance and working with governors and support staff. A case study approach is taken to provide practical and realistic problems and issues on which you can work. Some of the problems are fully worked out, so that you can see how they are handled and compare your practice with the ideas offered in this handbook. I have tried to include as many exemplars as I could find, because feedback from the first edition suggested that new headteachers find these really helpful, and there are some checklists, because these are particularly useful when you are new to the job. Some scenarios are included for you to work on as part of your NPQH or LPSH preparation.

1

A lot of the scenarios reproduced in this handbook are tried and tested through regular use to focus group discussion in training seminars for senior managers and in a few cases have been adapted or extended in response to course members' comments or experiences.

Whilst I have concentrated on the day-to-day concerns of headship, I have also tried to include an outline of relevant theory to help provide the theoretical understanding you need to support good practice. For example, in dealing with getting the best out of your staff, I include a synopsis of motivation theories, to help you understand what may cause someone to work well or to become demotivated. It can also be very useful to be able to classify behaviour or work out a problem using a problem-solving model or a management grid. It helps you to tackle a problem more objectively than perhaps you would otherwise.

1

PREPARING FOR HEADSHIP

You have been told that 'high-quality leadership is vital to success', so how do you make sure that you can deliver this essential commodity, and just how do you set about preparing yourself for headship? This chapter is designed to provide advice for those taking up senior positions in schools, and especially for new headteachers.

In their survey of new heads, D Weindling and P Earley (1987) highlighted the fact that most new headteachers felt they needed proper preparation for the post and that they would have liked more induction than they received. Now of course extensive preparation for headship is provided through the National Professional Qualification for Headship (NPQH) scheme, under the auspices of the Teacher Training Agency (TTA) and managed through regional assessment and training and development centres. The NPQH scheme has set out national standards for headteachers and helps you to identify and improve your skills in areas that need development.

Whereas you must use the most up-to-date NPQH pack to provide yourself with information about current requirements for headship, this book will help you with your preparation by providing materials, particularly case studies and discussion of situations that you may have to face as a new headteacher. In each of the chapters there will be case studies. You can either analyse these case studies individually and compare your own solutions with those offered in the text, or use them for group discussion. The case studies offer examples of good or bad practice and possible solutions to problems or ask you to provide solutions. Working on them will enhance your understanding of what the job is about and the book is useful both for those preparing to apply and for those who have recently taken up a post. Checklists and guidelines for handling particular tasks are also included where appropriate. In training seminars for senior managers, I regularly use some of the case studies featured in this book to focus on particular issues. I have used two main types of case study: 'For action', which requires you to offer solutions, and 'Exemplars', which provide an illustration, eg of a particular policy. Occasionally a case study will be labelled 'For reflection'. It will usually be a short quotation for you to think about.

What follows is a programme for preparing for headship. It consists of five elements:

1. Defining the role and its responsibilities.
2. Identifying the skills needed for headship.
3. Analysing your own skills, personal qualities and expertise.
4. Organizing your self-development programme.
5. Finding out about the school.

Only 'finding out about the school' is specific to those who have been appointed and are waiting to take up the post. The other components can be used as a general programme by which to prepare yourself and as an ongoing self-development programme once you are in post.

ANALYSE THE ROLE AND THE TASK AHEAD OF YOU

Analysing your role as a head or senior manager could be a valuable exercise for a number of reasons:

❑　If you are a candidate for headship you must expect to be able to answer questions on what the job is about, so you need to understand it.
❑　If you are newly appointed to a post it will enhance your understanding of what is required of you and help you to prepare.
❑　By identifying what the essential components of the job are, it will help you decide what you can delegate and what you must do yourself.

What does it mean to manage a school? The Education Reform Act of 1988 significantly changed the role of the headteacher in that it greatly increased the autonomy of a school, and heads changed from being predominantly the administrators of LEA policies and from handling a very limited budget to being the managers of the organization with much greater decision and policy-making powers and to being in charge of a totally delegated budget. The position of the LEA has declined in relation to the school and it is now the governing body that is the headteacher's main working partner. Thus, as a result of the legislation, the volume and importance of heads' and deputies' management tasks are greatly enhanced and it is essential to their own success and that of the school that they carry them out well.

What is the job about?

The National Standards for Headteachers provide a definition of the core purpose of the headteacher.

CASE STUDY 1.1 FOR REFLECTION

The headteacher is the leading professional in the school. Working with the governing body, the headteacher provides vision, leadership and direction for the school and ensures that it is managed and organized to meet its aims and targets. With the governing body, the headteacher is responsible for the continuous improvement in the quality of education; for raising standards; for ensuring equality of opportunity for all; for the development of policies and practices; and for ensuring that resources are efficiently and effectively used to achieve the school's aims and objectives. The headteacher secures the commitment of the wider community to the school, by developing and maintaining effective networks with, for example, other local schools, the LEA (where appropriate), higher educational institutions, employers, careers services and others. The headteacher is responsible for creating a productive, disciplined learning environment and for the day-to-day management, organization and administration of the school, and is accountable to the governing body.

TTA (1998) *National Standards for Headteachers*

CASE STUDY 1.2 FOR ACTION

To become a headteacher you will have to provide evidence of capability in the key areas of headship. Currently these are:

❑ strategic direction and development of the school;
❑ teaching and learning;
❑ leading and managing staff;
❑ efficient deployment of staff and resources;
❑ accountability.

For action

Compare the list of key areas of headship included in the National Standards for Headteachers with the description of a headteacher's management task given below.

5

Understanding the job description

What does managing a school actually mean? When you respond to a headteacher job advert, you will normally be sent a job description for the post, so probably the best way to start defining the head's task is by looking at a headteacher's job description, where your responsibilities will be listed. Although they are produced individually for each school, and reflect to some extent the preoccupations of a particular governing body, a lot of the same key functions will appear. Your job description could therefore read like the one in Case Study 1.3.

CASE STUDY 1.3 FOR ACTION

A headteacher's job description

Besthampton Education Authority
School: Bestwick Park High School
Job title: Headteacher

Relationships

Responsible to:
The headteacher is accountable to the school's governing body and, through the Director of Education, to the Local Education Authority.

Responsible for:
Pupils, teaching and non-teaching staff of the school.

Important relationships:
❑   pupils;
❑   parents;
❑   members of the teaching and non-teaching staff;
❑   the governing body;
❑   the school representatives of the teaching unions.

Important external relationships:
❑   officials of the LEA;
❑   the school's attached adviser;
❑   other headteachers;
❑   external agencies;
❑   members of the community.

Main purpose of the job

To be responsible for the internal organization, management and control of the school, to ensure that the school is managed effectively so that it contributes fully to each pupil's intellectual, moral, physical and personal development.

Main responsibilities of the job

1. Formulating, in concert with the governing body and the teaching staff, the overall aims and objectives of the school and policies for their implementation.
2. Determining and implementing a curriculum that is in accordance with the National Curriculum, the needs, experience, interests, aptitudes and stage of development of the pupils and the resources of the school.
3. Evaluating the standards of teaching and learning in the school and ensuring that proper standards of professional performance are maintained.
4. Determining and implementing a policy for the pupils' pastoral care, behaviour and discipline.
5. Participating in the selection and appointment of teaching and non-teaching staff.
6. Deploying and managing the teaching and non-teaching staff, and allocating particular duties to them in accordance with their conditions of employment.
7. Ensuring that all the staff have access to advice and training opportunities appropriate to their needs. This responsibility includes supervision of the school's appraisal arrangements.
8. Allocating, controlling and accounting for all the financial and material resources of the school, including the site and premises, that are under the control of the headteacher.
9. Promoting effective relationships and liaison with all the relevant persons and bodies outside the school.
10. Keeping under review the work and organization of the school.

Overriding requirements

A headteacher shall carry out his/her professional duties in accordance with:

❑ the provisions of the Education Acts and any relevant orders or regulations;
❑ the articles of government of the school;
❑ any scheme of local management approved by the Secretary of State.

For action

Compare this job description with the one you have been given. Compare it also with the National Standards for Headteachers' core purpose of headship and key areas of headship. What does this job description tell you about the nature of the management task in running a school?

The first thing it clarifies is *the purpose of the job*. It is your job to provide the pupils with the curriculum content and framework for learning that will give them the best opportunity for their intellectual, moral, physical and personal development, and you will do this a lot better if you are an effective manager than if you are not.

Using this job description it would be possible to divide the list of duties and functions into four main areas, which are detailed in the following four sections.

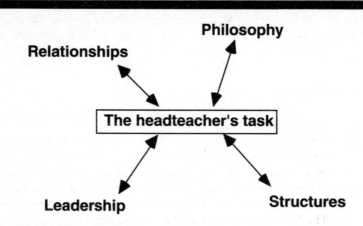

Figure 1.1 *The management task*

Creating the philosophy

This aspect of the job is concerned with ideas. It is the manager's task to set the aims and objectives for the school and create its ethos or corporate identity. This is sometimes described as 'managing the mission'. There are two components to this task: 1) creating the mission – by fashioning the goals; and 2) moving the mission – this involves winning staff commitment to the aims and policies and actually making them happen, and it is closely related to the other three main management tasks.

Establishing the structures

It is the manager's task to formulate the policies and deploy the resources that will translate the aims and objectives into reality and provide the curriculum, the system of pastoral care and the administrative framework that the school needs in order to function. In practice, a lot of this will be achieved by delegating responsibilities to deputies or to task groups, but you remain responsible for the organization and supervision and for ensuring that everything is actually done.

Managing and motivating the personnel

The job of running a school is all about people and relationships and most of this book is about managing people. You are responsible for the management and motivation of all members of the establishment – pupils, teaching staff, associate staff etc. You are responsible for the appointment, deployment and development of all members of the staff. You liaise with parents, the LEA and its associated agencies, the community and industry and you work in partnership with the school's governing body.

Providing leadership

It is the manager's job to provide leadership, direction and control. You are the director of the school with a considerable amount of power and authority. How you choose to use that authority will depend on your management style, but you are expected to use it. You will also be expected to negotiate on behalf of the school, represent it in critical situations and be accountable for its actions. As the headteacher, you are the person who will be first point of contact for any outsider.

How does your job differ from the deputy's?

If you are being promoted from a post as deputy or are looking for promotion, take your current job description and compare it with the new one. Analyse whether your existing role includes tasks from each of the

9

four areas identified above, or whether, as deputy, you have been given responsibility for one or more specific areas, eg providing the structures by managing the daily administration of the school. This analysis will help you decide how to tackle the job itself and focus your thoughts about your development needs. You may have had the opportunity to rotate posts as deputy but you may have spent several years concentrating on one area and need to firm up on areas of weakness. You may find, for example, that you need to spend some time learning about financial management, as this tends to be the province of the headteacher or the bursar.

Management and leadership

Of the four aspects of the manager's task described above, by far the most complex and abstruse is providing leadership. Defining leadership and analysing its characteristics has preoccupied writers on management over a long period of time, and it would seem a sensible next step to review the debate and consider some of the main arguments and approaches. This section is intended to give a flavour of the debate rather than to be a comprehensive survey, and its purpose is to encourage you to think about what leadership means and what kind of leadership you will want to offer.

Traits theory

One group of theorists concentrated on analysing leaders to see if it could identify distinct character traits. This resulted in labelling leaders as 'ambitious', 'charismatic' or 'decisive', but prolonged research failed to support the idea that there are sets of personality characteristics that recur in successful leaders. Setting historical personalities such as Joan of Arc or Alexander the Great or industrial leaders who had 'made it to the top' against a grid only served to highlight differences rather than similarities, and concentrating on personal characteristics of the leaders ignored the led and the situation.

Contingency theory

Contingency theory concentrated on the *situation*. The leader is not necessarily the person normally in charge, but when the crisis occurs he or she emerges to deal successfully with a difficult task or situation. Contingency theorists claim that it is the leader's capacity to understand the essential elements of a situation and provide the behaviours and paths out of the situation that distinguishes a good from a less good leader.

Another strand of this kind of approach is situation theory, where the situation has to fit the leader before he or she can work successfully. This approach does cover only some aspects of leadership and for that reason is regarded as unsatisfactory.

Styles theory

In styles theory the behaviour of managers is analysed in order to identify their predominant management style. Styles theorists claim that there are two sets of dominant behaviours in interpersonal relationships: 1) task-oriented behaviour and maintenance; and 2) people-oriented behaviour.

A task-oriented style of management is present when managers are likely to define and structure their own and co-workers' jobs towards achieving a goal. Direction, structuring and defining ways and means are characteristics of this style and it is sometimes described as 'management by objectives'. A people-oriented approach involves the manager relying on trust, mutual support, avoidance of conflict, and concern for the idea and feelings of others to achieve the organization's goals.

It was once thought that managers were either task- or people-oriented, but in fact most managers are not so clear-cut, though they usually have a bias one way or the other, and successful leaders are able to combine advanced behaviours in both styles.

Successful leadership is thus about managing both tasks *and* people. John Adair, working at the Sandhurst Military Academy in the late 1960s, developed the model with interlocking circles illustrated in Figure 1.3,

Task-oriented ◄————————► People-oriented

Figure 1.2 *The task–people axis*

Figure 1.3 *Action-centred leadership*

which he called 'action-centred leadership' (1973). It does not, however, address the issue of whether leadership and management, which are often regarded as interchangeable, are actually synonymous.

Is there a difference between management and leadership?

You can find plenty of definitions of what a manager does, eg 'Management is about getting things done with and through other people' or 'We see a manager as someone who:

❏ knows what he or she wants to happen and causes it to happen;
❏ is responsible for the performance of the unit he or she is managing;
❏ promotes effectiveness in work done and a search for continual improvement;
❏ sets a climate or tone conducive to enabling people to give of their best'. (Everard and Morris, 1996)

It is, however, much harder to find convincing explanations of the *differences* between management and leadership. Case Study 1.4, which follows, offers one view of how you can distinguish a leader from a manager.

CASE STUDY 1.4 FOR ACTION

Leader	Manager
❏ innovates	❏ administers
❏ develops	❏ maintains
❏ challenges the status quo	❏ accepts the status quo
❏ originates	❏ initiates
❏ focuses on people	❏ focuses on systems
❏ takes the long-term view	❏ takes the short-term view
❏ eyes the horizon	❏ eyes the bottom line
❏ inspires trust	❏ relies on control
❏ asks what and why	❏ asks how and when
❏ is his/her own person	❏ is the classic good soldier
❏ does the right thing	❏ does things right (Bennis, 1985)

For action

Think about Bennis's comparison of leadership and management. Do you agree with the comparisons made, and if not why not?

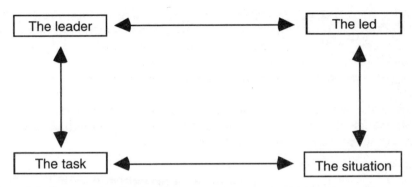

Figure 1.4 *Components of leadership*

Perhaps the difference between leadership and management can be better summarized as follows: 'The major difference between managing and leading is the leader's capacity to lift people up, to articulate purpose, to give reality to higher values, to resolve conflicting aims as a means to the fulfilment of the followers' (Hunt, 1986).

Providing leadership is an essential part of the manager's task, and for the purposes of this book I intend to treat it as an aspect of management consisting of four components, as illustrated in Figure 1.4.

Taking this view of leadership allows us to adopt the definition given by Hersey and Blanchard in 1982: 'Leadership is the process of influencing the activities of an individual or a group towards goal achievement in a given situation.'

Leadership styles

We must then address the issue of whether there is a particularly *effective* leadership style.

CASE STUDY 1.5 FOR REFLECTION

Jean is extremely direct in her dealings with people, the staff said approvingly. She is a good listener, gives you time to put your case and her decision is always fair. She is never influenced by any preconceived ideas, isn't swayed by personalities and doesn't have favourites. It is her rule to think about something for a few days because she does not like being rushed, and then to decide the issue on its merits, but then if she says 'No', there is no point arguing. You never have to worry that she will say something quite different to the next person who raises the same question, which is what they had found so irritating in the previous head. With Jean, you always know precisely where you are. Most of the staff like this very much indeed and think she is the best headteacher that they have ever experienced; a minority, however, although they like her personally, feel that too much power is centred in the headteacher.

Nigel had learnt his craft in an urban comprehensive when democratic management was in vogue and enjoys bringing teachers together in a collaborative management structure. He claims he manages through people, and from the front, back or sideways as appropriate. He would call himself a flexible manager. His staff, however, describe him as machiavellian, and he laughs with them and agrees. In Nigel's school to be called machiavellian is now almost a compliment. To gain support for his plans, he relies heavily on his skill at interpersonal relationships. In his approach to change, he does not give the impression of having a master plan — although some staff suspect that he might have one — but rather that he is pragmatic and proceeds one step at a time, finding ways around obstacles. Instead of leading all the changes himself, he often gets teachers who are trusted by colleagues to do so and they front the ideas or new initiatives. There is a lot of debate and discussion. Nigel always accepts the results philosophically, but usually the ideas are adopted and they seem to work. A great many of the staff like Nigel very much and enjoy working with him. They say it is never dull and that there is a lot of opportunity for growth and development because he is so receptive to ideas and likes to encourage staff to run with them. They also say he is supportive in the right ways if problems occur. A minority of staff, however, dislike the uncertainty.

The management styles, ie the working methods of these two teachers, could not be more different:

❏ Jean is direct and straightforward; Nigel is devious.
❏ It is clear throughout what attitude Jean is taking; it is unclear what Nigel really thinks or will do.
❏ Jean leads from the front; Nigel manoeuvres from the rear, often putting up other teachers to front his ideas.
❏ Nigel is more flexible than Jean. Once she has said 'No', there is no further debate.
❏ Jean is authoritarian; Nigel is collaborative.

Authoritarian managers are:	Democratic managers are:
❏ high on	❏ high on
– telling	– consulting
– instructing	– involving
– deciding	– accepting
❏ low on	❏ low on
– consulting	– directing
– delegating	– controlling
– team building	– setting structures

Nigel and Jean have very different management styles, but both are effective and successful managers. Jean is trusted and respected by her staff, who feel secure working for her. Nigel is popular with the majority of his staff, who enjoy the challenge of working with him.

The case study demonstrates that there is no one ideal management style or blueprint for good management. If it is to be effective, your management style needs to be appropriate to the institution, its personnel and the given situation. You see that this matches the definition of leadership given earlier in this chapter. Jean could face resentment in Nigel's school because his staff, who were used to and enjoyed his flexible approach, might consider her to be too authoritarian and feel that more of the staff should be involved in the decision-making process. Similarly Nigel would face major problems in dealing with Jean's staff, who were used to her more direct approach. It is important that you know what the styles are, and are able to recognize your own dominant style, so that you can see how it is perceived by the people whom you manage, and whether it is appropriate to the particular situation in which you find yourself. How to analyse your management style will be discussed in a later section of this chapter. Figure 1.5 shows the range of possible styles and their associated characteristics.

A rule of thumb

A new team, unused to working either with one another or with you, is likely to need a more structured approach than a well-established confident team that knows you well.

IDENTIFYING THE SKILLS NEEDED

If there is no ideal style, perhaps you should concentrate on firming up on the skills needed to be a successful headteacher. What are they and can

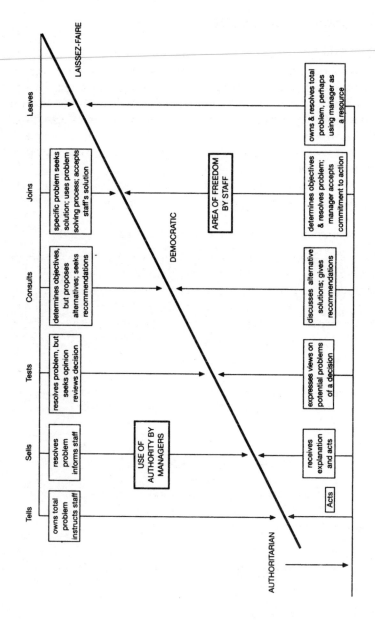

Figure 1.5 *Continuum of leadership behaviour*

they be learnt? We can identify the skills used by successful managers under three headings, as detailed in the following three sections.

Human – the interpersonal skills

If management is about getting things done with and through other people, highly developed interpersonal skills are essential. The most important interpersonal skills are listening, communicating and sensitivity to the needs of others and the organization, and you will find that several chapters in this book emphasize that you will need to make effective use of these skills.

Areas in which you will be expected to demonstrate strong interpersonal skills include those shown in Figure 1.6.

Technical – the knowledge and expertise skills

In educational management you need four kinds of technical skill:

1. Subject knowledge and expertise – you have to be a leading exponent of your own subject area in order to carry credibility in the staffroom.
2. Expertise in particular management areas, eg timetabling, finance or staff development. This is because as a member of the senior management team you will have been given responsibility for some specific management areas, eg resources or appraisal, and developed expertise

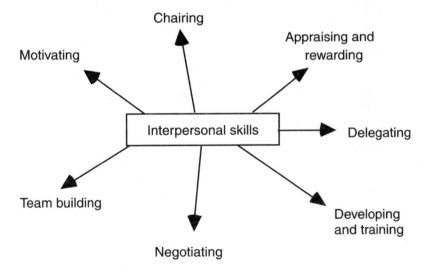

Figure 1.6 *Interpersonal skills*

in the particular area or areas, but as headteacher you will have oversight of *all* areas. Your technical understanding must be good enough to allow you to make informed judgements and decisions about what should be done.

3. You will need knowledge of the possibilities of ICT. It is more than just a useful tool for school administration and analysing and evaluating data on pupil and school performance to assist target setting and improvement. It can provide you with information about good practice throughout the educational world and with a network of contacts. You also have to ensure that your staff as well as your pupils can use ICT and that the National Curriculum requirements for ICT are met. Effective use of ICT in your school can make a positive difference to its success. You don't have to be a computer wizard yourself; you need an understanding of what ICT can do for the school and the ability to find someone with the expertise to ensure that ICT is in place and works. You may also need some entrepreneurial talent in identifying ways to keep the equipment up to date without unbalancing your budget.

4. You will need a good knowledge of current educational issues. This is because the SMT will have to respond to consultative documents and take the planning and policy decisions about these issues as they arise.

Conceptual – the planning and visionary skills

This means the ability to assimilate and process information in order to shape and reform it into a new structure. It also means the ability to take an overview of a situation and form judgements about it. This is sometimes called helicoptering. You will need good conceptual skills in order to:

❑ analyse and make judgements about a variety of data;
❑ set aims and objectives;
❑ formulate whole school policies;
❑ articulate the school's corporate values and beliefs;
❑ create an institutional development plan.

It is rare that any one manager is endowed to an equal degree with all those skills and abilities, so if you suspect that you lack some important skills, do not despair just yet, as there two ways in which you could improve matters.

First, you work in a team and not in isolation, and crucially the senior management team (SMT) is composed of people with a variety of different abilities and strengths. Everyone in the team does not need to be a good timetabler or financial wizard. Indeed, it would be a much greater problem for you if the team *was* too similar in its talents – resulting in tensions and conflicts over who does what. It is important to try to achieve a balance, to use the available talents most effectively and to think about the gaps whenever a vacancy in the team occurs.

Secondly, most of the skills that you require in order to be an effective manager can be learnt. Peter White, when Associate Director of the Industrial Society, summed it up: 'The great majority of those involved in managing schools would greatly improve their performance if they receive down to earth training in what a leader needs to be effective' (White, 1984).

As the Industrial Society is a provider of training, Peter White had a vested interest in promoting training, but I would agree that it is quite possible for a manager to improve his or her performance in a particular area of weakness. Obviously some areas are easier to improve than others. A lot of new heads, for example, are inexperienced in financial management, because the head in their previous school reserved this area for himself or herself. A lot of organizations run courses to help you improve your understanding of how to manage the budget and resources, and practice will help you improve your performance and develop your confidence. Similarly, there are plenty of training courses available to help you improve the management areas that depend on interpersonal skills, eg team building. You do have to be realistic, however: you can certainly find a course that will help you improve how you produce your school development plan or your chairperson skills, but creativity is much harder to develop.

ANALYSING YOUR SKILLS, PERSONAL QUALITIES AND EXPERTISE

Carrying out a needs appraisal

If you have followed the advice given in earlier sections of this chapter, you will already be well on the way to creating a personal development programme for yourself. By working out what the job is about and assessing your own skills and competencies against those needed to succeed in the post, you have carried out a needs appraisal, which should have given you a very good indication of where you would benefit from training and development. Doing this before you undertake NPQH training could get you on to the fast track.

Your purpose in analysing your skills, personal qualities and expertise is to identify your range of strengths and the areas that need improvement.

Further development should focus on the latter. NPQH questionnaires and needs appraisal sessions will help you do this exercise. Doing it before you apply for posts enables you to firm up in areas where you are weak, but there is also mileage in analysing and further developing your skills in the period while you are in limbo waiting to take up your new post. You will also want to do a needs analysis of what skills are essential to moving the school forward. You will have to wait until after you have been in post a little while, however, before analysing the SMT.

Forms of testing and assessment

Psychometric testing

There is a range of tests available. Most of these tests were originally devised for industry, but can be used by educational managers. If used properly, they can help us work out our basic orientation or dominant approach to managing a group or situation. This could help you determine how appropriate your management style is and whether it needs any modification in order to be more effective. A common feature is use of a questionnaire (filled in by the individual, and sometimes by colleagues), the results of which are filled in on a grid and the results analysed to show your orientation.

Governing bodies regularly use psychometric testing in headship assessment to complement formal interviewing. It provides an indication for the governors of your dominant style and the results can be set against their person specification for the post. Feedback on your results is usually provided by the consultancy firm used. If you fail to get the post, the feedback can be a useful guide for your development, and, if you are successful, it could be a valuable exercise to use the time between being appointed and taking up the post to reflect on the feedback and to do some relevant training.

Professional assessment

Professional assessment, usually conducted at an assessment centre, has also become an important component of headship testing. It too complements the interview process. During the testing, detailed notes are made on your actions and interventions. You participate in a range of multi-purpose exercises, some on paper and some through simulations, and you are watched and recorded by observers, usually ex-headteachers. Again, whether or not you succeed in getting the job, the feedback can be useful for you.

NPQH assessment

The National Standards for Headteachers programme is the main vehicle for headship assessment, training and development. Professional assessment has become an integral component of headship training. It was developed originally to meet a specific gap in the senior management training market, ie to assess senior managers' competencies in a range of skills and to provide a development programme tailored to an individual's needs, and it quickly developed into a 'training for headship' course. For NPQH, you complete assignments largely based on work you do in your own school, and you are assessed. The routes to NPQH are described below. The governors will be looking for your NPQH accreditation if they are seriously to consider you for a headteacher post. It 'signals readiness for headship, but does not replace the selection process'. There will still be the interview and there will regularly be tasks to complete as well. The materials studied during NPQH, however, should help you to cope well with these tests and tasks.

What are the National Standards for Headteachers?

National Standards for Headteachers define the knowledge, understanding, skills and attributes required for the key tasks of headship. 'Schools need headteachers of ability, wisdom and vision. Excellence at the top will raise standards throughout. That's why the national professional qualification for headship exists – to prepare the next generation of school leaders' (DfEE, 1999).

How does it operate?

There are now three stages to this development programme:

1. Aspiring headteachers NPQH – initial training stage. The NPQH assessment and training has become the main route to headship. If you are selected, you complete a needs assessment process and then undertake training and assessment at the regional training and development centres and assessment centres or through distance learning modules. If you are using supported open learning (SOL), you are expected to attend a day school for each module undertaken. There is a standard programme, which can take up to three years, and an accelerated programme for those judged 'close to headship', particularly for those who have had experience as acting headteachers. If you are following

the standard NPQH route, you will study the core module on strategic leadership and accountability and up to three further modules. There is assessment relating to each key area and a final assessment. If you are following the accelerated route, you can be considered ready for your final assessment within one term.

2. Newly appointed headteachers – the Headlamps induction phase (headteachers' leadership and management programme). You are provided with a mentor and funds to purchase relevant training in areas identified as needing development. Most commercial training companies are 'Headlamp approved'.

3. Serving headteachers – the In-service phase (leadership programme for serving headteachers). The programme aims to improve your own personal effectiveness and help you bring about school improvement. You are linked with a senior business partner to work on general issues of leadership and management.

Applying for NPQH

You normally have to demonstrate several years as a qualified teacher and that you have good experience in leadership and management, eg as the head of a major department, in order to be considered for the NPQH. Non-teachers are considered. They have to show similar management experience.

To be included on an NPQH programme you will have to show that you have experience in all the key areas listed on p 5, so don't wait until you have been a deputy for several years before you start preparing yourself to apply; make sure that you build up experience in each of the relevant areas. You will also need to show evidence of continuing professional development, which is why you need your own programme of development.

How you complete your application form is crucial, so make sure that you give it your full attention. Pick your referees carefully so that you get all the support that you need to get on to the programme. If you are unsuccessful, there is an appeals procedure for unsuccessful candidates, but you would probably do better to improve your application and try again.

Funding NPQH

If you are at an LEA-maintained school, a foundation school or a city technology college, you can apply for central funding. If your bid is successful, the LEA (local education authority) or the assessment centre may agree to fund all or part of the cost. LEAs receive money for NPQH through the training grant (Standards Fund). Applicants have to apply for this, and LEAs select according to the merit of the candidate and where they expect need to arise. Thus in some areas it can be easier to get funding to train for primary headship than for secondary because there is a dearth of candidates for primary headteacher posts.

As well as central funding, you may get some support from your school. As some assignments are school-focused and are useful for the school, you can make a good case for partial funding. You can also seek sponsorship from industry. If all of these fail and you have to fund your own training, there are career development loans (deferred bank loans) available.

Getting hold of the information

The programme is regularly modified in the light of problems experienced by new and aspiring headteachers and to meet their needs, so you will want up-to-date information. Probably the best way to start is by obtaining copies of the National Standards pamphlets, as they have a number to telephone for further information, addresses of the assessment centres and information about how to apply, but you need a pamphlet to get these numbers. The local education office and job centres should have information about these opportunities and a phone number to contact – you may have to persevere to obtain it. The Internet, however, is probably the best way to access the most up-to-date information about current provision, how to apply and costs of the training programme.

ORGANIZING YOUR SELF-DEVELOPMENT PROGRAMME

As part of your preparation for headship or your induction, you will want to continue your professional development.

Learning from a manager

As a preparation for taking up my headship I did an industrial placement. The firm arranged three separate days for me during which I met managers at different levels in the company. I actually went to different plants, which also helped me appreciate differences in nuances in running the same kind of thing but with a different team. It was a fascinating experience and I learnt a great deal from it. It really made me think and focus on how I respond to my own responsibilities. I learnt from both the things that were similar and those that were very different in industry. Later I did some shadowing of their Managing Director, which I also found very helpful.

New headteacher

Talking to managers in industry can be a very worthwhile experience. You will notice that this headteacher claims to have learnt from both the similarities and the differences, and found it valuable to see the same thing being done on more than one site. What is often very useful is the opportunity to meet a variety of managers, either in one firm or from a few firms, especially when the sessions come fairly close together. Shadowing a manager for a day or two can also be beneficial.

Making best use of your mentor

LEAs provide their new headteachers with a mentor, a more experienced headteacher working in the same LEA who can act as a guide and support for the less experienced colleague through the first year in post. Most new headteachers who have been given this form of support have found it very useful indeed. It provides them with someone they can consult when faced with difficulties and who can act as a sounding board for ideas. It can also be therapeutic to have someone to talk to in moments of stress, who will understand what the problem is about and who may have experienced similar problems in the not-too-distant past.

Appraisal

Once you are in post, using appraisal to focus on strengths and weaknesses or specific skills could be a more effective way of analysing your development needs than either of the above methods. You can concentrate on one or more of the competencies. Headteacher appraisal has to involve two appraisers, one of whom is another headteacher, and the other an adviser or consultant. They will collect data from your colleagues, observe you in action and discuss the results with you. This is certainly the most cost-effective method and it could be very valuable. You may find that you want to link it to one of the other methods, eg some team analysis. Belbin's team roles analysis is discussed in Chapter 2.

CASE STUDY 1.6 FOR ACTION

This exercise is probably most useful after you have been in post a term or two. Choose a skill or competency, eg decisiveness. Mark yourself either on a bar chart or on a 1–5 scale. Choose five members of staff and get them to mark you in the same way as you have graded yourself. Compare the results to see if:

❑ you exhibit a consistent pattern;
❑ you are perceived in the same way by all sections of staff;
❑ you have flattered yourself.

Discuss the results and the development implications with your appraiser or your mentor head and, if necessary, plan a training programme.

FINDING OUT ABOUT THE SCHOOL

Weindling and Earley's survey, mentioned at the beginning of this chapter, also revealed that it was often very difficult for new headteachers to visit the school while their predecessor was still in post and all too visibly didn't want them around.

CASE STUDY 1.7 FOR ACTION

She kept me out of the school until September 1st. I was only able to visit it once after I was appointed before I actually took up the post, and then she wouldn't let me talk to anyone on my own. It was impossible to get a clear impression or gather the information that I needed. It made preparing for the job very difficult indeed.

New headteacher describing his treatment by his predecessor

For action

What advice would you give this new headteacher and why?

The quotation above is an extreme example. You may not find it as difficult as this new headteacher did to gain access or information, but for a whole variety of reasons you may not be able to visit as often as you might wish, and any information provided may not be precisely what you are seeking. Whatever you do, however, try not to create an unpleasant atmosphere by imposing yourself on anyone who is reluctant to see you or give the impression that you are trying to take over before the present head has left. Even if you take a softly-softly approach there is still a lot you can do to prepare yourself.

Analyse the documents

A school's documents and brochures could be a very useful aid in helping you analyse the state of the school. You will probably have been sent some of these when you were a candidate for the post and they will have given you an initial impression of how things stood and helped you to decide whether or not you wanted to proceed with your application. Now, as the head designate, you can ask for a complete set of the school's most important documents and you will certainly want to see the school development plan, which is often not given to candidates, as they are expected to offer their own vision of the school's future. Don't forget to ask for the most recent Ofsted report and the school's action plan in response to the report. You can use the documents to get an impression of how the school operates, whether it is on track after Ofsted and to assess how well the school presents itself through its documents and brochures.

Meet the attached adviser

If you are new to the area and are joining an LEA-maintained or foundation school, it might be possible to arrange a session for you with the school's attached or link adviser at the education office. This would inform you about the school's relationship with the LEA and about the LEAs priorities and facilities, and its attitude to current issues. If a meeting is impossible before you take up the post, arrange it early in the first term and, in the meantime, you could make use of the LEAs policy documents on current issues as a means of informing yourself. If you are to be the head of a school in an area run by a firm of contractors, find out what form of consultancy is used by the school – does it buy a package from the local or another LEA, use a consultancy service or attempt to struggle through, relying on the expertise of the governors?

Meet the chair of governors

If the opportunity arises for a session or sessions with the chair of governors, seize it. He or she is likely to want to spend some time with you even if the present head is less than welcoming, and will have an agenda of issues. The sooner you familiarize yourself with these, the better. If the current head is operating blocking tactics, you may have to visit the chair of governors at his or her business premises.

Gathering information from the existing head

The best-placed person to help you gen up on your new role is obviously the existing headteacher. You can expect a minimum of one visit, but hopefully you will be able to arrange a number of sessions working together, and arrangements may be made for you to meet a number of key people, such as the bursar to find out how the school's finances are organized. Obviously the existing head will have his or her own gloss on things, and may want to see the current system continue, but he or she cannot actually legislate for the future and, while in post, is the person with the most detailed knowledge of the way things operate. As one new headteacher recently commented, 'One of my main problems is that too much of the information was only in the previous headteacher's head, no one else knew what was going on and she didn't record it, or she shredded everything when she left. There is nothing in the file.'

Find out about mentoring arrangements

As part of the induction entitlement for new headteachers, you will be allocated a mentor. It might be useful for you to have an initial meeting with your mentor before you take up your post.

Meet the personnel

Don't worry if you can't do much about meeting the personnel before you actually start in post; you will have plenty of time for that once you have started the job. Make sure, however, that you don't give the impression that you have kept away because you are not interested in your new colleagues; make it clear to them that you don't want to impose and that you are allowing your predecessor the space to depart gracefully.

Explore the locality

It can be very useful and informative to visit the streets or estate nearest to the school and meet and talk to some of the local residents and shopkeepers and perhaps visit some of the clubs, churches and other local organizations. You will want to build good relations with those who live and work in the immediate vicinity of the school and you will begin to learn how the school is regarded locally. In these ways you can gather information about the school and begin to analyse its current state of development. It will enable you to do a lot of thinking and planning before you start.

What kind of things do you need to think about?

❏ What state are the budget and the buildings in?
❏ What do the job descriptions and any meetings you have had so far with the senior management team (SMT) indicate about the tasks they undertake and their contribution (separately or as a team) to the running of the school? How does this fit into your vision of things?
❏ How did Ofsted view the school in the last inspection?
❏ What seems to you to be the most urgent problem to tackle on your arrival?
❏ To what extent are you going to have to educate the governors into taking a greater or different role in school affairs?
❏ Do you need to arrive with a preset agenda or can you afford to be a gradualist?
❏ What are you going to do in your first week or term?

CASE STUDY 1.8 FOR REFLECTION

Making your mark

I made my mark by sacking the cook. My first real challenge was to do with the quality of the meals served in the school canteen. In the first few weeks of my headship, virtually all the letters of complaint that I received from parents were about how awful the food was. I tried some of the meals myself and the parents were right: the food really was dreadful. I checked what my powers were and then I phoned the contractor and said that I wanted the cook replaced immediately. They argued a bit, but I insisted and, with a different cook, the meals improved enormously and parents rang up to say how much better it was.

Headteacher recalling her first challenge

After all this rigorous preparation, you will be eager for the challenge of actually doing the job. Now read on.

2

MANAGING THE SENIOR MANAGEMENT TEAM

THE ROLE OF THE SENIOR MANAGEMENT TEAM

The senior management team (SMT) is the executive group who give leadership to the school. They do the main planning, determine the policies and carry out the daily running of the school under the leadership and guidance of the headteacher. The SMT has evolved into its present pre-eminence since about the early 1970s with the development of large comprehensive schools in which the headteacher could no longer undertake personally all the tasks associated with managing the school. 'It is becoming increasingly impractical for any one person to encompass the diversity and work necessary to manage and organize a secondary school' (Torrington and Weightman, 1989b). 'What has emerged markedly is the existence of a policy and management team, comprising deputy headteachers and occasionally other senior teachers, under the chairmanship of the headteacher' (Todd and Dennison, 1978).

The SMT has thus become an important feature of educational management with a central role in running the school. 'Senior management's task is to review the effectiveness of the school in delivering programmes, to manage resource distribution and to propose and manage change' (Murgatroyd, 1986).

Although surveys of management in schools (eg Torrington and Weightman, 1989b) are agreed about the importance of the task to be carried out, they also point to a clear discrepancy between how the team should function and what its members actually do, and they have been highly critical about 'the reality of school management'. The most frequent criticisms are:

❑   There is underutilization of team members – too much free time and not enough to do.
❑   The work done by the senior teachers and the deputies is not perceived as important by the staff.

❏   They are given trivial or administrative tasks that fill up their time, but which could be done by a clerical assistant.

❏   They have no clear role.

❏   Many of their responsibilities are very nebulous, eg 'liaison with…' or 'oversight of…', etc.

❏   They fail to operate as a team.

The Secondary Heads' Association (SHA) survey of deputy heads *If It Moves…* (1989) reinforces this impression, as some deputies were carrying out as many as 50 or 60 miscellaneous tasks, which included furniture moving and cleaning the graffiti off walls. This seems to have happened for two reasons. One reason is historic, reflecting the way that the SMT has developed. As demands upon the school have increased, new responsibilities have simply been added on to the existing workload of the deputy, or a third or occasionally a fourth deputy post has been added to the team (occasionally in the wrong place) and this additional team member picks up a miscellaneous collection of jobs – normally the tasks that no one else wants.

The other reason is more fundamental. The head decides what to delegate to the SMT and, in many cases, has retained the personal management of initiatives that could have been delegated to a deputy. This may reflect the head's lack of confidence in the abilities of his or her team members, or a desire not to lose direct contact with staff. Sometimes it is simply the reluctance to share power. Whatever the reasons, the effect on the image of the SMT has been unfortunate, because in some schools it has led to it being perceived as an ineffectual and unnecessary institution, whose members do little and are being carried by other staff. 'Seldom did we find a situation in which the deputies had full jobs and never did we find a situation in which three deputies were actually needed' (Torrington and Weightman, 1989b).

There has been some improvement since the 1990s, especially as schools responded to Ofsted criticisms, but it is still the case that in a lot of schools, especially some primary schools, the SMT's management role is underdeveloped. As new tasks arrive, one of the deputies is expected to take on the new responsibility, usually without a strategic rethink of the overall workload. (Case Study 3.1 gives an example of what can happen when a conscientious deputy is overloaded.)

Torrington and Weightman's utterly damning comment obviously reflects adversely on the deputy heads and senior teachers described in the survey, because a job is what you make of it, but far more seriously it reflects on the headteacher as a team leader. It is essentially the role of the deputy head to undertake those tasks and responsibilities delegated to him or her by the head, and there are limits to how far a deputy can be expected to manage upwards. The head is the manager of the SMT, and enough evidence has now emerged to suggest that some senior management teams are being very poorly managed. 'When all decisions, procedures, communications and systems are focused on the head, serious weaknesses of management and organization occur.'

A good senior-management team can make all the difference to how well a school performs but, to be effective and fulfil its functions, it needs the right kind of leadership. Too many teams are poorly run because the head keeps all the real power, because they lack any cohesion and do not function as a team at all, or because the lack of real leadership has resulted in the team losing its sense of purpose and direction. The team should be one of your most valuable assets, so you should try to make the best use of it that you can. What then are the skills that you need and how should you set about creating a strong and effective senior management team?

For reflection

Management skills and personal qualities needed to lead a team

❑ Analytical ability – to identify team needs and characteristics. You could of course get a consultant to do this for you, or use Belbin's team roles analysis (see below).
❑ Chairperson skills – to co-ordinate activities, manage meetings, arbitrate, negotiate, etc.
❑ Communication skills – the ability to share information clearly. The team needs full information at all times, and the ability to listen actively to others.
❑ Willingness to delegate power and demonstrate trust in others. This is linked to the ability to recognize and encourage talent or expertise in team members.
❑ Skill in developing or providing opportunities for the professional development of the team members.
❑ Leadership skills – as head your task is to give a clear lead to the team and to be decisive when necessary.

Belbin's team roles analysis

In *Management Teams: Why they succeed or fail*, RM Belbin (1981) claims that one of the key determinants of a team's success is the nature of the interaction in terms of the qualities brought to carrying out the task. He argues that status, technical knowledge and experience are not necessarily the most significant determinants of an individual's contribution. In fact what he calls 'alpha teams', ie teams composed entirely of high achievers, may perform significantly less well than those made up according to Belbin's criteria for effective task achievement. Belbin identifies eight role types, which refer to the potential contribution of the individual in terms of behaviour or roles rather than knowledge or status. The roles he identifies are:

❏ **Chair/Co-ordinator**: controls and directs the team; is able to make best use of its diverse talents and balance contributions in order to secure the goals and objectives. *Characteristics*: stable and dominant.
❏ **Shaper**: pushes the team towards an action, sets objectives and looks for outcomes. *Characteristics*: dominant, extrovert, anxious.
❏ **Plant**: innovates, generates new ideas and approaches, problem solver. *Characteristics*: intelligent and introvert.
❏ **Resource investigator**: the team's contact with its environment, generates ideas and resources. *Characteristics*: intelligent, stable and introvert.
❏ **Monitor-evaluator**: analyses problems and evaluates contributions. *Characteristics*: stable and introvert.
❏ **Completer-finisher**: ensures attention to detail, maintains schedules. *Characteristics*: anxious and introvert.
❏ **Company worker**: capable of converting plans into action, working systematically and efficiently. *Characteristics*: stable and controlled.
❏ **Team worker**: supports and reinforces, improves communications, fosters team spirit. *Characteristics*: stable, extrovert and flexible.

Belbin's analysis of team roles is used quite frequently on management courses and is probably known to you. Each member of the team fills in an individual questionnaire, which is then analysed to identify the dominant team roles adopted by each member of the team. Members of the team then do the same exercise for one another because it will highlight whether a team has a complete range of roles or if there is an imbalance or overlap, eg if there are too many plant or ideas people competing to manage the developments, or if an important role is missing entirely. In Case Study 2.2, which appears later in this chapter, there are too many company workers and completer-finishers and not enough plants or shapers, so when a vacancy occurrs in the management team, the headteacher wants to look for specific talents.

If you do use Belbin, it is important to remember that people take on different roles in different teams or as the need arises, and that people rarely have only one dominant role.

BUILDING THE TEAM

By this stage in your professional development the description of team development given below should be well known to you, and only the briefest résumé is included here. The National Foundation for Education Research (NFER) survey of new heads undertaken by Weindling and Earley (1987) has not dated significantly and its findings inform the thinking in this chapter.

Organizational research has indicated that team development typically displays four stages: *forming*; *storming*; *norming*; *performing*.

Forming is the first stage in which the team is put together. In order to get off to the best possible start, industry has used a variety of aptitude and personality tests to select suitable team members so that they are compatible and effective. As a head you will inherit an existing team, whose composition you may be able to alter over a period of time. This is not quite as bad as it sounds: the NFER survey of the first two years in post of heads appointed in 1982–83 found that 51 per cent of the sample were able to appoint one new deputy within the two-year period, and this trend has been maintained. Often a deputy waits until a new head is in post, perhaps works through the first year to help the new head take over and then retires.

Storming is the stage of team building characterized by tensions and low morale as team members test one another out and jockey for position. The honeymoon period is over, but there has not been time to build up trust or confidence in you as leader. Latent fears and anxieties come out into the open, and co-operation and good will are at their lowest. You will eventually build a stronger team if the problems have been aired than if they remain submerged.

Norming is the stage of development when the team begins to come together and 'gel'. This is sometimes described as welding and it can be very rewarding – the members learn to work together and you can test out and establish which are the most successful working procedures. It also means that you can delegate far more to the team than in the early stages of its formation. The NFER survey found that it took a year for most of their new heads to begin to delegate much work. Earlier in the process they had been reluctant to trust deputies whose strengths and weaknesses were still an unknown factor. Learning to know and to work with one another is an important stage in team building.

Performing is the stage that represents the target for the team's style of operating. The two most common cultures are club culture, in which the team revolves around its charismatic leader, and task culture, in which the team's commitment to the common task binds it together. Which culture you use will depend very much on your own leadership style. In both these cultures this stage of team development is characterized by a high level of trust and support among team members, who are prepared to be open and honest with one another. The team is confident and able to build on the strengths of its members in order to achieve its objectives. Its self-confidence makes it possible for it to be self-critical and willing to accept outside advice when difficult issues arise.

The process described above clearly takes some time, though some teams come together more quickly than others. As head you are the team leader and your role in team building is crucial. How easy or difficult it will be will depend on how compatible you find your team, and your own skills in welding incompatible or unwilling team members into a fully functioning unit. Although I cannot offer you a blueprint for team building, remember that skills can be learnt or improved and that what you should use are what you feel to be the most appropriate methods to weld together your particular team.

There can, however, be problems. The NFER survey of new heads makes it clear that the heads in their sample rated coping with a weak member of the management team amongst the most serious of the difficulties that they encountered in their first year in post. Some of the problems derived from the fact that the team was appointed by the previous incumbent and reflects his or her management style, which is often very different from that of the new head. If the deputies have been in post for a long time, and are not used to a participative management style, it can be very difficult and possibly inappropriate to try to get them to change their ways.

Most frequently encountered problems

❑   members who lack flexibility – sectionalism or inability to adapt to new roles;
❑   a deputy who has been promoted beyond his or her ability;
❑   overlap of roles;
❑   burn-out;
❑   historic appointments, eg the head of science is a senior teacher but does not take a senior management role;
❑   personality clashes between members of the team;
❑   loyalty;

❑ jealousy – one of the deputies is a disappointed candidate for the headship.

The following quotation from the NFER survey encapsulates this situation: 'The senior management team is certainly not as I should want it. I would never have appointed the second and third deputies, as neither, I think, is really up to the job.'

What can you do about this kind of situation? The most commonly applied strategies seem to be:

❑ Redefine the responsibilities of the members of the team. Be careful if you use this strategy, as it can lead to more problems and there are examples of deputies taking out grievance procedures against a head who forced them to change duties against their will. Nevertheless, if handled with firmness and sensitivity, redefining responsibilities can make a significant difference to how the team operates.
❑ Use pressure or tough measures against individuals to force an incompatible member of the team either to co-operate or to opt for early retirement. This can be very divisive for a school – use with extreme care.
❑ Use secondment, particularly with jealous or incompatible deputies. Sending them on an MA course, for example, gets them out of your hair for at least one year and improves their promotion chances.
❑ Use short training courses to raise awareness. These are useful when the person lacks the right experience or technical knowledge, but is developable.
❑ Use advisers or industrial consultants as mediators and facilitators. Sometimes this involves residential team-building sessions off-site, eg at a hotel or an industrial training centre.

There are no easy answers, but exploring ways in which you can get the best out of the team available and building up trust over a period of time are the methods most likely to result in success.

CASE STUDY 2.1 FOR ACTION

1. 'I realized that you can't wait for people to leave, you have to work with what you've got...' (headteacher in NFER survey).
2. 'The manager selects a few members of his team... but tolerates the vulgarities of many others. One could almost say that picking one's own people is an abdication of management, a part of the art of being

able to organize and co-ordinate the contributions of different types of people, including those one does not get on with. This involves the manager adapting his style and approach to the various expectations and needs of others, rather than being able to work only with kindred spirits, hand picked for their compatibility' (Torrington and Weightman, 1985).

3. 'It wasn't easy, but I managed to persuade her to give up her deputy head role. We had to find a way in which this did not affect her pension, because it was another year before she went, but at least I could move forward in building a team that could do the job' (headteacher talking about how she made changes to the SMT).

For action

Compare the approaches taken – what problems do you have and what approach is most likely to work with your own team?

The extended case study that follows explores some of these issues more fully.

CASE STUDY 2.2

THE SMT AT BESTWICK PARK HIGH SCHOOL

Yvonne Perkins

Yvonne had been deputy head for five years, with responsibility for the daily administration of the school and constructing the timetable. It had not been Mr Smythe the headteacher's practice to take his deputies into his confidence or to consult them about decisions. Yvonne's task had been to ensure that things ran smoothly, which she did very well. She was efficient and conscientious, and performed every task meticulously. She was respected by the staff because of her competence and because she always treated them fairly. She had no favourites, and could be relied upon to find a way to allow them to go on courses or to have time off when needed. She was cheerful, unambitious and almost unflappable. She was not greatly interested in educational theory, and was largely unsympathetic to the innovations demanded by current educational legislation. She nevertheless felt it was her duty to make such innovations work. She held a central position in the life of the school. Staff regularly dropped into her office for a chat or to consult her about a problem, as she was a sympathetic listener who would respect a confidence and could be relied upon to offer some useful advice.

Fred Brown

Fred had originally been deputy head in a school that had amalgamated with Bestwick Park. He was a martinet, whose autocratic regime was feared as much by the staff as by the pupils. He was in charge of the pastoral system, and it was his custom to hold short briefing sessions fortnightly to instruct his team of year heads. Otherwise he avoided meetings as he viewed them as a waste of time. The year heads tended not to tell Fred about problems unless absolutely necessary. As a result, he was largely unaware of what was happening from day to day in the school. His rigid approach had originally meant that discipline was tight, but in recent years his very remoteness had resulted in a breakdown of uniformity. The year heads tried to apply their own solutions to issues that arose but, not working as a team, their styles and standards varied. Fred was determinedly ignorant of current educational trends, and hostile to change. Under James Smythe, who did not demand much of his deputies, Fred had done relatively little. His general approach suited Mr Smythe, who regarded him as an excellent deputy. When Mr Smythe retired and Brenda Gatlin was appointed to the headship, Fred had two or three years to serve before his own retirement.

Mike Wade

Under Mr Smythe, Mike had been the senior teacher in charge of examinations and Inset arrangements. He had been in the school for a number of years and was in his early 30s. He was a bright, well-informed young man, who enjoyed a challenge; he had plenty of ideas, especially about developing Inset. He had received little encouragement from Mr Smythe, who was determined that the growth of Inset should not lead to the introduction of a staff development policy, which he equated with appraisal, an initiative to which he was hostile. Mike tended to be the member of the

SMT who would be given responsibility for introducing those new initiatives the head could not avoid altogether. Mr Smythe was reluctant to give Mike a free hand. Mike's facility for thinking on his feet and his enthusiasm for his ideas and schemes could sometimes make other staff feel threatened. He was also rather shy, and appeared more aloof than he really was. He had come to feel both frustrated and taken for granted. He felt the outsider on the management team, yet his position as a senior teacher isolated him from the majority of the staff. At the time James Smythe's retirement was announced, Mike was considering applying for posts elsewhere. When Mrs Gatlin was appointed, Mike thought that he would wait a bit longer and see which way the wind blew.

Sarah Holly

Sarah had been in post as senior teacher in charge of the sixth form for two years, and was in her mid-30s. She enjoyed her status and ruled the sixth form with a firm hand. She was confident and efficient, regarding herself as fully on top of a difficult job, but she worked within closely defined boundaries, interpreting her responsibilities narrowly. She rarely took a whole school perspective, but viewed initiatives from the perspective of the sixth form or her own position. She was willing to stay after school ended, but she was never available before the register bell in the morning and regarded herself as off duty during breaks. This created problems for people who needed to consult her. Pupils rarely saw Sarah, and did not often consult her about their problems because they felt that she was insensitive and her manner curt and unsympathetic. They worried about the university references that she wrote for them, fearing that she would not do them justice – but here they did her an injustice. When faced with a problem, she worked very hard to help the pupil, badgering the relevant authority until something was done. When faced with a real difficulty, she still tended to consult Mike Wade, as he had been head of sixth form before her and had guided her through her first year in post. People said that Mike had all Sarah's ideas for her. She was not a fast worker, but once she was on task she was extremely thorough and would persevere until she felt satisfied with the result. Her determination to get her own way and total conviction that she was in the right in any argument were sometimes expressed in an aggressive manner, which could make her an unpleasant person to cross, but as long as you played to her rules, she was a friendly and helpful colleague.

Lawrence Payne

Laurie had been appointed to the senior management team some three years previously as senior teacher to introduce computerization and manage some of the innovations now demanded of the team. He was highly qualified and it was said that he had interviewed well. Many staff were hopeful that he would provide the element of dynamism lacking in the SMT. However, once he arrived, he appeared ponderous and gave the impression that he found life and its attendant tasks a burden. He was preoccupied with his mathematics teaching, which seemed to leave him little time for his senior management responsibilities. He was a slow worker, never on top of things and found it difficult to meet deadlines. At senior management meetings he offered no constructive ideas or suggestions. He looked to Mr Smythe to tell him what policy he ought to adopt in any situation, which suited the head but greatly disappointed a lot of staff who had hoped for more from this appointment. After a few months they wrote Laurie off as a nice conscientious chap, but hardly a whizz-kid. Laurie's general attitude seemed to imply criticism of Bestwick Park's practices, and suggest resentment of the weight of the tasks that he was being asked to undertake. After three years Laurie had stopped talking about his previous school, and had integrated well into the staff, who liked him but laughed gently at his ways. Bestwick Park data were slowly getting on to the computer, but it was clear that, although a loyal subordinate, he lacked all leadership qualities.

This SMT had served James Smythe's purposes well. It was sound, reasonably effective and loyal, and he would not have wanted a more innovative team. For Brenda Gatlin, who wanted senior managers who could give leadership to the school in a period of change and innovation, this team presented a problem. She could not, however, dispense with it and start afresh with people of her own choosing, and she had to face the fact that the majority of the team could be with her for some years to come. She therefore needed to make the existing team perform as effectively as possible, so with the help of her mentor head she analysed the strengths and weaknesses of the individuals in order to see how far they complemented one another and work out how to make the best use of the talent available.

Analysing the team

In Yvonne Perkins, Mrs Gatlin had a deputy who was an experienced and capable administrator, liked and respected by the staff. Her ability to construct effective procedures and desire that things should work well were assets for the team. Unlike Mr Smythe, Brenda Gatlin expected to consult her deputies regularly. Yvonne was well informed about what was going on in the school; she knew what would work, how to make it work and what would be popular or unpopular with staff, and her advice to staff was always sensible. Using Yvonne as a sounding board could have the knock-on effect of raising her awareness of current issues, giving her a better understanding of why changes were being made and making her more sympathetic to the changes themselves. Brenda Gatlin was likely to be out of school much more frequently than Mr Smythe had been, both because her perception of her role was very different from his and because the number of headteachers' meetings had itself increased. Mrs Perkins was well fitted to deputize for the head on these occasions, and enhancing her role in this way could improve her job satisfaction. Mrs Gatlin could also give some thought to how she could build on Yvonne's counselling work with staff.

Fred Brown constituted a major problem for the new head, because he was totally hostile to everything that she stood for and was not developable. It was a short-term problem, however, because in two or three years he would retire. When Brenda began to analyse the problem of Fred, she realized that there were in fact two interrelated issues: Fred's position in the team and the pastoral system.

A number of options were open to her:

❑ redefine Fred's role – put someone else in charge of the pastoral system and find Fred other duties;
❑ force Fred to change the system;
❑ pressurize Fred into taking early retirement (forcing him to change the system could have this effect);
❑ sit it out.

Sensibly, she discussed all the options and likely outcomes with her mentor head.

Taking Fred off the pastoral system could allow her to make the changes she wanted, but humiliate Fred and increase his personal hostility to her. She might need to use this option if changing the pastoral system was her most urgent priority. Finding Fred other duties would itself constitute a problem, and funding such a change could be expensive.

Forcing Fred to introduce changes he detested and did not understand was unlikely to work. Even if he did not deliberately sabotage things, he lacked the necessary skills to be a successful manager of change. Pressurizing Fred into early retirement would require both toughness and perseverance. It would entail making constant demands upon him so that he would feel so threatened by and uncomfortable in the situation that he would choose to go. There was no certainty that this strategy would work and it could have adverse effects, because treating Fred harshly would win him sympathy from other staff and could affect their attitude to Brenda. Others might decide that they did not wish to work for this kind of headteacher.

Sitting it out seemed initially the weakest solution, and would be if it meant that she ignored the problem or pretended it was not there. She would certainly have to discuss the situation with Fred, because the timing of his departure would be crucial to her development planning. Her terms should be that she would not interfere with him provided that he went sooner rather than later. It would take some skill in negotiation, as Fred would probably interpret it as weakness, especially because he was dealing with a woman headteacher. This option would only be viable if she put reforming the pastoral system into Year 3 of her five-year development plan and published it so that the staff knew changes were in the pipeline.

The real issue is thus how long she can afford to wait.

Michael Wade is potentially an extremely valuable member of the team and is certainly the most talented. He is a good teacher, well versed in current educational theory and capable of carrying through the development work that Mrs Gatlin believes is essential for the school if it is to hold its own against competition. Undervalued by Mr Smythe, Mike is considering leaving and clearly wants and deserves promotion. If she is to keep Mike, Brenda must address this situation, and should have a job appraisal review with him. She has a third deputyship in her gift, and although she may not be able to afford three deputies in the long term, it could ease the situation until Fred retires. Promoting Mike would give him the status to lead the developments she wants, and could benefit them both. She may need to support him through some management training, especially in interpersonal skills, and to help him overcome his shyness. She may also need to help him cope with the inevitable staff jealousies arising from internal promotion.

What do you do about a dud appointment? The good interviewee is not always the best choice when it comes to doing the job. Lawrence Payne constitutes a real problem for Brenda. He is slow and has no ideas to offer, but is a conscientious and methodical worker who will earnestly undertake anything he is given. He also has computer skills, which the team lacked before his appointment. Now Brenda must get value for money from him. There is no point putting him in charge of development work, which needs leadership skills he cannot offer; she has to concentrate on using and developing his strengths. Completing computerization is clearly the first task, as the school is backward in this respect. It could be a sensible move to have Laurie work closely with Yvonne Perkins. It would give him training in working on options, timetabling and daily administration, and give her a much-needed back-up in a colleague with computer skills. Yvonne is a creative administrator, so she could set the parameters, while he could create and run the programs and do a lot of the routine work for her, which would free her up to take on other tasks as they arose. One of the advantages of this strategy is that Yvonne is extremely efficient. She would set the deadlines and expect Laurie to meet them. She is a good manager of people, and Laurie is less likely to become resentful of the pressure to increase his productivity working with her than he would be working with any of the other members of the SMT. He could also contribute to financial planning, working the budget program for Brenda and managing the bursar, who implements the financial decisions. Adopting this strategy could remove a time-consuming task from Brenda's workload. Laurie is ripe for a job appraisal review delivered in the context of the changing demands of school management. The issues of the volume of work tackled and time management would have to be addressed and would need sensitive handling, but she could offer him a time management course, and the changes to his job could be put to him as a way of raising his status.

Sarah Holly would have been surprised to learn that Brenda considered Sarah to be her most difficult problem. Sarah's inflexibility and her narrow approach, combined with her outbursts of aggressive behaviour when things did not go as she wished, did not accord at all with Mrs Gatlin's own preferred management style, and she foresaw clashes ahead. Brenda wanted a head of sixth form who could take a whole school view when necessary and not think only about the interests of her own section. She also disapproved of a member of the SMT defining her responsibilities so narrowly and not being available to deal with her pastoral responsibilities when pupils needed her. Sarah would have to learn who was boss, and that Mrs Gatlin would be setting the terms of reference.

What also worried the head was that major changes had to be made to the sixth form curriculum shortly. Mrs Gatlin suspected that Sarah would not be able to provide the kind of creative leadership that the development programme would need. Training had raised Sarah's awareness of the issues, but it was likely that the real planning would have to be done by a team that included Mike and some of the most promising sixth form tutors. If Mike was to sustain the brunt of the work, there was all the more reason to give him the status to put Sarah down when she became difficult. If the preliminary planning was done by a task group led by Mike, then Sarah should be able to cope, because her 'completer-finisher' skills should enable her to flesh out the proposals and implement them.

We have considered how Brenda Gatlin could develop the individuals in her team. The next step is to think about how she could weld her team together. At Bestwick Park, the team know one another better than they know the new headteacher, so Mrs Gatlin needs to think of strategies to bind the team to her.

Some ideas for welding the team

Review how regularly and in what ways the team meets

A briefing or information-sharing session every morning before school could be very useful. Superficially it keeps the team members informed of what is going on in the school and helps them understand how other members of the team spend their time, but its real value is that it creates a short working session for the head with her team every day. If this isn't possible, she should think about what ways she can devise to bring the team together on a regular basis.

Make the meetings more participative

Under Mr Smythe, senior management meetings had almost been briefing sessions or monologues by the head. Mrs Gatlin could use the agenda to ensure that all members contribute, either through a review of the week, or by introducing items for which they are responsible. More on senior management meetings can be found in Chapter 11.

Involve the SMT in decision making

Mrs Gatlin is planning to share more of the planning and policy making with the team. This could help her weld them together as she shares her ideas and plans with them, asks them for their ideas and involves them in the decision making.

Have regular working sessions with individuals

Mrs Gatlin can do this either through dedicated time each week or by working on a particular task. This regular contact will help the new head get to know the team members and begin to build up a relationship with each of them. It is important, however, to beware of developing a closer relationship with some members of the team than others as this leads to jealousies or friction, so a strategy could be to pair the team for some tasks so that they work with one another as well as with the head.

Avoid public disagreements

If Mrs Gatlin wants to build loyalty, she must beware of criticizing any members of the SMT in front of the others or, even worse, behind their backs to other members of the team. Public disagreements could affect both the morale and the image of the SMT and disaffected team members could retaliate by airing their disagreements with the head – she would not want this situation to develop.

Confront the problems

Working round a weak, disaffected or difficult member of the team can create its own problems. If, for example, Sarah Holly persists in taking a sectional view, and becomes aggressive or unco-operative if things don't go the way that she wants them to, Mrs Gatlin is going to have to deal with her and demonstrate to the team who is boss, otherwise Sarah will impose her views on the team and prevent progress.

Avoid criticism of the previous regime

If the new head is too critical of her predecessor's methods and practices, she will find it harder to win the team's loyalty. These people were the old head's team and criticisms of the previous regime will implicitly be criticizing his team, who implemented his policies. She has the freedom to change things, but it is wise to talk in terms of the needs of the future rather than the deficiencies of the past.

Review the accommodation

Mrs Gatlin would be well advised to have a look at whereabouts in the school the various members of the team are located and think about what effect this has on how they function as a team. Deputies are often in charge of particular buildings, which helps maintain discipline and protect property, but unless regular meetings are built into the week, physical separation of this kind can lead to isolation of a member of the team, or to difficulties in creating an effective team.

Programme a residential weekend for the SMT

A weekend away together could be beneficial for the SMT, speeding up the process of team building through enabling the team members to spend a lot of time together working on a task. Mrs Gatlin will, however, need to think carefully about when this would be of most use to her. If it is too soon, it may not achieve much; indeed it might heighten the storming stage if too much time together brings latent conflict out into the open, so it would probably be most useful when the team have begun to accept that the new regime means different working methods or when there is a major task to tackle. An obvious example would be a weekend away to write the school development plan for the next five years.

Make the time to take an interest in the team

Taking an interest in the team means more than just providing them with some professional development. It means remembering their birthdays and asking about their health or families. Listening to and remembering what they tell you indicates whether your interest is genuine or not. Occasional social events such as inviting the team to dinner at your house or a local restaurant once a term can also pay dividends.

Make the team feel valued

Providing encouragement and tactful support when a team member experiences difficulties in leading changes that test his or her management skills to the limit, giving some praise for a job carried out well and remembering to say thank you for a task that has involved someone in a lot of work will help a new head build up loyalty. Above everything else, if you want to create an effective management team, it is essential to make the individual members and the team as a whole feel valued. Remember praise must be specific and sincere if it is to work.

HOW DO YOU KNOW WHEN YOU HAVE ARRIVED?

The following checklist of characteristics of a good team is reproduced from *Middle Management in Schools: A survival guide* (Kemp and Nathan, 1989), because it applies as much to a school's senior management team as to the department or task groups for which it was originally devised.

An effective team

Shares clear objectives and agreed goals

❑ It agrees on what the team is trying to do and its priorities for action.
❑ It agrees on what differences are tolerable within the team.
❑ It clarifies the roles of team members.
❑ It discusses values and reaches a general consensus on the underlying philosophy of the team.

Has clear procedures

❑ for holding meetings;
❑ for making decisions;
❑ for delegating responsibility.

Reviews its procedures regularly

❑ It reassesses its objectives.
❑ It evaluates the processes that the team is using.
❑ It does not spend too much time dissecting the past.

Has leadership appropriate to its membership

❑ The leader is visible and accessible.
❑ The leader utilizes the strengths of all the team members.
❑ The leader sets the mission – models the philosophy of the team.

Has open lines of communication

❑ Team members talk to one another about issues and not just to the team leader.
❑ It recognizes each person's contribution.
❑ It gives positive and negative feedback.
❑ People are open-minded to other people's arguments.
❑ It welcomes ideas and advice from outside.
❑ Members are skilled in sending and receiving messages in face-to-face communication.

Has a climate of support and trust

❑ People give and ask for support.
❑ Team members spend enough time together to function effectively.
❑ Team members' strengths are identified and built on.
❑ There is respect for other people's views.
❑ The team relates positively to other teams and groups.

Recognizes that conflict is inevitable and can be constructive

❑ Issues are dealt with immediately and openly.
❑ Members are assertive but not aggressive.
❑ Feelings are recognized and dealt with.
❑ Members are encouraged to contribute ideas.
❑ Conflicting viewpoints are seen as normal and dealt with constructively.

Is concerned with the personal and career development of its members

❑ Regular reviews are carried out with each team member.
❑ The leader looks for opportunities to develop each member.
❑ Members look for opportunities to develop one another.
❑ Members look for opportunities to develop their team leader.

If you want a shorter list, then there are two tests that you could apply: 1) the volume and quantity of work being done by the team, indicating how well it is functioning; and 2) how the team is perceived by the staff – the cherry on top of the cake attracts attention and there is always some mole who will be prepared to give you a progress report. It is safer to take soundings from more than one source.

CASE STUDY 2.3 FOR ACTION

INTEGRATING A NEW DEPUTY INTO THE TEAM

Making the choice

When Fred Brown retired, Brenda Gatlin, the headteacher at Bestwick Park High School, appointed a new deputy to the SMT. She wanted someone who would give strong leadership to the pastoral team and who was capable of giving the school's pastoral system a complete overhaul. She also wanted to strengthen her own management team. She felt that she had several plodders who needed strategies worked out for them, and that this was occupying too much time. Now that she had the opportunity to make an appointment of her own, she wanted a high flier who would add both drive and intellectual rigour to the team. Thus ability and potential were more important to her in making her selection than pastoral experience.

From a good field of applicants, the selection committee chose Derek Farr, a young man in his mid-30s, who had been head of science in his previous school. His subject qualifications were good – he had a doctorate in physics from a leading university. His previous headteacher spoke highly of his innovative work as head of science, and Mrs Gatlin liked his enthusiasm, the way he talked about the projects he had run for his pupils and his desire to widen his experience through managing a school's system of pastoral care. She did not expect him to be an expert in pastoral matters, but she hoped she had found a fast learner and creative thinker who would have little difficulty in transferring his skills to a different sphere of management and a different school.

How to manage the induction

Over the past two years Brenda had spent a lot of time building her management team, and she appreciated that introducing a new member to an established team should have its difficulties. She was particularly concerned that the team members should not regard the new deputy as having a special relationship with her, as this could affect team spirit, yet she needed to provide induction for Derek, who would clearly need some support through his first couple of terms.

Providing a mentor

Her solution was to make Mike Wade, who had recently been promoted to the vacant third deputyship, Derek's mentor. This would provide Derek with the guidance he was likely to need without making him too dependent upon the head. Mike's general responsibility was to oversee staff and curriculum development in the school, and this could prove helpful for Derek who was to be the leader of a major development. Mike was also near in age to Derek, and his own recent promotion was likely to make him sympathetic to Derek if difficulties occurred, and there could be advantages for Mike in giving him someone of ability to work with, as hitherto Mike had done almost all the creative planning for the management team. The head realized, however, that this move could create division in the team if, through working so closely together, Derek and Mike became isolated from the others. She would have to make sure that there was enough group activity or opportunity for change of partners to prevent this from happening, and she made it clear to the existing team what Mike's role was to be and that it fitted in with his responsibility for the induction of the other senior staff that she appointed.

The new deputy experiences difficulties

What she hadn't anticipated was that Derek would find the change of school and role very difficult to manage. He seemed much more hesitant than she had expected and gave her and others the impression that he was out of his depth. 'He looks as if he wants to retreat into a corner and have a quiet weep', the head said to Mike during a review of his work with Derek. 'He was much more assertive at interview. Could I have mistaken his character and ability so completely?'

Analysing the problem

Mike, who was taking the brunt of supporting Derek and realizing that a great deal of support was needed, reflected on the problem. Derek was clearly finding the change of school and all the new demands very difficult to manage. Why was that? What could be done about it? Mike decided that a lot of it was probably a confidence problem. As head of science, Derek had been an expert in his field, totally on top of the technical aspect of his job. Here in a new school, where he had to prove himself, he was the least knowledgeable and experienced member of the pastoral team. At the same time he had been presented with a highly complex and extremely difficult management problem. He had to carry out a complete overhaul and restructuring of the pastoral system with a team who were not yet welded together and had not accepted him as a leader. The size and complexity of the problem was clearly bothering the new deputy. Talking to Derek made it clear to Mike, who liked Derek, that the new deputy was simply not clear where to start or what his priorities should be and was anxious not to make mistakes that could be damaging for him. Mrs Gatlin, who had waited patiently for Fred Brown, was impatient for Derek to deliver results. He did not want to disappoint her but, because he did not know her very well, he was not sure what she wanted and her obvious irritation when he appeared hesitant was not helping. She was beginning to feel that in Derek she had another senior manager who wanted to be told what to do, and as this was the last thing she wanted, so she kept telling him it was up to him. It was therefore becoming increasingly difficult for him to discuss things with her at all.

Managing upwards – dealing with the headteacher

Mike decided to tackle Brenda first, because he felt that the head's failure to establish a good working relationship with her new deputy was a major part of the problem.

'I think unintentionally you have created part of the problem yourself', he said to Brenda as tactfully as one can tell the headteacher that she is partly to blame. 'Your desire to give him the space to be creative was good in itself, and something that later on he is likely to come to value, but perhaps it was too soon. He does not know you or the school well enough to be sure what is likely to be acceptable and he does need to know what is wanted, particularly when the proposed changes are extremely sensitive and will affect everyone in the school. He is entitled to some guidance, and it is hardly his fault that some of the others lean on you too much. Making me his mentor has a lot of advantages, and I am enjoying it. I like Derek very much and think he has a lot of potential, but you need to build up a relationship with him yourself. I also think he would appreciate the opportunity to acquire some of the technical expertise that he is so conscious he lacks. Can't we find him a principles of pastoral care course?'

Managing sideways – reassuring Derek

Mike took a different approach with Derek, for whom he had a lot of sympathy.

'All this worrying is getting you nowhere. What you need to do is to use some basic management techniques to help you stand back from the problem and get it into perspective. Doing an analysis of the issues will help you distinguish the wood from the trees and decide what your priorities are. No one really expects you to solve it all in one fell swoop. What you have to do is decide what the main issues are and in what order you want to tackle them; then the problem won't look anything like so bad. Working on it together will help, and creating a programme will itself show people that you have the matter in hand. They would prefer a realistic staged approach to change than an ill-thought-out rush.'

After a few working sessions, it became obvious that working together and using the problem-solving approach had paid off. Derek tackled the pastoral system from first principles, working back from desired outcomes to possible routes to achieve them and produced a well-drafted paper suggesting a possible new structure together with a programme for implementation. This very much pleased the head, who had taken on board a lot of the criticism that Mike had levelled at her about her approach and now realized that she had been unrealistic in her expectations of Derek. She now understood that there had to be a learning period before he became a fully integrated member of the team and an effective senior manager. Derek thus found her more amenable, willing to help him and generally easier to talk to, and his own growing confidence in turn helped him in giving leadership to the year heads and to begin to enjoy the challenge of getting fractious and sometimes unruly horses to water. The head thought the more of Mike for being straight with her, and wanted to reassure him that he had not offended her, so she sent for him and thanked him for his advice and for the time he had spent in helping Derek.

'Now I know that you can manage upwards and sideways as well as leading the more conventional teams', she said.

For action

❏ What issues in terms of team management and development are raised by this case study?

❑ What had gone wrong?
❑ What techniques had Mike applied in dealing with the problem?
❑ What advice would you give the headteacher and on what grounds?

Devise an induction programme for a new deputy joining an established team.

3

DELEGATION

CASE STUDY 3.1 FOR REFLECTION/ACTION

Mary had always been a conscientious deputy, who willingly undertook any task given to her by the headteacher, and generally handled it effectively. Her relationships with staff had always been good: she treated them fairly and they respected her competence. Now she was often irritable. Work seemed to be taking her longer, and she complained about deadlines. Mistakes began to occur quite frequently in the arrangements she made for daily cover and room changes, and she was very short with anyone who pointed out the errors.

This had been going on for some months, when George, the headteacher, observed a particularly acrimonious incident. Electricians were in school, necessitating some room changes. Two members of staff were mistakenly allocated the same room, but when they went to report the mix-up, they were harangued by Mary for interrupting her. When she failed to remedy the situation, the two staff members began to shout at each other. George decided it was time to act, but when he tried to introduce the subject, he found it difficult; Mary became very tense and seemed reluctant to admit that there was a problem. George probed as gently as he could, asking if it was the menopause causing the trouble or whether there were some home difficulties that he did not know about. Tact had never been his strong point, and it was the reference to the menopause that finally pierced Mary's front that nothing was wrong. She was utterly incensed.

'It's just like a man to hit on the menopause as the reason why things are going wrong. If you really want to know what's wrong, I'll tell you. It's not my fault. Just because I was a willing and efficient worker, you loaded me with every new job that arrives on your desk. You don't think about what

I'm doing already, or who might be appropriate to do the job. I wouldn't dream of refusing to do anything you have asked me. It isn't that the jobs are so difficult in themselves. With the time to think them through, I could do each of them well, but I just don't have the time these days to concentrate on running the school as I used to do. It is not surprising that I make a few mistakes. It's more surprising that I get the work done at all.'

For action

- ❏ What issues are raised by the case study?
- ❏ What mistakes had George made in dealing with his deputy?
- ❏ What hadn't he understood about delegation?
- ❏ Why might he benefit from Equal Opportunities Inset?
- ❏ What advice would you give George and on what grounds?

Mary's problem is that she has been given more work than she can cope with effectively, and this is having an adverse effect upon her performance and her relationship with other staff. It often occurs in schools that new tasks are simply added on to a deputy's workload as an additional responsibility, rather than that the job description is reviewed and the tasks distributed fairly. George's method of delegation is to offload anything as it arrives on to his reliable and hitherto uncomplaining deputy. What is needed here is that some of Mary's current functions should be delegated to other people.

WHAT IS DELEGATION?

The *Concise Oxford Dictionary* defines delegation as 'entrusting authority to a deputy', a definition with which Mary would have totally agreed. For you as a head or a school manager, in practice it means handing over tasks for which you carry ultimate responsibility to another teacher with that teacher's agreement.

The main reason for delegation is that the job of running a school is too big for any one person to manage alone. However many hours you work, you still cannot do it all yourself. There are too many tasks and too many people to deal with, so the workload has to be shared out. For this reason, as schools expanded in size and tasks multiplied and became more complex and diverse, a senior management structure evolved, so that there is a group of experienced staff who can deal with all the work involved in managing and organizing the school. There are other reasons, however, why some tasks and responsibilities should be delegated:

- ☑ It prevents job overload and leaves managers with more time for thinking, planning and evaluation.
- ❏ It makes it more likely that all the jobs are done effectively.
- ❏ It promotes initiative and creativity by giving someone the opportunity to undertake a new and demanding task.
- ❏ It extends the skills and experience of those who take part and contributes to professional development.
- ❏ It provides training opportunities.
- ☑ It motivates by providing opportunity and challenge.
- ❏ It gives people confidence because they have had to demonstrate their capability to undertake a difficult task, and helps provide a sense of personal worth.
- ☑ It encourages corporate loyalty by promoting a sense of common purpose.

Although delegation is central to the successful management of a school, surveys such as John Sutton's (1985), carried out for the Secondary Heads' Association, indicate that many heads are reluctant to delegate or do it badly.

CASE STUDY 3.2 FOR ACTION

An example of the problem that I have with the new head occurred only last week. She was out of school for a couple of days. On the second day a problem arose. I sorted it out and announced the arrangements to the staff. The head returned the following morning. Her first reaction, publicly in the staffroom, was 'You can't possibly do that! It will have to be changed.' It's always the same. If I deal with an incident, she can't bear not to interfere and she has to show everyone that she's the head and I am only the deputy.

Complaint overheard at a deputy heads' conference

For action/discussion

- ❏ What issues are raised by this case study?
- ❏ What does it indicate about the head's attitude to delegation?
- ❏ What advice would you give this new headteacher and why?

REASONS WHY MANAGERS ARE RELUCTANT TO DELEGATE

❏ Managers tend to think that they are indispensable and they often want to hold on to all sources of power.
❏ Upbringing – we are educated into thinking that we must do everything ourselves.
❏ Guilt – people feel guilty about delegating or that they have failed in some way if they delegate any of their responsibilities.
❏ Fear of taking risks – there may be a lack of confidence in our subordinates or the SMT.
❏ New headteachers particularly need time to settle in and to get to know and trust the SMT.

'We usually tend to overrate rather than underrate our importance and to conclude that far too many things can only be done by ourselves. Even the very effective executives still do a great many unnecessary, unproductive things' (Drucker, 1970).

The problem with delegation seems to be largely one of attitude, but it has to be understood that the prior condition for effective delegation is a positive attitude. This means starting from the idea that delegation is a good thing in itself and will benefit you, the delegatee and the school. You also have to want to delegate and be prepared to take the risks involved.

What is implied in delegation?

Delegation requires courage, judgement and faith in others, because we still remain accountable for what they do. In these circumstances, it is not always easy to give people the right to be wrong. However it is worth remembering that we shall be judged not so much on what we do, but what we inspire others to do. Our aim ought to be dispensability, not indispensability and we should not fear it.

White, 1983

Genuine delegation means:

❏ allocating responsible as well as routine tasks;
❏ possibly surrendering things that you enjoy yourself;
❏ accepting that a job will be done differently from how you would do it yourself;
❏ trusting others to do what you are ultimately responsible for;

❑ willingness to accept failure as well as success;
❑ careful planning.

HOW SHOULD YOU DECIDE WHAT TO DELEGATE?

Deciding what to delegate could involve you in some considerable heart-searching. In the end you will have to resolve two issues: the kind of tasks colleagues should undertake in order to widen their experience and promote their professional development, and whether there are categories of tasks that are suitable or totally unsuitable for delegation.

You could start by reviewing what you do – your responsibilities, activities and functions. You may want to refer to your job description or you could simply list your activities over a period of time so that you can get an indication of how you spend your time. Then divide the activities into categories; some examples are: routine (eg planning and organizing regular events such as parents' meetings), supervisory jobs, liaison outside the organization, strategic decision making. There are obviously many others.

Classifying your tasks in this way will help you to offer your colleagues a range of different kinds of activity, which is the fairest way to approach delegation. Delegation entails increasing your subordinates' workload and, to retain their good will, you must not simply unload a lot of your more time-consuming and irritating jobs. Delegating a whole lot of clerical or administrative tasks may meet one of your objectives, ie it will provide you with more time to think and do other aspects of your job more effectively, but it will not help the development of your team, so it is important to provide them with some elements of choice.

You might also want to analyse where regular tasks come in the annual cycle, so that, for example, you don't load one person with several heavy tasks that all need a lot of work at the same time.

CASE STUDY 3.3 FOR ACTION

Using the job description given in Chapter 1, try applying these tests to see which of your responsibilities are the most suitable for delegation:

❑ Which of the tasks on my list could be done by someone else as well if not better?
❑ Would those tasks provide a good opportunity for the professional development of a colleague?

❑ Which tasks should be managed by the senior management team acting as a team?

❑ Which tasks should remain my personal responsibility and not be delegated at all?

If you then decide not to delegate a task, it might be helpful to apply two further tests:

❑ Are you retaining a particular task merely because you enjoy it?

❑ Is it appropriate in this particular school to delegate this task?

CASE STUDY 3.4 FOR ACTION

Jenny, newly in post as a deputy head, found the customs and practices of her new school differed sharply from those of her last school. In her previous post as a senior teacher and head of sixth form, she had regularly dealt with parents who wanted a consultation about the progress or welfare of their child. Only the most serious problems had been reserved for the headteacher to deal with, and even then Jenny had been very closely involved and was present whenever parents of her year group came in to see the head. She had also organized and taken the leading role in interviewing prospective entrants to the sixth form and their parents. Now, in the more senior post of deputy head, she found herself excluded from seeing parents and, as the head's practice of interviewing every prospective student personally meant that Jenny barely saw him for three weeks (with a knock-on effect on his communications with her and the staff as a whole), she felt the need to protest. 'Surely interviewing prospective sixth formers is a task that can be shared among the members of the senior management team', she suggested. 'Not here', said the head. 'In this school the parents expect to see the head. Interviewing prospective sixth formers together with their parents is a task that I simply cannot share or delegate. It is a vital part of my public relations function. If I stopped doing it, we should lose so much good will.'

For action/discussion

❑ How valid do you think the head's case is that to delegate any part of this task would be inappropriate and counterproductive in this school?

- ❑ What might it indicate about this headteacher's attitude to delegation?
- ❑ How should the head deal with his new deputy who feels strongly that it is a waste of her experience and highly developed interpersonal skills if she is denied access to parents?
- ❑ What advice would you give this headteacher and why?

The case study highlights the point that in different institutions different areas of responsibility might be considered inappropriate for delegation and it raises the further question – are there some areas of responsibility that should never be delegated?

Recent writers on this subject stress the developmental view of delegation and the need to provide the delegate with freedom of action. If delegation means 'giving people the right to be wrong', then the delegates must be given tasks that allow them a full measure of responsibility and authority.

My advice on the thorny question of how much you can delegate is that you can delegate most senior management responsibilities successfully as long as you go about it the right way, but that there are three categories of task that it could be unwise to delegate:

1. vital jobs that only you can do;
2. tasks requiring confidentiality or particular sensitivity;
3. new or ill-defined tasks that may prove very difficult or that have a much higher than average failure risk.

CAN DELEGATION BE LEARNT?

A significant test of good management is the effectiveness of delegation.

Sutton, 1985

You may not be a natural delegator, but it is not difficult to improve your skills, as the following guidelines show.

Guidelines for effective delegation

❑ Negotiate about what is delegated, never impose it.

❏ Provide a variety of types of task or the opportunity to rotate tasks.

❏ Select the person best suited to carry out the task – you want him or her to succeed.

❏ Use delegation as an opportunity to widen someone's professional experience.

❏ Build on an existing enthusiasm or interest in a new development; delegation will get it off to a good start.

❏ Don't be selfish in your attitude to delegation – this means:
  – Don't unload your least favourite jobs.
  – Don't unload difficult jobs that you wish to avoid.
  – Do not simply relieve your own overload by transferring it to someone else. That person will either have a nervous breakdown or look for another job.

❏ Delegate as much as you can – be ruthless with yourself.

❏ Clearly define the job or task that you are delegating – this means working out a job description and ensuring that the person receiving the task knows what is expected of him or her.

❏ Make the terms of reference clear, ie how much responsibility, freedom of action, etc are you delegating? Clarifying the position could prevent ill feeling later.

❏ Provide any necessary resources and guidance. You cannot expect someone to know instinctively what he or she should do.

❏ Decide what the deadlines should be and make sure that too short a deadline does not make it impossible to complete the task.

❏ Make regular progress checks to provide opportunities for feedback and to maintain an appropriate level of control. Bear in mind that whereas regular appraisal will contribute to the success of the job (and is not inconsistent with delegation), frequent interference will contribute to its failure.

❏ Determine the objectives and targets together with the delegatee, and then allow the freedom to carry out the task. How the delegatee does it is up to him or her. Your concern is for results not for routes.

❏ Do not take decisions or make changes that undermine the delegatee's authority or position.

❏ Recognize success with public praise and provide sympathetic support for failure.

Effective delegation is about encouraging creativity – this means:

❏ welcoming new ideas, however apparently unworkable;

❏ not telling the delegatee how to do everything;

❏ discouraging unthinking imitation of the previous postholder, or of you;

❑   supporting new ideas with resources and training;
❑   matching responsibility to creativity, ie by increasing the level of responsibility and scope to create in line with the delegatee's professional growth.

What should you do in case of failure?

Providing the procedures for reporting and monitoring, and trying to ensure that the right person has been chosen for the job are your best safeguards, but even so trouble can arise. You want to give the delegatee freedom of action and to interfere as little as possible, but you don't want him or her to fail disastrously. Such a result would damage the delegatee personally and damage the school as well; it would also make future delegation more difficult. So what can you do when you pick up vibes that things are going wrong?

Your aim is to help the person as unobtrusively as possible. The first thing to do is to try to assess how serious the problem really is. If it isn't too serious, a warning in time could avert disaster. The regular progress meetings will probably provide you with your best route through which to tackle the issue, because this is your programmed opportunity to discuss the task with the delegatee, so if you handle it tactfully, it shouldn't seem like interference. You will have to assess whether the problem is occurring because of the difficulty or complexity of the task undertaken or because of the method adopted by the delegatee. Sometimes you will find that an input of additional resources or time allocation will rectify the situation and improve morale. Often talking through and confronting the problem will help to resolve it. The really difficult situations tend to centre on personality clashes, and here you will need all the sensitivity at your disposal to retrieve the situation. Only if there is utter disaster and no alternative do you resort to taking over publicly. In the end the final responsibility is yours. If the delegatee succeeds, he or she deserves and should receive the credit. If he or she fails, the blame and the ultimate responsibility are yours.

Delegation issues

CASE STUDY 3.5 FOR ACTION

Bob had been responsible for the timetable in the school for at least 10 years. A mathematician, he had always enjoyed the job, which built on his subject skills. He was careful to consult people about their needs, and was thorough and systematic in his approach. Hitherto he had coped ably with even the most unreasonable demands made by departments. Now the changes brought about by recent legislation and DfEE directives are putting his considerable skill as a timetabler to the test. He is also very reluctant to use the computer package suggested by the governors, one of whom is a director of the computer company concerned, which is prepared to supply the software free and to assist in training Bob or whomever the school nominates. Bob says that he has tried computer-aided timetabling in the past and found such systems too rigid, particularly in dealing with the large contingent of part-timers. Other staff, however, suspect that it is Bob who is too rigid. Some of the younger staff have expressed an interest in learning to timetable and have offered to help Bob with his increasingly difficult task, but he prefers to work alone. He says that having someone else there affects his concentration, but really he doubts others' ability to handle such complex tasks as curriculum analysis or the school timetable. When he was recently asked to run an Inset session on how the timetable was constructed, he refused, saying that he thought it was a complete waste of time. Now the head has said that Bob is failing in his role as a developer, and Bob, who has never seen himself as a developer, feels very hurt and aggrieved about this criticism.

For action

1. You are the headteacher. Bob has been your loyal deputy since you took up the post three years ago, supporting you during a difficult settling-in period when you faced hostility from a number of the staff, but he has always been very traditional in his view of management. How do you get him to review his approach to his task and to consider delegating some aspects of it? How do you persuade Bob of the advantages to the school of establishing a shadow structure or to undertake his role as a developer?
2. What issues arise from this case study? What advice would you give this headteacher in dealing with the situation and why?

CASE STUDY 3.6 FOR ACTION

'What was the point of the head giving me this major initiative to implement, if he isn't prepared to let me do the job?' Peter, the deputy head, was letting off steam in the pub after work one night with a close friend. 'I didn't ask for the job. He begged me to do it. He said that I was the only person he could trust to handle it because it was going to be difficult, but once I agreed and took on the job, it was as if he just couldn't bear to let it go. He calls me in, questions me closely about every action I have taken, and then rejects or reverses everything, including things that he insisted on having last time round. I don't know where I am from one moment to the next. He keeps insisting that he has the school's best interests at heart, and that he has to monitor things so closely because of the sensitivity of the issue. I think that he is actually scared of the implications of the change and terrified of provoking the unions. I think that he has panicked and got it all out of proportion, and for me he is a much bigger problem than the unions. I'm sure I've got enough good will to get a pilot scheme going, if only he would get off my back. Every time I call a meeting of the working party, I have to tell them that he's rejected everything again and that we are back to square one. We can't make even the smallest decision without reference to the head. It's an impossible position to be in. It makes me look utterly ridiculous. I'm not really in charge. I'm just some sort of stooge and they all know it.'

For action/discussion

❑ What is going wrong with this piece of delegation?
❑ What advice would you give Peter?
❑ What advice would you give the head and why?

CASE STUDY 3.7 FOR ACTION

The headteacher of Uptown High School has been giving a lot of thought to the roles and responsibilities of the senior management team. Some of the appointments are historical, and some very senior members of staff are receiving senior teacher allowances for leading a subject area. The budget will not allow this kind of luxury; moreover, the number of tasks to be undertaken has mushroomed with the flurry of DfEE directives that followed in the wake of recent legislation. She feels it is unfair to expect the middle managers to take on greatly increased responsibilities if the senior managers do not increase their load. She has therefore drafted a working paper putting forward a scheme in which the senior management team responsibilities would be restructured so that, although the deputies would still do considerably more than the senior teachers, each member of the team would take on responsibility for a strategic area. She presented this paper to the team at a senior management meeting and suggested that they consider her ideas, but that before they were discussed as a package, the members of the team should come to see her on an individual basis to discuss how it affected each of them. Her deputies liked the proposed changes, because for some time now each new task had been added to their already lengthy list of duties, and to them the new scheme gave a badly needed coherence. Her interview with one of the senior teachers, however, revealed a very different reaction to her proposal. 'No, dear', said the senior teacher, 'I read your proposals, but I really can't see my way to doing any of the things on your list. I have thought about it, but I just can't do any more. It takes me all my time to run the department. I'm sorry, but I can't help you.'

For action

Why do you think this senior teacher has refused the delegation, and what do you think the headteacher should do about it? Suggest some strategies that the headteacher could adopt.

4

MANAGING THE MISSION

One of the most important aspects of the senior management role is planning and policy making, sometimes described as 'promoting' or 'managing the mission'. It is an emotive image, suggesting that the headteacher is some kind of visionary dedicated to carrying out his or her educational mission. The concept of a headteacher as a missionary does have its own distinct charm, but after one has laughed a little, there is some mileage in following the idea through.

DEFINING WHAT IS MEANT BY 'MISSION'

If you are promoting the mission, you are trying to establish a corporate philosophy or system of shared values for the school. There are three stages:

1. You *create* the mission by fashioning a set of goals for the school, which are published as a mission statement – in practice, this often means the school's statement of aims.
2. You *move* the mission by winning commitment to it and motivating the staff to support its implementation.
3. You *manage* the mission by formulating the policies and deploying the resources that translate the aims and objectives into reality.

Mission statements are more commonly used in industry than in schools, and the case study that follows gives an example of a set of company values.

CASE STUDY 4.1 FOR REFLECTION

High Grade Stores expect all personnel to demonstrate their support to our two linked value statements:

❏ *Our values in relation to the customer*
- Treat service as a priority
- Listen
- Be open and honest
- Understand his or her needs
- Be supportive, caring, flexible, professional and dedicated
- Build good, positive relationships
- Value his or her satisfaction/happiness
- Be fundamentally in tune with the business

❏ *Our values in respect of one another*
- To own and commit to our values
- Use principles of teams, not tribes, and openness and trust to resolve conflicting priorities
- Combine responsibility with accountability
- Be supportive, caring, flexible and dedicated
- Be open and honest – listen
- Build good positive relationships
- Learn from mistakes – no one is perfect
- Lead rather than be driven by events
- Give one another feedback
- Identify with overall High Grade goals

It would not be difficult to translate this list of values into similar statements for a school, about our values in respect of the pupils, one another and the community.

You would probably find it more useful, however, to produce two complementary statements: a code of conduct for all personnel and a set of aims and objectives for the school.

The purpose of undertaking this kind of exercise is to formulate a set of agreed principles, which would underlie all future planning and policy making. It is a major exercise to undertake because it makes the school rethink its whole philosophy and ethos, and involves a lot of lengthy discussion. It tends to be a strategy employed by a new head within a year or so of taking up the post when he or she wants to refocus the school's thinking, so it could be an appropriate way for you to give the school a shake-up and remodel its philosophy.

CASE STUDY 4.2 FOR ACTION

Bestwick Park High School – Statement of Aims

The following aims are based on the belief that all pupils are of equal value and concern:

❑   to provide a secure and caring community where a multiplicity of needs and interests are catered for, and where pupils are encouraged to aim for excellence in everything they undertake;

❑   to ensure that all pupils reach their full potential;

❑   to develop each pupil's talents to the full so that he or she can lead a life of personal satisfaction and fulfilment;

❑   to promote self-discipline and an understanding of the needs of others within the community;

❑   to involve the parents and the community in its everyday life;

❑   to encourage the ability of pupils to make reasoned decisions and to participate in those concerning their school community and society in general;

❑   to assist pupils to understand themselves and relate to the world in which they live;

❑   to ensure that equal curricular opportunity is genuinely available to both boys and girls, and is positively encouraged;

❑   to eliminate sexism whenever it occurs and create an anti-sexist environment in which girls and boys have real equality of opportunity;

❑   to equip each pupil with the basic skills needed to function in the complex society of today;

❑   to ensure, since we are a multi-cultural, multi-racial society, that all children are educated towards an understanding of and commitment to that society;

❑   regularly to monitor and evaluate our curriculum, results and development.

Bestwick Park High School – Code of Conduct

The one rule for all of us in this school is that everyone will act with courtesy and consideration to others at all times. This means that:

1.   You should always try to understand other people's point of view.
2.   In class you should make it as easy as possible for everyone to learn and for the teacher to teach. (This means arriving on time with everything you need for that lesson, beginning and ending the lesson in a courteous and orderly way, listening carefully, following instructions, helping one another when appropriate and being quiet and sensible at all times.)
3.   You should move quietly and sensibly about the school. (This means never running, barging or shouting, but being ready to help by opening doors or standing back to let people pass and helping to carry things.) In crowded areas, please keep to the left.
4.   You should always speak politely to everyone (even if you feel bad-tempered!) and use a low voice. (Shouting is always discourteous.)
5.   You should keep silent whenever you are required so to be.
6.   You should keep the school clean and tidy so that it is a welcoming place of which we can all be proud. (This means putting all litter in bins, keeping walls and furniture clean and unmarked, and taking great care of displays, particularly of other people's work.)
7.   Out of school, walking locally or with a school group, you should always remember that the school's reputation depends on the way that you behave.

For action/discussion

Define this school's mission. What were the main principles underlying the Statement of Aims and the Code of Conduct?

STRATEGIC PLANNING

Your role in managing the mission will involve you in a great deal of strategic planning, and you may prefer to use this term (rather than referring to what you do as managing the mission) because it implies a far more down-to-earth approach. Another reason for using the term strategic planning is that it is a much wider concept, as it brings together and integrates all the various management aspects and activities.

What does strategic planning involve?

Strategic planning means wide-ranging and long-term planning, seeking to establish appropriate objectives and matching these objectives to the available resources in the most efficient and effective way.

Figure 4.1 *Strategic planning*

Why do we need strategic planning?

Prior to the Education Reform Act of 1988, maintained schools had to operate entirely within the policies of the LEA, which determined their numerical size and future and, apart from capitation, schools could make no decisions about the deployment of their resources. Now a maintained or foundation school (like any independent school) is fully responsible for its own destiny, and explicit overall direction is essential.

Strategic planning consists of four processes:

1. **analysis or audit** – when the school analyses its strengths and weaknesses, and assesses its own needs;
2. **planning and decision making** – generation and evaluation of options;
3. **implementation** – putting the plan into action;
4. **evaluation** – checking the success of implementation, and reviewing targets.

ANALYSIS

Your first task is to carry out a needs analysis as the basis of your planning. It asks two questions: firstly, 'Where are we now?', the answers to which should provide an audit of your current provision; and secondly, 'What do we expect to have to do next year/over three years, and can we cope?',

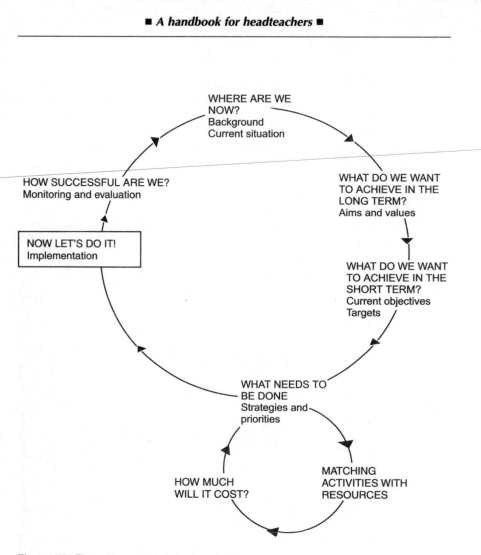

Figure 4.2 *The processes of strategic planning*

which assesses how far your current provision matches your expected requirements. You have to look both *backwards*, to check how far targets in last year's plan have been met, and *forwards*, to project likely pupil numbers and the demands that these will place on available resources. You will have to do this exercise quite precisely, otherwise you could be way out with costings and this could make nonsense of your plans. Your analysis of how things stand will help you assess what you can afford. Your development plan should be led by objectives not by the budget, but the budget cannot help but be influential.

You will also have to analyse some of the less tangible resources to assess the strengths of the school, which will also help you to deal with future demands. You will have to make some judgements about the school's value system and about how the school is valued by the 'consumer' – the local community, pupils and parents. Case Study 4.3 is an example of a questionnaire to parents to help a school assess whether parents thought the school was successful in what it was doing. Designing this type of questionnaire always presents problems, and you may wish to compare this example with the one currently issued by the Office for Standards in Education (Ofsted) to parents before an inspection. Monitoring the extent of the response could also produce an indicator that could affect your planning.

CASE STUDY 4.3 FOR REFLECTION

Bestwick Park High School – parents' viewpoint questionnaire

Section A – Yourself and your children

1. How many children do you have at the school? (Please include both past and current.)
2. Journey to school – time and method of transport.
3. Local papers – which do you read?

Section B – About the school

Please comment on the following:

1. receipt of information – newsletters, booklets, etc;
2. visits to the school;
3. information about your child/children's progress;
4. homework;
5. discipline in/out of lessons;
6. canteen facilities;
7. educational facilities – IT, sports, workshops, etc;
8. pastoral care;
9. welcome and reception.

Section C – Your feelings about the school

1. Possibility of greater involvement with the school.

---

2. Priority listing of the school's aims (list included).
3. Why did you choose this school?
4. Would you choose it again?
5. What changes would you most like to see?
6. What are the best things about this school?

Section D – Any other comments

Your analysis may also usefully include a trawl among pupils, teachers and parents for what they consider *special* about the school. This might sound a bit precious, but it can produce some interesting results. Remember, if you do produce a list of this type, it must stand up to Ofsted inspection.

CASE STUDY 4.4 FOR REFLECTION

What is special about our school?

❑ academic excellence and rigour;
❑ extension of the gifted;
❑ support of those in difficulty;
❑ development of the whole individual;
❑ caring and disciplined environment;
❑ an ethos that encourages creativity;
❑ highly qualified, professional and committed staff;
❑ an active Inset programme open to all members of the school community;
❑ a consultative management approach.

This list reflects the results of a selective school's trawl of pupils, staff and parents.

PLANNING AND DECISION MAKING

This stage starts with the generation and discussion of a lot of possible ideas and options as the senior management team seeks answers to the question 'What should go on the planning agenda for the long- and short-term future?' The needs analysis will have produced some of the ideas now under discussion, others will have come in as bids from departments or individuals, and others again will arise from externally imposed changes. This last group of demands may not fit in easily with the school's plans, especially if it means that the government has totally changed its mind about some important aspect of education, but nevertheless will have to be superimposed on the plans, whatever you might think or feel.

Not all the challenges facing the school can be responded to immediately, so the next task is to decide which issues should become priorities for the following year, and which developments should be phased in over a longer period.

How should you go about determining priorities?

Determining priorities means making a decision about which issues are most important and placing them in a time sequence. Applying this formula means that you have to focus your attention on what is absolutely essential for the survival, prosperity and effectiveness of the school. Criteria for evaluation could include:

❑ Suitability – how far does a possible course of action respond to what the analysis told you?
❑ Feasibility – how far can you resource what you propose? How many of the items can you afford to resource now, which could you afford next year and which are simply too expensive to envisage at all?
❑ Acceptability – how far will the development be acceptable and to whom?

The conflict between wanting to construct a long-term development plan for the school and the educational constraints that were turning planning into a yearly operation seems to have been resolved by schools constructing a three-year management and development plan, which is prioritized on a three-year cycle of implementation.

Consultation about embryo plans can be helpful, and there are various ways of doing this. There is no best method; rather it is a matter of what suits your school. However, if you want Ofsted or Investors in People approval you will need to show that you have consulted widely over the whole school community. In a maintained school, the area education officer or the link adviser may come into the school to discuss the plan with you, and there is also plenty of commercial consultancy available, but if you buy into this kind of package, you need to ensure that you receive value for money.

The school management plan is in reality the governors' management plan, but they cannot produce it in isolation. The different departments or cost centres will need to submit their requirements. Usually bids are made to the curriculum and finance committees, but in practice these committees are likely to be guided by the headteacher and SMT about which new initiatives to support, and probably the SMT will do some of the initial drafting. The governors' finance or curriculum committees will contribute to the plan by submitting ideas and recommendations or by imposing constraints, and it is wise to have some representatives from the governing body on the planning group.

An exemplar of how to organize departmental input into the development plan is included below as Case Study 4.5.

CASE STUDY 4.5 EXEMPLAR

Bestwick Park High School – planning guidelines

Each department:

- ❏ submit development plans;
- ❏ submit cost centre bid;
- ❏ submit professional development plans;
- ❏ all to be cross-referenced to whole school development plan;
- ❏ bid to be submitted by...;
- ❏ outcomes shared with all staff.

Working out the resource implications:

Departmental/cost centre planning sheet

Department/centre

Annual recurring costs

Teaching resources

KS3

KS4

KS5

New courses/qualifications

Consumables

Furniture

Equipment

Training

DRAFTING THE SCHOOL MANAGEMENT/WHOLE SCHOOL DEVELOPMENT PLAN

The school management plan – a corporate planning document – has become the school's main policy and planning vehicle. Once the contents have been agreed, the drafting of the document is usually delegated to one member of the group, either to you as the headteacher or to a deputy with expertise in drafting. You are likely to have to amend the draft a number of times through the consultation process, as your knowledge of budgetary constraints becomes clearer and following a full governors' meeting. Once it has been adopted, it becomes the school's main policy instrument for the time period that it covers and will be central to any review of your school carried out by the LEA or Ofsted.

CASE STUDY 4.6 FOR ACTION

EXEMPLAR OF A DEVELOPMENT PLAN

Bestwick Park High School – development plan

This plan follows on from the plan for last year. Most of our objectives for the previous year have been achieved. An interim evaluation is attached as Appendix 1. Fuller statements in support of our information form a series of appendices to be found at the end of our development plan.

Aims

Our statement of aims is attached as Appendix 2.

Survey of the current situation

This year the school has 890 pupils on roll, which is an increase of 36 pupils over last year's figure of 854. There are 50.35 full-time equivalent teaching staff, of whom 44 are full-time and 11 are part-time. The staff also includes 3 language assistants, who are shared with another local school, and 14 ancillary staff, of whom only 3 are full-time. Five members of the ancillary staff are funded by short-term contracts, and there is a site manager and an assistant caretaker. Full details of our staffing structure may be found in Appendix 3.

The curriculum continues to provide broad and balanced courses leading to nine GCSEs at 16+. There have been substantial changes to our menu of post-16 courses, and we have maintained a variety of non-examined courses – see Appendix 4.

The buildings have been redecorated externally, but the backlog of internal redecoration and minor repairs remains a concern.

Objectives

1. to raise standards in all areas;
2. to increase our knowledge base through various value-added schemes;
3. to work towards a greater variety of learning and teaching methods, and to enable differentiation;
4. to seek ways of maintaining and where possible increasing pupil numbers at both 11+ and 16+;
5. to develop a marketing strategy that will enable us to achieve objective 4.

Curriculum development

❏ to provide IT within the curriculum at Key Stages 3 and 4 – to bring us in line with current requirements;
❏ to introduce a new technology GCSE syllabus;
❏ to increase curriculum time for RE in accordance with DfEE requirements;
❏ to modify our curriculum arrangements for years 12 and 13 in the light of new requirements.

Other initiatives

❏ to expand our Initial Teacher Training scheme to take eight students per year;
❏ to introduce an industry mentoring system for year 10 and 11 pupils.

Resource requirements

Our curriculum forecasts show that we are largely able to service our National Curriculum requirements at both Key Stages 3 and 4, but there will be a need to strengthen staffing in technology and RE to meet increased demand. This may need to be done by retraining or by employing part-time staff on short-term contracts. The increased use of a wide range of technological facilities has placed heavy demands upon our ancillary staff, and we need to think how we can fund increased technician time.

At 16+, major resource implications followed the changes to the curriculum. Larger-sized classes for the A/A-S levels affect room requirements, and we shall need to increase our 16+ budget for books, equipment and consumables. Last year we decided to resource these changes over a two-year period and this is manageable within our existing budget plans.

Staffing

Staffing at Key Stages 3 and 4 is adequate for our needs. Changing to IT within the curriculum enables some saving and allows one member of the science department to return to teaching science full time. Staffing for the 16+ courses, however, will be strained by the new requirements and we shall have to think about where we can make savings elsewhere.

Materials and equipment

We shall continue to need to resource the National Curriculum as it enters a new period of its development.

The increasing use of IT across the curriculum has placed a heavy demand upon our existing equipment. In the short term we shall purchase three more machines from our IT equipment fund. In the longer term we shall have to replace existing equipment and renew the network, which is fully extended and showing signs of the heavy use it receives. Developing a strategy for the future funding of IT is a priority.

Buildings and site

The growth of the school and changes at 16+ have meant that we urgently need additional laboratory space. Plans have therefore been drawn up to convert a classroom in the new wing adjacent to the science area. The conversion should take place in July and August of this year.

To compensate the humanities faculty for the loss of a classroom, we have decided to partition the old dining hall, which is no longer used for school lunches now that we have the new canteen. This work will provide two additional classrooms for the use of the humanities faculty.

The building needs to be redecorated in a planned, systematic way, and the buildings subcommittee has been asked to prepare a five-year plan for redecoration. We have also begun a phased programme of furniture replacement, which will be monitored by the buildings subcommittee.

In the longer term it is clear that the life of the huts is limited, and plans are being prepared for six new permanent classrooms.

Training needs

❏ Inset will be needed to support the introduction of the new technology GCSE.
❏ Differentiation pilots will need development time.
❏ Considerable Inset will be needed to support our 16–19 developments.
❏ Supporting changes to the National Curriculum over time remains a major Inset need.
❏ Mentoring training for our subject mentors and professional tutor.
❏ NQT training.
❏ Management training for new/struggling middle managers – twilight course.
❏ Technical updates and sessions on new developments/government directives for the SMT.

Financial plan

The improvement in our pupil numbers has led to a slight increase in our estimated income for next year, but this is more than counterbalanced by the sharply increased cost of staffing after the recent pay award. Although we contemplate being able to cover our costs in the coming year, if we maintain staffing at its present level we have very little money to invest in badly needed resources.

Our priority, therefore, is to devise a strategy to raise substantial additional funding. In order to achieve this objective, we have set up a governors' subcommittee to undertake the task.

A standstill budget using last year's prices has been prepared and is attached as Appendix 4. We can only provide a provisional budget, as the revised LMS formula is not yet available to us.

Methods of evaluation

1. By outcome – evaluating whether our targets have been achieved.
2. By process – to assess how far along the road we have gone with each initiative.
3. We shall target one area each year for detailed evaluation. This year we intend to evaluate our Inset programme.

For action

What critical comments are the Ofsted inspectors likely to make about this development plan and for what reasons?

Bestwick Park High School's development plan is a rather discursive, chatty document, which would benefit from revision in line with the Audit Commissioners' pertinent suggestion that management plans should become less wordy and align more closely with budgetary plans in their format.

Rather than being listed as an appendix, the school's aims should be numbered and cross-referenced against initiatives, as Ofsted will want to know which initiative supports which school aim. Moreover, the school's aims are not the same thing as the aims of the development plan.

In Bestwick Park High School's plan there is some confusion between aims and objectives. 'To raise standards in all areas' is surely an aim rather than an objective, because objectives are the strategies that will help the school achieve its aims. 'To develop a strategy to fund IT' is a clear and urgent objective, yet is only to be found in the section on the financial plan.

This is a one-year development plan, but schools are now expected to provide a three-year plan, with projects prioritized according to urgency and importance and the time span of the initiatives clearly stated, eg 'Develop the library as a resource area – priority 1, start Year 1 (staged three-year programme), Aim 2, Objective 3'.

There is reference to a budget being attached, but the fact that it is a standstill budget is worrying, and there are no costings anywhere in the development plan, which is a major omission. Nor is there any sign of an action plan or plans to clarify how the initiatives are to be implemented.

CASE STUDY 4.7 FOR REFLECTION

Headings for a three-year management and
development plan for Bestwick Park High School

1. Numbered list of the school's aims (referenced throughout the plan).
2. Three main aims for the next stage of the school's development.
3. List of objectives (where do we want to be in three years' time?).
4. Our current position in relation to the objectives.
5. Action plan (to show how we plan to arrive at the objectives).
    Headings for this part of the plan could include: objectives; key personnel; resource implications; Inset implications; outcome.
6. Evaluation procedures.
7. Appendix: detailed financial plan/budget (the Audit Commission emphasized the need for the budget to be included as part of the development plan).
8. Appendix: chart of the staffing structure (see exemplar in Chapter 6).

IMPLEMENTING THE PLAN

Implementing the plan can be harder than constructing it and involves both moving and managing the mission. In order to carry out the management plan successfully, you have to get the details right and communicate them clearly, you have to delegate responsibilities and you have to win the commitment of all those involved. Implementation is a key management task and it is important to get each step right.

Ten steps to successful implementation

Allocate the responsibilities

The first step is to determine who should take responsibility for the various initiatives set out in the plan. Make sure that you allocate responsibility to the most suitable member of the team. You will not always get a choice, eg the introduction of a science initiative will be co-ordinated by the head of science, but you *can* choose which of your deputy heads is given oversight of the management of appraisal or differentiation.

Win commitment to the plan

If you do not win commitment to the plan, it has no chance of success. Winning commitment means that you have to 'sell' it to the staff, and convince them that it is the right way to move forward. It becomes easier to convince people that this is the case if they see that there are clear benefits for the school, its pupils and themselves, that the task is manageable and likely to succeed and that ownership is shared with the staff – a top-down programme will be difficult to implement. You are most likely to win commitment for particularly difficult activities if you have delegated the task to a manager with the ability to enthuse others.

Make the task achievable

To make the plan succeed you need to create a *framework* for effective implementation. In addition, breaking the task down into a series of stages or 'bite-sized chunks', each with its own target, makes the overall task less daunting and brings a taste of success each time a stage is accomplished.

Set realistic deadlines

'More haste less speed' is wise advice. If you carry through a major change too rapidly, without sufficient preparation and time to solve the problems that arise, you are likely to fail, so give yourself and your staff enough time to do the job properly. It is demoralizing for them to have to keep trying to meet deadlines that they know they can't achieve, and an even more demoralizing experience to keep having deadlines put back. Making the deadlines realistic helps you to succeed.

Establish clear lines of communication

Clear lines of communication are essential to effective implementation. Everyone needs to be aware of his or her own responsibilities and of reporting and demarcation lines.

Communicate the programme

It is important that the plan should not be a secret document known only to the SMT. Its contents need to be communicated to the staff as a whole and it is a sensible move to keep a copy of the school management plan available in the staffroom so that the staff can see the priorities for the year ahead and where their own activities fit into the scheme of things. Staff grumbles about not knowing what is going on in the school do not always go hand in hand with a real desire for information, and you may find that you will need to hold awareness-raising sessions to raise the profile of some major new initiatives.

Carry out regular progress checks

You design the programme, but then you have to rely on others to carry it out, so you need to know how well the various initiatives are doing, and this means carrying out regular checks on their progress. A term some-times used for this activity is 'taking stock'. One method of recording progress is to use an action plan progress sheet (an exemplar is included as Figure 4.3). If the check reveals that the initiative is making slower progress than anticipated, or that it is experiencing difficulties, you will need to act swiftly to rectify matters.

Support and facilitate

An important aspect of your role as a senior manager is to support and facilitate change and development. The enthusiasm that often accompanies the launch of an initiative tends to wear off when the going gets tough. Inquiring sympathetically about the progress of a development can both reveal the mood of a team and reassure a worried team leader that you haven't forgotten him or her. It can also provide an informal opportunity to discuss how an initiative is progressing.

You should make time specifically for a session in which the progress of the initiative is discussed, and it can be helpful occasionally to attend part of a team meeting. Normally one of the deputies will be assigned to support the initiative, but some input from you indicates your personal commitment to the development.

If problems arise, you (or the relevant deputy) are in a position where, because of your experience and your senior position, you can take an overview so that the problem is assessed and put into perspective, and you can offer advice or support (eg by providing the time for Inset, improving the resources or reappraising the targets, deadlines or roles within the team).

Praise

You sustain motivation and commitment by making development possible, and you support progress by offering encouragement when things are difficult and praise where it is due. Never be fulsome or insincere – this is counterproductive. A warm and encouraging comment, which shows that you understand how much has actually been achieved, or some public support for the initiative can make all the difference to morale and indicates to staff that their hard work is really appreciated.

Report progress

Feedback is an essential part of successful implementation. Reporting progress at least once a term ensures that there is no secrecy and helps to involve people outside the immediate team. There is no need for this to be a lengthy procedure. Its aim is to keep people in the picture and to make sure that the development programme remains high-profile. A longer annual report will probably form part of the evaluation process and will be directed to a number of different audiences including the governors.

Implementing the plan – a checklist

❑ Have you clarified the responsibilities and lines of communication?
❑ Are the targets and deadlines realistic and achievable?
❑ Is the programme adequately resourced?
❑ What training/Inset has been provided?
❑ Are the benefits/advantages clear to all those involved?
❑ In what ways are the SMT supporting implementation?
❑ Have progress checks been carried out for each target?
❑ Who is responsible for the progress checks? What reporting procedures are used? Do they include all those involved?
❑ What problems are indicated as a result of the progress checks and what remedial action is being taken?
❑ In what ways do the progress checks influence the construction of next year's plan?
❑ What management lessons have been learnt from designing and implementing this plan?

EVALUATING THE PLAN

Evaluation is concerned with assessing the success of the plan and helping the school to take stock of what has been achieved.

The progress check described in Figure 4.3 is a monitoring operation, which makes an important contribution to the evaluation process. It is a

---

Priority title:

Member of staff responsible:

Other staff involved:

Governors involved:

Report on progress:

a) Frequency

b) Mode of report (written, verbal, etc.)

c) By whom

Deadlines:

Details of staff Outcomes	Progress indicators	Other action
Inset required	What evidence will be sought? How, when, by whom?	

Figure 4.3 *A progress checking sheet*

mini-audit or formative evaluation, providing valuable data about your progress towards achieving the objectives described in your plan.

The indicators included in your action plan will also help you see whether you have reached your destination and, if some of them are process indicators, they may help you analyse where you are on your journey. The analogy of a journey is helpful here because evaluation is about assessing to what extent you have arrived, ie achieved the objectives set out in the plan.

You will need to carry out an annual evaluation, which involves more than simply checking off whether individual targets have been met or indeed how many of them have been achieved. You will have to think about what overall effect carrying out this plan has had on the school, how far the school's aims have been furthered and what was the impact on the pupils' learning. How you do this will vary according to the evaluation procedures established in your school, but the results of the evaluation will probably form a written report presented to staff and governors.

Evaluation should always lead to action, and evaluating the extent to which the management/development plan has succeeded should influence the next three-year planning and policy-making cycle.

CASE STUDY 4.8 FOR ACTION

Downtown Primary School – monitoring, evaluation and review

Definitions

❑ Monitoring – progress check by a collection of data on starting-points and your position after time. *What is happening? What are we doing? What are the patterns?*
❑ Evaluation – making comparisons and judgements. *How does this fit in with our intentions? How does this compare?*
❑ Review – making decisions about whether to change our plans. *What shall we do about this? What, if anything, do we need to change?*

Key points

❑ Monitoring provides less subjective evidence. However, clarity is essential in deciding what will be monitored, evaluated and reviewed.
❑ Monitoring, evaluation and review provide many opportunities for celebration.
❑ Monitoring must be fair. In practice, this means that there is a set procedure with aims and objectives clear to all.
❑ The system must allow results to influence future action.
❑ It is not possible or desirable to monitor all things at all times.

Key purposes – why do it?

❑ accountability, ie the proving of quality by individuals and teams, externally and internally;
❑ self-accountability through self-evaluation, ie the improving of quality;
❑ promoting the 'learning school' by involving people and developing them by providing feedback that can help them improve their own performance or that of their department;
❑ identifying trends in effectiveness over time;
❑ providing the basis for further development;
❑ doing it to ourselves before others do it to us (eg Ofsted).

Table 4.1 *Monitoring and review programme*

What will we review	When	How	Who will be responsible?
Levels of attainment	Twice yearly – September and July.	Review and set targets.	Head, deputy head, SMT.
	Termly self-review cycle	Governing body meeting considers results.	LEA/link adviser, governing body.
	Monthly at staff meetings.	As in school self-review document.	Co-ordinators, classroom teachers.
Progress	End of term 1 and June	Sample of pupils AA, A & BA, check levels – assess improvement and pace.	Overview deputy head, subject co-ordinators.
Attendance	Weekly.	Review weekly attendance percentage and certain pupils.	Head/deputy head, EWO, LEA/link adviser.
		Governing body meetings.	Governing body.
Punctuality	Weekly	Termly target number of lates.	Deputy head/head, EWO, LEA/link adviser.
		Governing body meetings.	Governing body.
Quality of teaching	Monitoring cycle through year.	Develop monitoring programme.	Oversight of deputy head.
	Linked to appraisal programme	Subject co-ordinators, SMT and link adviser.	Subject co-ordinators; reviewed by governors termly.
Behaviour	Half-termly	Time out sheets. Head reviews incidents and sets targets.	Head and classroom teachers.
		Selected pupils monitored by classroom teachers.	Governing body reviews termly.
School targets	September, July	Review achieved percentages against targets.	Governing body with head and link adviser.
Parental involvemnt	Termly	Review how to improve involvement.	Head/deputy head, parent-liaison governor.
Classroom display and organization	Termly	Check every classroom once a term.	Deputy head/head.
		Discuss display at staff meeting – highlight exemplars of good practice.	
Leadership and management	School self-review cycle	Follow guidelines in cycle.	Head/SMT, governors, LEA/link adviser.
Curriculum areas	According to SDP cycle	Co-ordinators released to make classroom observations, sample work and check planning.	Subject co-ordinators and head.

For action

The monitoring and review programme described above is a good attempt to provide a clear overview. How might you improve it? Compare it with practice in your own school.

MAKING A BID FOR A SCHOOL SPECIALISM

Making a bid for a school specialism, eg to become a technology college, is not dissimilar to drafting your development plan. If you want further advice about how to manage this important task, contact the Specialist and Affiliated Schools Network. Their address is 23rd Floor West, Millbank Tower, 21–24 Millbank, London SW1P 4QP, or you can access information through the DfEE or via the Internet.

5

MOTIVATING THE STAFF

In the education system it is the human resources that consume the most investment.

Everard and Morris, 1996

The task of the manager is to achieve results through people – you must become a successful *motivator* of people. Managing, motivating and developing the staff occupy three chapters of this book, which indicates how much of your time will be spent in dealing with the staff of the school. In the past, however, staff management has been something of a poor relation, as educational managers have focused on achieving the task of educating the pupils, and staff management would probably have consisted merely of 'the recruitment, administration and deployment of staff'. Now, effective staff management is seen as the key to quality education and an essential component of running a good school, and it is the job of the headteacher and the senior management team (SMT) to create and maintain the conditions and atmosphere in which people can work with a sense of purpose and give of their best.

The case study that follows illustrates what can happen if the SMT are not sensitive managers of people.

CASE STUDY 5.1 FOR REFLECTION

For some years the staff at Cheerly High School had been shielded from Geoffrey's worst failings by Joyce, his competent deputy head, but she had finally got a well-deserved promotion and Geoffrey promoted Ian, the head of boys' PE, to the vacant deputyship. It was rumoured among the staff, because two apparently better-qualified women candidates had been passed over, that Ian owed his promotion to his long service to the school, his assiduous cultivation of Geoffrey, Geoffrey's keen interest in sport and the fact that Ian, at 50, was fast becoming a liability to the PE department. Ian tended to rush headlong into things. He was impatient both with the theoretical (which he considered a complete waste of time) and with worrying about details, which he thought people could work out for themselves. He prided himself on being decisive and on not changing his mind. The staff, on the other hand, considered many of his decisions as arbitrary and irrational, and he was regarded as autocratic, insensitive and sexist. Events organized by Ian tended to be chaotic and came to be dreaded by any member of staff who had to participate. It rapidly became very difficult to get any volunteers to help with anything, because the staff knew that the activity or function would be ill organized. Geoffrey would not be available to provide support or leadership, so they would have to pick up the pieces, and afterwards Ian would blame them for the disaster. Staff meetings became contentious because Ian took comments personally, and staff began to dread these sessions and to make excuses to avoid them.

Going directly to Geoffrey, however, didn't help the situation. Geoffrey was much less aggressive than Ian and said 'Yes' to everyone, but he wouldn't implement your scheme, and certainly wouldn't have any recollection of the conversation having taken place. His priority was a quiet life. It was no good resorting to memos or to putting your ideas in writing, because Ian had no patience with pieces of paper and Geoffrey simply lost them. Trying to implement the changes the school needed to bring the school into line with current National Curriculum requirements was generally regarded as hopeless and, after three attempts to get the senior management team to consider his scheme for integrated junior science, the head of science began to look for another post. The *Times Educational Supplement* was now in great demand in the staffroom, and staff turnover increased dramatically. A senior teacher post became vacant and the two women passed over for the deputyship were urged by their colleagues to apply. But they saw no point in applying, believing the school only had 'jobs for the boys'.

There were clear signs of teacher dissatisfaction at Cheerly High School:

❑ People stopped volunteering to help with activities or functions.
❑ Meetings became contentious.
❑ Teachers stopped putting forward ideas for curriculum development.
❑ The *TES* was much read in the staffroom.
❑ Staff began to look for other jobs.
❑ Women teachers were reluctant to apply for internal posts.

The reasons for this dissatisfaction were also clear and included:

❑ Administrative incompetence – poor organization and attention to detail created an expectation of disaster and led to reluctance to participate.

❑ Unpleasant working conditions – the deputy was aggressive and took things personally. There were a lot of rows, a 'them and us' atmosphere grew up and a lot of staff began to take a low profile in order to avoid being involved in unpleasantness.

❑ Inability to pick up on grass-roots ideas – no serious attention was given to the ideas put forward by the departments or by individual members of staff, with the result that people became very discouraged.

❑ Lack of encouragement or support – Ian rejected ideas because he could not be bothered with them, and Geoffrey provided no support for teachers dealing with difficult situations. Inevitably this had an effect on good will and morale.

❑ No appreciation for effort – Ian blamed the teachers for his mistakes and their efforts were never praised or rewarded.

❑ Promotion opportunities seemed to have little connection with merit or effort – this was particularly demotivating for female staff, who perceived the situation as 'jobs for the boys'.

❑ No one knew what decisions meant – the headteacher was indecisive, and the deputy head was too decisive. The head said 'Yes' to everyone, and the deputy said 'No' to everyone.

Everard (1986) commented that he found in education more examples of inhuman, downright incompetent management than in industry, and the example of Cheerly High School encapsulates this view.

Most schools are nothing like as bad as Cheerly High School, and the Education Acts of the 1980s and 90s have forced heads to become better managers of all their resources, but it is probably true that whereas a lot of attention has been focused on improving the quality of education for the pupils who receive it, far less attention has been paid to providing supportive structures and improving working conditions for the adults who deliver it.

Motivating the staff

In most schools:

❑ Some people work hard; others do the minimum amount.
❑ Some want freedom of action; others want a highly structured environment.
❑ Some work virtually alone; others work almost all the time in groups.
❑ Some are satisfied; others are perpetually discontented.

Yet they work in the same institution. What is it that causes some teachers to work extremely hard and others to do the minimum amount? To find the answer, we shall have to review the main ideas and theories about motivation and also consider the findings of research into current practice. This section is intended as a summary and a starting-off point from which to think about ways in which you could make your management of staff more effective. For a more detailed consideration of motivation you should use more theoretical books on organizational behaviour.

WHAT DO WE MEAN BY MOTIVATION?

The two quotations below provide us with a basic definition and starting-point from which to consider motivation.

CASE STUDY 5.2 FOR REFLECTION

Definitions of motivation

Motivation is made up of a number of factors of which the most important are the perceived value of the outcome to the individual and the correlation between that outcome and the effort necessary to achieve it. Motivation is therefore about action and is the product of determination, ability and performance.

Davies *et al*, 1991

Motivation arises from arousal and choices in the individual – a desire to allocate time and energy to particular goals in exchange for some expected result or reward. More generally motivation is the degree to which an individual chooses to engage in certain behaviours.

Hunt, 1986

MOTIVATION THEORIES

The most popular motivation theories have been needs theories, in which goals, aspirations, values and behaviours are collected into motives, which are called drives, needs and wants. They are based on the premise that motivation depends on the relationship between the potential drive of an individual and the nature of his or her needs.

One example of this kind of thinking is Maslow's theory of needs. Maslow (1954) suggested that we could make needs into a hierarchy and predict the order in which individuals could satisfy their needs. The strength of this model is based on one level becoming dominant as another is satisfied. Thus according to Maslow only unsatisfied needs motivate. Maslow's hierarchy is traditionally represented as a pyramid, as shown in Figure 5.1. The hierarchy is explained as follows:

❑ **Physiological** – hunger, thirst, sexual drive, etc. Unless these are satisfied, little further progress can be made, because these needs come to dominate one's whole existence.
❑ **Safety** – these drive out the baser instincts of an individual as he or she seeks shelter, warmth, clothing, etc.
❑ **Social** – the desires for companionship, acceptance, the regard of others, etc are less selfish needs than the physiological and security needs because they combine giving with receiving, and so they are regarded as being on a higher plane than the first two.

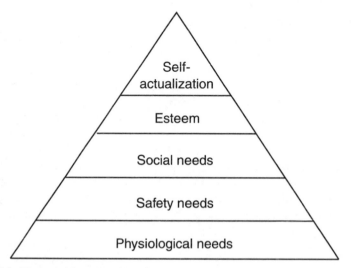

Figure 5.1 *Maslow's hierarchy of needs*

❏ **Esteem** – the drive to externalize one's inner feelings or creativity in some way.
❏ **Self-actualization** – this forms the apex of Maslow's pyramid because only through self-fulfilment can an individual realize his or her true humanity, and this cannot be achieved until all the other contributory and more partial needs have been met. Self-fulfilment through work should thus be a key aim of the institution.

While most physiologists accept that people do find some goals so attractive that they will pursue them with considerable energy, many of them do not accept Maslow's theory of a rigid hierarchy because they consider it too simplistic.

Frederick Herzberg attempted to overcome the problems associated with Maslow's hierarchy of needs by developing a more sophisticated analysis of attitudes to motivation and work, and he developed a distinction between satisfiers and dissatisfiers, which he called hygiene factors (Herzberg, 1974). Dissatisfiers could include:

❏ administration;
❏ relationship with section head, supervisor, head of department or senior manager;
❏ working conditions;
❏ salary;
❏ relationship with colleagues;
❏ status;
❏ job security.

The problem with using hygiene factors is that dissatisfiers make people very disgruntled and demotivate, but removing them is not a motivator. This is reinforced by research into current practice. 'When teachers are satisfied with the management of their schools they do not mention it, because good management is not in itself under normal circumstances, a satisfier in its own right' (Nias, 1980).

Every deputy head who has ever handled cover for absence arrangements will identify with the findings from Jennifer Nias's research. A crop of errors in cover or the overuse of any individual will quickly result in a rush of complaints; success in dealing with cover may help to keep industrial action at bay, but it will not enthuse staff and it is rare for a deputy to receive any thanks for managing cover consistently well.

That does not mean that you should not remove the dissatisfiers, but rather that when you have done so, you will not have solved the problem of motivating your staff.

Following on from the work of Maslow and Herzberg, a whole range of motivation theories has emerged:

❑ **Goals and expectancy theories** – providing staff with specified goals for them to work on will increase their motivation. This has led to an emphasis on management by objectives and much target setting.
❑ **Intrinsic motivation** – leaders can foster conditions within an organization that build up intrinsic motivation, though it has been found that some extrinsic demotivators (such as poor pay) can affect this adversely.
❑ **Behaviour modification** – the use of positive reinforcement can substantially increase motivation.
❑ **Working in small groups or teams** – this can help teachers feel a sense of belonging and commitment.

No single motivating factor has been found to have a dominating effect, and some behavioural psychologists now suggest that there are a number of factors that influence how people behave at work. For example, JW Hunt (whose *Managing People at Work: A manager's guide to behaviour in organisations* (1986) is a useful resource for headteachers who want to read some theory in an accessible format) researched some 10,600 cases, and identified abilities, experience, goals and values, and expected rewards as the most important factors in influencing how people behave at work.

His research led him to develop the opinion that our backgrounds provide us with themes or patterns that reappear in values, beliefs and goals, and he identified eight recurring goal categories: comfort, structures, relationships, recognition and status, power, authority, creativity and growth.

Each individual has his or her goals, which may shift over a period of time. Our goals tend to relate to the situations in which we find ourselves and the cues of the people around us – our subordinates, peers and managers are all important triggers. Research findings also indicate that people at different levels in an organization seek different goal satisfactions and that the most motivated workers, not surprisingly, are those who identify with the organization's own goals. 'If individuals have the necessary abilities and experience and their goals are the same as the organization, then provided that they find the rewards attractive, and have the energy, they will work hard to achieve the goals.'

As managers, we need to understand that there is a whole range of factors that affect motivation and, more importantly, we need to be able to respond appropriately to people's individual needs.

What are the implications for you as a manager and motivator of staff? One message that emerges very clearly from the research work on motivation is just how important it is to have an effective and proactive approach to staff management. I now consider what this means for you.

CASE STUDY 5.3 FOR REFLECTION

Providing a supportive environment

This aspect of staff management addresses the comfort, security and structure needs of your staff.

'Comfort' includes providing reasonable working conditions. Many teachers work under dire conditions – in many staffrooms there is room only for a social area, and there is nowhere available for the teachers to prepare or mark and not all schools are able to provide all their middle managers with offices, however small.

> Staffrooms are typically too small, poorly furnished, untidy, badly laid out, with coffee making facilities which would disgrace a dosshouse. . . Yet the staffroom is the hub of the school community, where information is traded, working relationships are forged and innovation generated, as well as drooping spirits revived, books marked, letters written and hosts of everyday tasks of teaching being completed.
>
> Torrington and Weightman, 1989a

One of the most common demotivators is when teachers think they have not received adequate support from senior staff in maintaining discipline or setting a standard.

> The children are not motivated to work and are easily distracted. There's no help from the senior staff. If you send a pupil who has been difficult or disruptive to any member of our senior management team, the pupil is back in your classroom a few minutes later, and this makes it much more difficult to control the class than before you sent the pupil out, so we try to cope, but it isn't easy. The management team here doesn't take a stand on anything. Even if they said that homework should be done, it would be a start. But we also need to demonstrate clearly to those children who failed to produce homework that some follow-up action would be taken. If the pupils could see that the senior

team were prepared to support us, it would be so much better. As it is some staff have given up trying to enforce a standard.

Extract from a teachers' discussion (illustrating that a perceived lack of support can also deter staff from persevering with a difficult task)

Job security is also a worry for staff in schools, both teaching and non-teaching.

Every so often one of the governors comes and talks to us and suggests that one of us should go. There are three of us and really they only want to keep two. They are not making us any offers, they just keep up the pressure, though if they did make a reason-able offer, Marjorie, who's in her late 50s, might take it. The head says that I should be safe, because I am his secretary, but I was the most recently appointed, and I'm worried about my position here.

Head's secretary discussing staffing issues

This extract illustrates that working in a school is no longer the safe and secure job it used to be. The competitive market-place, depleted rolls and cost-conscious institutional development can all lead to redundancy, and redundancy issues affect the morale of a wider group than those directly affected.

They told us that seven teachers had to go that year and we all knew that it was more than natural wastage could absorb. Of course I worried about it, even though I knew that I was relatively safe because I taught a shortage subject. There was a dreadful atmosphere in the staffroom. I think a lot of it came from the uncertainty. In the end enough people left and they did not have to make anyone redundant, but it affected morale badly and the whole relationship between the staff and the management team.

Teacher recalling falling rolls in an inner-city school

Handling redundancy successfully while maintaining staff morale is an extremely difficult management exercise requiring a great deal of sensitivity. It is explored more fully in Chapter 10.

CREATING A FEELING OF BELONGING

The best organizations are run in such a way that the staff as a whole regard themselves as part of a corporate team. Achieving this task will draw on all your skills as a leader and your ability to create a corporate spirit. Chapter 4 discussed ways of creating a corporate philosophy that clearly articulates the values of the organization. This philosophy needs to be understood, accepted and owned by staff, if they are to be motivated. This will involve you in an ongoing planning dialogue involving the whole staff and regular restatement of the philosophy to hammer it home.

> What is so different about working in this school, now that Philip is head, is that for the first time we really know where we are going and we're all pulling together. In the past it was like a lot of individuals who happened to work in the same building; now we are like one big team, and even the pupils seem to recognize that they can no longer play us off one against another.

If a survey of your staff can consistently produce that kind of comment, you are succeeding as a motivator.

MOTIVATING THROUGH TEAMS AND TASK GROUPS

Participating in group activities can also contribute to motivation, because it too creates a feeling of belonging. Both in industry and in education there has in recent years been a movement to management through teams. In schools, subject departments have always existed, though it is only in the past decade or so, with its emphasis on change necessitating curriculum development, that the sheer volume of work has forced an increase of team activity, and schools have created co-ordinators to lead development work for new curriculum areas and for cross-curricular activities. These teams, which have had to focus on working out solutions for the delivery of an aspect of the curriculum, eg technology, are a form of task group, an organizational style that Handy and Aiken (1986) identified as 'the teachers' own preferred culture': 'Teachers with very few exceptions saw themselves as task culture aficionados.'

This kind of group has to undertake a demanding or challenging task, often with a tight deadline. It draws on the talents and abilities of its members and, although there is usually a group co-ordinator or team leader, it is not a hierarchical unit, but more a team of colleagues, co-operating on a project. It is the nature of the relationships formed through the team, the interaction of the personnel and the common task, goals or targets that provide the motivating force.

The task group formed for a specific purpose and chosen from volunteers or those with the relevant talents is the easiest team to enthuse or motivate. The ongoing department team, whose members may well be approaching new developments with much less enthusiasm, will need more nursing and encouragement, and pastoral teams, with some determinedly unenthused tutors, need most motivating if they are to achieve the objectives set out in the school's mission statement.

Some training for your middle managers both in team building and in managing change and personnel would probably equip them better to deal with this complex and difficult task. Effective well-motivated teams are the product of hard work and good leadership by their co-ordinator, who has to gain the commitment of their members.

A warning note

Creating enthused task groups can sometimes be counterproductive to organizational unity, as it sets the group apart from the rest of their colleagues and this is something that senior management need to monitor in case resentments build up. It also may motivate small groups but it could splinter an organization, as it focuses loyalty on the team and its task rather than on the organization.

MAKING STAFF FEEL VALUED

This involves recognition of effort and valuable work, feedback and reward where appropriate, but most of all it involves *positive* feedback.

Our general observation is that most managers know very little about positive reinforcement. Many appear not to value it at all, or consider it beneath them, undignified or very macho. The evidence from excellent companies strongly suggests that managers who feel this way are doing themselves a great disservice. The excellent company seems to know not only the value of positive reinforcement, but how to manage it well (Peters and Waterman, 1982).

The case study that follows illustrates that some heads clearly understand the value of positive reinforcement and do know how to manage it in order to create a strong team spirit among their staff.

CASE STUDY 5.4 FOR ACTION

Open day

The open day means a lot of hard work for the staff. I always go round the rooms before the parents start to arrive so that I know what each department or unit has contributed. I have a word with as many teachers as possible at that time and comment positively on something in the display. Staff get a lot of our current year 7 pupils involved. When the year 7 team go round the primary schools in the summer term, there are always a lot of comments from next year's pupils about how much they enjoyed open day; this only happens because of the work the staff have done.

At the first staff briefing after the open day, I thank everyone and mention any positive feedback we have received. I also take feedback from staff. We discuss how successful new ventures have been, and I ask for suggestions for the following year. I take criticism on board, and act on it. Staff know we can be honest with one another. Sometime during that week I have a word with staff who have contributed a great deal to the success of the day, and I specifically mention what it is that I valued in their contribution, following it up with a short personal note of thanks.

For action

List the strategies adopted by this headteacher in order to make the members of his staff feel that their efforts are valued, comment on their effectiveness and suggest what else he could do. How do you convince your staff that this is not just a management ploy but that you are sincere?

REWARDING INDIVIDUALS THROUGH PAY AND PROMOTION

Pay and promotion of course are the most obvious ways of making an individual feel valued, because it shows everyone that the recipient is regarded as worthy of reward and is a recognition of merit or effort.

Pay and promotion, however, are two-edged swords. Choosing one person means rejecting a lot of other people. Pay is a particularly fraught area.

For many years there was little room for manoeuvre because of national scales. To make matters worse, falling rolls or a stable staff who had reached the top of the scale or who had already received any allowances that you had in your gift blocked promotion opportunities for others and left you with nothing to offer staff who clearly deserved reward. Now pay arrangements that necessitate salaries being reviewed annually give you flexibility and, in theory, you have much more opportunity to reward deserving staff and show them you value their efforts. In practice, you are restricted by the tightness of the budget and may find yourself having to deal with one of the worst possible scenarios, which is a climate of raised expectations that cannot be met. The nomination of advanced skills teachers, a small group of practitioners selected because of their excellence in the classroom is a particularly difficult area to manage. Badly handled, it can make these teachers unpopular with their colleagues, while demotivating those who have no hope of ever being selected. Having a governors' pay policy with the criteria clearly established has become essential, but still does not solve all the problems in using pay to encourage staff. Rewarding a small number of individuals may motivate a few staff and encourage them to identify with the goals of the institution, but it is equally likely to antagonize and cause dissension and disenchantment among the majority. Indeed, where a teacher is not favoured or it is handled insensitively, pay can be a dissatisfier.

CASE STUDY 5.5 FOR ACTION

I don't understand why George is suddenly getting an allowance. There are three other teachers in the languages department doing identical work to George. What has George got that the others haven't? They are pretty annoyed about it.

Teacher's comment on a colleague's good fortune

For action/discussion

What does this comment indicate about how the pay policy is being applied in this school, and what advice would you give the headteacher?

CASE STUDY 5.6 FOR ACTION

Bestwick Park High School: an extract from the governors' pay policy

General principle

The governing body will endeavour, within its budget, to use the national pay scales and discretion available to them as the 'relevant body to recruit, retain and motivate' teachers of quality to ensure the best possible delivery of the curriculum. Consideration will also be given to the non-teaching staff. The governors will be mindful of the need to create and maintain high morale among the staff in order to achieve the best response from pupils.

When considering the enhancement of the pay of any staff, the staffing committee should be aware of existing differentials and ensure that any proposed variation is based on relevant evidence and seen to be just, and will ensure that all decisions are properly communicated to staff. The criteria will be as follows:

❏ responsibilities beyond those common to the majority of teachers;
❏ outstanding classroom ability;
❏ employment to teach a subject where there is a shortage of teachers;
❏ employment in a post that is difficult to fill.

For action/discussion

Comment on the Bestwick Park policy statement. What do you think should be the main principles of a school pay and conditions of service policy, and what is the best way of setting one up so that it does not provide a dissatisfier?

Pay policies are discussed more fully in Chapter 10.

JOB SATISFACTION

This strand of your staff management policy positively motivates because it addresses the needs of power, status, growth and creativity. It is the product of good will and an understanding of individual needs and opportunity. These are some of the ways in which you can provide staff with the opportunity for fulfilment through work:

❏ leadership opportunities – co-ordinator roles, chairing working parties, carrying out a specific task or leadership of a task group;
❏ successful delegation, which gives the individual the freedom to interpret a role or task in his or her own way;
❏ participation in a challenging or stimulating new development where there is opportunity for creativity;
❏ participation in a team where the task is high priority, high status and well resourced (some pilot projects find themselves in this enviable position);
❏ promotion to a new post or the chance to undertake additional responsibilities;
❏ redesignation of an existing post, eg change of responsibilities to prevent staleness and provide new challenges.

All of these examples provide the opportunity for individual growth and development either through new or enhanced responsibilities or through membership of a vibrant team.

CASE STUDY 5.7 FOR REFLECTION

The first half-term that we delivered the new technology course, we were really hyped up. We'd head for the staffroom at break or lunchtime after we had had a lesson with the group in order to compare notes and reactions with the other members of the team. The whole approach was new to us. It was very exciting, but also very demanding. None of us had done assignment-based learning before. We had to learn to let go and allow the children to take control. We found that we really had to think on our feet, but it was exhilarating. What really surprised us was that whereas at the beginning some members of the team had not been totally convinced that all this effort was worth while, now the whole team really pulled together, and these staff became as involved as those who had been committed from the start. They said that now that they could see how much the children were enjoying it and how much they were achieving, they suddenly saw the point of the whole enterprise.

> Teacher describing the introduction of
> assignment-based learning in her school

The example demonstrates how a growing belief in what they were doing motivated this team and brought in those who were initially unconvinced of the value of the initiative. It also helped create a sense of excitement and a strong group identity.

CASE STUDY 5.8 FOR ACTION

Who would have thought it of Janet? We all thought that she was just coasting through the twilight years of her career; then came this edict that we had to implement appraisal, and the head put her in charge of it, because she was experienced and sympathetic, but not a threat to anyone, because she wasn't in the senior management team. She really blossomed. It seemed to bring out all kinds of qualities we would never have guessed that she had. In next to no time she had all the staff involved in some form of appraisal with no trouble at all. No other school in the county got off the mark as fast as we did. I wouldn't have believed it if I hadn't seen it for myself. How did the head know how to choose her?

Teacher describing how appraisal
was introduced into his school

This example shows how finding someone a challenging task can unexpectedly motivate, but of course it has to be the right task and the right person. If Janet hadn't possessed the skills and personal qualities to do the job, the results could have been very different.

For action

What are the lessons of Case Studies 5.7 and 5.8 for you as a new headteacher?

CASE STUDY 5.9 FOR ACTION

When John, the head of year 9, had to have an operation, Nora offered to take over the management of his year group. She did the job unpaid for half a term and then was given an acting responsibility. She put a lot of time, thought and effort into the job, introducing some ideas of her own that seemed to go down well with both the year team and the pupils. Although she had plenty of ideas, she was sensitive about procedures and consultation, and careful not to erode John's position. When John did take up his post again, he immediately eradicated every trace of Nora's tenure. Around that time another year-head post became vacant and Nora applied for it. She was not among the short-listed candidates, and could not understand why her successful experience had not earned her an interview. From being a willing volunteer, within a few months she had become one of the school management's most vociferous and hostile critics.

For action

How would you set about remotivating Nora? What advice might you give the headteacher in Nora's school?

KEY QUALITIES

Openness

Regular and open communication should be a part of your approach to management. It is perhaps the most important motivational factor. A continuous dialogue between the senior management and the staff is essential. Finding simple, clear means of letting the staff know what is happening, no matter how trivial, makes them feel part of the school, whereas if they feel that they are being kept in the dark about important things happening in the school, it will be difficult to win their co-operation. Lines of communication and reporting should be clear to all concerned. Communication should include consultation, which needs to be genuine, and the results of the consultation should be communicated without delay so that the staff know that a decision has been taken, how it has been taken and what the decision is.

Concern and interest

It is more difficult for you to know a large staff as well as a middle manager can know his or her much smaller team, but studying the staff files when you take up your post and learning something about each person and what he or she is doing would help to get you started. It is important that you demonstrate your knowledge of and concern for the people you manage. A few well-chosen words, which indicate to hard-working members of staff that you have noticed the work they are doing, that you are interested in the progress of their current project, or that you are aware of a problem or of difficult home circumstances, are likely to repay you a hundredfold in terms of good will. The qualities that you really need here are a keen awareness of what is going on in your school and a sensitivity to vibes about people or contentious issues. Some headteachers rely on 'moles' in the staffroom for information, but this can be a dangerous practice.

Accessibility

Associated with concern and interest is accessibility. Having to book an appointment with the headteacher a week or so in advance to discuss a fairly minor matter, or having that appointment repeatedly postponed, does not promote good will. Some heads make a point of being in the staffroom for at least five or ten minutes each day, so that is the opportunity for informal contact. If someone wants to see you urgently, then, if at all possible, make time on the same day at least for an initial contact.

Willingness to listen

'She never really listens to what we say' or 'He's really only interested in what he wants to tell us' are all-too-frequent comments made about the senior managers in our schools and they are quite damning indictments because they show a fundamental lack of interest in the affairs of the people being managed. All too often we only hear what we want to hear from a conversation or we are so determined to show that we are right and insist on having the last word that we dominate a conversation or meeting, and fail to be attentive to others. The ability to listen carefully, showing interest in what other people are saying to you and with an awareness that makes you sensitive to the nuances of a situation, is an essential skill for any manager.

Consideration

Treating staff well leads to low staff turnover and encourages internal applications for vacant posts. Treating people with consideration means not making unreasonable demands on them, eg by holding lengthy or unnecessary meetings, or expecting them to do something at a moment's notice. It means providing good working conditions and consulting rather than imposing whenever possible. Treating people generously in respect of their private requests helps to create a reservoir of good will.

Ability to counsel

As a senior manager you will have to deal with a lot of situations that require counselling skills or the ability to resolve conflict. If your counselling skills are not naturally strong, you can always work towards improving them through counselling courses. It is, however, important to remember that you are a manager, rather than a social worker or psychiatrist, and it is therefore your task to look towards finding solutions for problems.

Fairness

You have to be careful not to create 'haves' and 'have nots' by appearing to favour one individual over another. You have to demonstrate even-handedness, while managing to reward merit. Publishing the criteria you use to determine capitation, rather than a list of how much each department gets, is one way of avoiding interdepartmental jealousies. You should also be careful about becoming too dependent upon any one member of the senior management team – this can be very divisive.

Support and encouragement

So much development work is being undertaken these days that supporting change has become one of the senior managers' most important functions. It means that you have to give generously of your time and is linked to accessibility. Supporting and encouraging staff can entail acting as a sounding board, or providing guidance and advice to a hard-pressed middle manager trying to deal with a sensitive situation in his or her department.

Appreciation

Always give credit where it is due and make a point of giving praise when it is deserved. For example, a member of staff, who may have spent hours preparing a display, will feel valued when the senior manager makes the effort to visit it and makes some positive comment to the teacher or technician concerned. Remembering to say 'Thank you' or 'You did that well' shows people that their efforts are appreciated. Making the praise specific – 'I really like that because. . .' – helps to convince people that you are sincere and have actually noticed what they are doing. Try not to be grudging, half-hearted or too fulsome.

Decisiveness

If taking decisions worries you, you will not enjoy being a senior manager. Taking sufficient time to make a sound decision is one thing; indecisiveness is quite another. Putting off making difficult or potentially unpopular decisions will soon lose you the respect of your staff. The meetings that most undermine morale are those that end without any decisions being taken. How democratically those decisions are arrived at is a matter of your own management style, but the point is that people want issues to be *resolved*.

Leadership

As a senior manager, you are expected to set standards. If you spend a lot of your time at rotary lunches, claiming that you are managing the school's external relations, you will quickly lose all credibility. Basically you have to lead by example. This means being in first and out last at an evening function that you have made compulsory for the rest of the staff. It means not delegating the really difficult things to your deputy, not conveying an unpleasant decision to someone through a note. It means offering to sit some lessons yourself when staff absence is high, and it always means being prepared to take the blame when things go wrong.

CASE STUDY 5.10 FOR ACTION

Most teachers feel undervalued by their fellow citizens. Partly they are sharing in the situation of other employed people, as there has been a general levelling out of status differentials, if not of pay differentials. But the particular situation of teachers' low self-esteem has been aggravated by the acrimony of long-running industrial action and widespread dissatisfaction with government policies on education. The feeling of low appreciation from outside makes it more important for teachers to feel valued by their colleagues and to be valued inside the school.

At the same time as teachers feel less appreciated by the world outside, the innovations to which schools are being asked to respond, generated largely by the same world outside, have multiplied in recent years. Bolam (1986) listed as many as 40 current changes (innovations, policy initiatives and developments) that have to be managed – and that was before the National Curriculum, LMS and more recent legislation. Seldom will all these apply simultaneously to a school, but never before have secondary schools had to cope with so many changes, many of them major. The fact that most of these changes are landing on schools from outside means that staff feel little or no 'ownership' of them. This not only reduces the likelihood of changes being implemented effectively, it also demoralizes by creating a sense of being at the mercy of others. Many of the changes require staff to adjust their working practices, and nearly all of them are generating increased workloads. Most schools are suffering from innovation overload, just at a time when staff morale is – generally speaking – lower than it has been for some years.

Staff are responding to the situation in different ways; some by withholding commitment, some by withdrawing from out-of-school activities, some by increased militancy, some by reduced militancy, some simply bow their heads and resolve to work harder – again – like Boxer, the horse in *Animal Farm*. We encountered many staff who seemed stoically to have decided to concentrate on doing their best to tackle the major, inescapable tasks that face them.

Torrington and Weightman, 1989a

For action

❑ *Management and Organisation in Secondary Schools*, from which the above extract was taken, was a product of the 1980s. If you were writing that extract today what changes would you have to make to bring it up to date? To what extent have the demands on teachers and their reactions to them altered?

❏ What would be the main staff management issues for you as the head of a school? How would you address them?

❏ Draft a staff management policy for your school.

CASE STUDY 5.11 FOR ACTION

Appraising yourself as a motivator

As motivation is a complex and difficult area to manage, it could be useful to focus an appraisal on it. Appraisal usually starts with the collection of data about performance. One way that you could approach this is to rate your own performance as a motivator in the key areas already discussed and then see how some of your colleagues rate you. You could use the findings as the basis of the appraisal discussion and to help you set targets. You will want to collect data from a number of colleagues at different levels in the organization. Scoring could be out of 10. As with any test of this kind, the first thing tested is your own self-confidence – are you brave enough to try it?

How well do you rate your performance checklist

❏ saying thank you to colleagues;
❏ showing concern for someone's well-being;
❏ giving encouragement;
❏ praising work well done;
❏ constructive criticism;
❏ supporting other people's ideas;
❏ handling conflict situations;
❏ listening sensitively;
❏ ensuring that people are informed and understand;
❏ counselling.

MANAGING APPOINTMENTS

As headteacher, you need to attract and retain staff with the right qualifications, experience and personal qualities to enable the school to run as efficiently as possible. How well staff are recruited will have an overall effect on the quality of education provided. This chapter examines the procedures and issues involved in making appointments and provides some exemplar materials.

A member of staff has just been to see you. He has received a letter saying that his application for early retirement has been approved. You will have a staff vacancy for the following September. Your first move should be to consult your school management/development plan. Has it anticipated this development? How does this vacancy fit into your staffing plans for next year? Will falling rolls or financial difficulties mean that you simply cannot afford to replace this member of staff, or does this resignation come as a longed-for opportunity to restructure and replace overstaffing in this subject with increased staffing in a more popular subject? You can no longer consider any appointment on its own; you have to relate it to your overall staffing structure and to your budget. An exemplar of how to move to an ideal staffing structure is included as Case Study 6.6.

FORMING THE SELECTION PANEL

Once you have decided that there is a post to fill, you will need to decide your method of selection, and this will necessitate involving the governors. Governors must deal with the selection of headteachers and deputies and may wish to be involved in the selection of other staff, so you should at least consult them. The appointment panel will be identified in the policy document on staffing or appointments (see Chapter 10) so this should not change every time that a vacancy arises. A change of head, however, could lead to change in the way appointments are managed. There are three options available for appointments for all teacher posts other than deputies: selection by the headteacher, selection by a panel of governors and selection by a panel consisting of both governors and the headteacher.

It is unlikely below deputy level that you would need to raise the matter at a full governors' meeting. In most schools the vacancy would appear as an item on the agenda at the personnel subcommittee (which handles all the personnel and staffing issues) and it would be discussed there. This gives you the opportunity to advise the governors as to what is the most sensible procedure to adopt. You will probably find that after a year or so a formula is likely to have emerged. If it is a senior post, head of department and above, the governors will usually want a considerable degree of involvement. If it is a part-time post, or a member of the support staff, they are likely to decide to leave it to you, and if it is a main grade teacher, it will vary whether or not they want a token presence.

For the purposes of this chapter, let us imagine that it is a senior post, eg a deputyship, and the personnel subcommittee decide to set up a separate selection committee consisting of three or four governors. What are the duties of this panel?

The duties of the selection committee

❑ drawing up a job description and a person specification;
❑ deciding how the post should be advertised;
❑ preparing details about the school;
❑ deciding criteria for shortlisting;
❑ making the shortlist;
❑ dealing with references;
❑ organizing the interview;
❑ conducting the interview;
❑ deciding who is the best candidate for the post.

In practice, a lot of the work, especially drafting and preparing the details about the school, is likely to be delegated to you as head, but the selection committee will want at least to approve the drafts, eg of the job description, and must discuss the thorny issues such as the criteria for shortlisting.

EMPLOYMENT LEGISLATION

At this stage it is sensible to consult the legislation relevant to the appointments procedure. Nobody will expect you to know or remember it all, but

111

the volume and complexity of recent legislation is such that you should take account of it. Remember that you must not only comply with education legislation, but you must also conform to British employment law and EU employment legislation. If you are an LEA school, this could be a good time to have a chat to your LEA officer or adviser, for a reminder of likely pitfalls. It could also be a good idea to make one of the personnel committee responsible for this aspect of staff selection and he or she could build up expertise and a file of information.

There are three main areas of potential discrimination in selection that are covered by employment law. They are disability, race and gender. We shall also look briefly at age and religious discrimination.

Disability

People with disabilities have the same rights under employment law as able-bodied employees, and employers of 20 people or more are required by law to employ 3 per cent registered people with disabilities. An employer unable to fill this quota, however, may apply for an exemption permit and, in practice, prosecutions for non-compliance have been rare, if not unknown. If you need additional information about employing people with disabilities, then you should consult the local Disablement Resettlement Centre through the local jobcentre. You would also get information there about the grants and services available to assist people with disabilities obtaining and retaining employment.

Race discrimination

The term 'race' includes race, colour, nationality, ethnic and national origins. It is illegal to discriminate on grounds of race at any stage of selection, and appeals against an employer for racial discrimination are quite frequently taken to industrial tribunal, so this is an area in which you should tread very carefully indeed.

Direct discrimination

This means treating a candidate less favourably than others because of his or her racial group, eg asking Asian or Afro-Caribbean candidates a question about when they came to the UK, or about their ability to produce the standard of written English required for the post, when no other candidate is asked these questions. This could lead to a claim of racial discrimination. It is likely that such a claim would be upheld by an industrial tribunal, and it might also lead to the awarding of damages. For this reason you have to be very careful about the way you ask questions at interview.

Indirect discrimination

This means creating conditions or requirements for the post that implicitly restrict the kind of applicant. 'Applications invited from UK graduates' is one example of a condition with which a far smaller proportion of applicants from one racial group can comply than can another. Again, unless a justifiable reason for the condition could be found, a claim of indirect racial discrimination would be upheld by a tribunal.

In limited and specific circumstances, however, discrimination on grounds of race is permissible, ie where it is essential to select candidates of one particular race, but you will have to prove the need. For example, a Chinese restaurant may be allowed to select only Chinese waiters on grounds of authenticity, or Asian social workers only may be appointed to assist Asian families. This need is described as a genuine occupational qualification (GOQ).

Gender discrimination

It is illegal to discriminate on grounds of gender or marital status in terms of the arrangements for filling posts, the conditions on which the employment is offered and the non-offer of employment. As with race discrimination, the ability to claim sex discrimination against an employer at industrial tribunal is quite wide.

Direct discrimination

This means unfavourable treatment that is directly linked to the sex or marital status of the person concerned, and applies whether or not there was the intention on the part of the employer and even if there is some justification. It is often tied to assumptions about gender or stereotypes. For example, it is most unwise to ask questions about a woman's marriage plans, when she is planning to start a family or her child-care arrangements if you don't ask the same or very similar questions of the male candidates. Discrimination is about singling one person or group out from others and disadvantaging that person or group by the questions you ask or the arrangements you make. Even if it is important to your perception of how the candidate can cope with the demands of the post, as with a one-parent family with a small child, you may not single that candidate out by asking direct questions at interview.

Indirect discrimination

This form of discrimination is about imposing a requirement or condition that acts to the detriment of applicants of one particular sex, and applies if it means that a smaller proportion of the applicants of one sex can comply. An example of this form of discrimination is to ask for say 10 years' experience for a promoted post, while also requiring the applicant to be under 35. Such a requirement would disqualify a lot of women who had taken time out for family reasons and would count as indirect discrimination.

Justifiable discrimination is permissible on limited and specific grounds, ie where special care, supervision or attention is needed for members of one sex. It will justify women teachers for girls' PE, and a GOQ is used in the same way as for racial discrimination. A GOQ should not simply be assumed, so, to make sure you have got it right, discuss the perceived GOQ first with your LEA officer or adviser or, if you are a foundation or private school, refer the matter to any consultant you are using to help with the appointment. Voluntary schools may consult the Diocesan Board of Education or its equivalent.

Age discrimination

It is not illegal to discriminate on grounds of age, though, as shown by the example used above, it can easily become linked to gender discrimination. It is usually unwise to be too precise about age in the advertisement as it could adversely affect the field.

Religious discrimination

There should be no reference to religious belief when selecting for county schools, but the position in voluntary-aided and special agreement schools is quite different and it is common practice to refer in some way to religious beliefs when seeking staff for posts in these schools. Even here, however, you must ensure that the need to appoint an applicant of a particular religious belief or outlook is genuine and necessary. For some posts, especially headteacher of a church school, there is a strong case for arguing that the applicants should be communicant members of that particular faith and when this occurs it should be clearly stated in both the advertisement and the particulars of the post.

To safeguard yourself, you should show clear evidence of intent to operate a fair selection policy, ie by drawing up clear procedures of how all appointments in the school will be made and including in this a firm statement that you are an equal opportunities employer. An example might be: 'There shall be no discrimination against any applicant for any post in Bestwick Park High School on the grounds of race, sex, age or religion.'

JOB DESCRIPTIONS

You can use a job description to outline the responsibilities and main duties of the post. It gives the prospective candidate information about the post and you can use it at a later date for appraisal or regrading.

A job description is likely to contain many of the features given in Case Study 1.3, as well as teaching and other duties, contract details and salary applicable to the post. In other words, it tells the applicants in broad terms what the post involves. It will help them to decide if the job is attractive, so it is important to get it right.

When a post becomes vacant, you do not of course need to use the existing job description. This may be the opportunity to review the functions of this post, because over a period of time the demands change. The job description may not have kept up with what work was actually being done, so check to see to what extent it matches the job as it is now. On the other hand, you may want something slightly different this time round and this is your opportunity to include new components or change the balance of the responsibilities.

Make sure that you have included the flexibility to make changes to the duties or teaching commitment later on if necessary, without affecting the grading of the post. All job descriptions should include a saving clause, eg 'These duties will be reviewed and revised as necessary.'

You will need to get the right balance between being too general and too detailed. A simple example of this kind of thing is to be too specific about the *kind* of equipment a technician will be expected to operate, when what matters is that he or she will need the expertise to operate a *range* of equipment.

A clear job description will help you attract the kind of candidate that you want. An example of a job description is given later in this chapter as Case Study 6.11. You will also find a bursar's job description in Chapter 12.

PERSON SPECIFICATIONS

The person specification is a supplement to the job description and should give you a pen picture of the ideal candidate by providing a statement of the attributes, characteristics, qualities and abilities of the person required for the job. The person specification is usually not sent out to the candidates with the job description, but it is used by the members of the selection panel to help them choose the most suitable candidates for the short list.

A person specification is likely to answer the following questions:

❑ **Qualifications** – is a graduate essential for this post? What particular knowledge, skills and abilities are needed?

❑ **Experience** – does the candidate need experience of A level teaching? Is it important that he or she has taught in a school that is similar to yours in organization or ethos? Is this post suitable for an NQT?

❑ **Broad age range** – is it a good idea to specify an age range, or will this create problems?

❑ **Special requirements** – for example, must the post holder offer a subsidiary subject, definite commitment to a multi-cultural approach or willingness to help with extra-curricular activities?

CASE STUDY 6.1 FOR ACTION

The selection panel are considering the advertisement for a teaching post. They have written 'Applicants will preferably be between 25 and 45.' You are horrified, not only because this is a shortage subject, but because you suspect it could be challenged. A governor protests, 'We don't want an NQT if we can avoid it, but we need someone with a bit of experience, who can help move this department into the 20th century. Older than 45 in this subject and you will be totally out of date. Why can't we advertise for what we need? Putting an age range isn't illegal, is it?' He is right that it isn't illegal, but you know that age discrimination is inadvisable because it is unfair employment practice and you could lose a case if it were to come to tribunal. It would also restrict applicants and you want to attract as wide a field as possible.

For action

What issues are raised by this case study and how would you go about dealing with this problem? What arguments would you use to persuade the governors to change the wording of this advertisement?

SELECTION PROCEDURE

The criteria for selection

Establishing clear and agreed criteria will help you demonstrate why unsuccessful candidates were not short-listed or selected if the appointment should be challenged. These should include, in addition to what is in your person specification, additional relevant training, outside interests relevant to the job and interpersonal skills.

Prepare the information the candidates will need

Sending the appropriate information to the candidates will help you attract suitable applicants. You want to encourage a potential applicant to apply by making the information user-friendly, but you also want to ensure that the right people apply, so you need to provide information about the type of environment in which he or she will work and how the workplace is organized so that the applicant has enough information to decide whether or not the job is suitable.

The pack you send out should include a copy of the job description and details about the school. (It is sensible to develop a description of the school to use for all appointments.) Including an organizational chart can also be helpful for candidates because it gives a clear immediate picture of where the applicant will fit in. Finally, get the department or section of the school concerned to provide information about the department or section in which the applicant will work.

Other information should be available on request, but as it is expensive to send out a lot of paper, you should send out sufficient information initially to attract the applicants you want. Additional information can be provided for short-listed candidates. Some candidates phone up and ask for copies of anything and everything ever produced by the school – resist this kind of unnecessary demand and think about what it tells you about the candidate! You may also want to use some documents as tasks in the selection procedure, so think carefully about what you send to candidates in the initial stage.

Advertise the post

The costs of advertising are substantial. This makes it important to target your advert carefully. Remember that the advert is the way possible candidates get their initial knowledge and understanding of the post on offer, so, while stinting on the wording may save you money now, if it is not clear to potential applicants what the job is and what kind of person is required, you are likely to attract a very small field and may have to read-vertise, which is not cost-effective.

The advert should concentrate on job title, salary, brief description of work or duties, indication of the kind of person who would best fill the post, location, benefits package and assistance given to the successful candidate, how to obtain an application form and application details, and the closing date.

No advert should be worded in such a way as to give the impression that applicants of one particular race, age or sex are preferred. Beware of gender-specific job titles, eg headmistress. It is always wise to include a statement that makes it clear that the school has a fair recruitment policy and that applications are invited from all sections of society.

CASE STUDY 6.2 FOR ACTION

Bestwick Park High School – head of science – CPS plus 4

Following the retirement of Mr B Proudlove after 25 distinguished years of service, the governors wish to appoint a well-qualified and experienced scientist to lead the faculty. A preparedness to lead from the front by example and an understanding of the likely needs of students of this successful and oversubscribed suburban school are essential. The ideal candidate is likely to be in the 30–40 age range and a graduate of a British university.

For action

What are the main mistakes in this advertisement? What advice would you give the headteacher and the personnel subcommittee?

Woodlands School – head of science – CPS plus 4

An ambitious head of science is required for September, ready to take a significant step towards school leadership in a rapidly growing and improving school. This is an excellent opportunity for an aspiring teacher to lead the management of an enlarged department. Woodlands High School is committed to individual progress and quality development for all its stakeholders.

For action

What is the message of this advertisement, ie what impression does it
want to give the candidate and does it achieve its aim?

What you put in your advertisement is not your only problem. You also
need to think very carefully about where and when to advertise. If you
advertise at the wrong time or not widely enough, you could be wasting a
lot of money.

You will have to decide whether to advertise nationally, locally or by a
combination of the two. The vacancy for a head or deputy must be advertised nationally throughout England and Wales. The main method is to
use the specialist press. Make sure that local advertising does not exclude
local church or ethnic papers. If the post is suitable for a first-time applicant, you may want to do a trawl of the universities. This will increase the
number of good applicants and you may find it useful to develop links
with particular colleges who get to know your needs. This method should
supplement the main methods of advertising and not substitute for them.

Ensure that you advertisement is non-discriminatory. Failure to do so
could lead to a complaint being brought, which could be upheld by an
industrial tribunal. 'Word of mouth' recruitment is one example of recruitment that might save you money on advertising and bring you a candidate whose virtues and attributes are known, but could result in you and
your governors being taken to tribunal by someone who claims that the
appointment was unfair because it was not advertised properly. In these
circumstances it could be very difficult to justify your actions, so beware!

CASE STUDY 6.3 FOR ACTION

The librarian had announced her resignation. It was only a part-time post,
and the secretary suggested to you that one of her clerical assistants, who
was also a parent, could easily take over the job, combining it with her
existing post. Mrs Chattin is a lively person with a lot to offer. Her children are now nearly grown up, so she could take on a full-time post. You
think it is a good idea, and so does the chairman of governors when you
mention it to him, so you go ahead and offer her the job. Then you begin
to receive letters of complaint. There is a furious one from a parent who

is a trained librarian, claiming that she would have jumped at the opportunity of working for the school if the post had been advertised properly; and another threatens to take the governors to tribunal because the job wasn't advertised and the writer hadn't known it was available.

For action/discussion

What mistakes were made in managing this appointment? What advice would you give the head and governors?

There are specific circumstances, however, when internal-only advertising is justified. This is when the school is involved in reorganization or merger with another school. The governors could justify not advertising posts because of the need to protect the employment of existing members of staff.

Make sure that posts advertised externally are also advertised internally, even if you are unlikely to appoint an internal candidate. Again this is a safeguard for you against trouble later.

Attracting candidates

The LEA package of benefits and assistance was designed to help attract candidates, but nowadays few governing bodies have the resources at their command to maintain this kind of incentive, so the post itself or the reputation of the school has to be the attraction. Setting the salary or grading the post at the right level to draw candidates is vital.

CASE STUDY 6.4 FOR ACTION

The school was expanding and I thought it was only fair to create a second in the English department because it is compulsory to 16 and attracts large groups at A level. We reached this decision at the autumn meeting of the personnel committee and decided to go ahead with the appointment during this academic year rather than to wait for September, as it could be tied into the vacancy arising in the department for the spring term. In the meantime I mentioned to the main scale teacher whom we appointed last year that we would be creating this post, and asked him if he would be a candidate. He's quite good and I wouldn't object to his appointment, although obviously I wanted to advertise properly. I was taken aback, however, when he said, 'No, for such a small allowance, it's not worth my while.' Then when we did advertise the field was very weak and in the end we didn't appoint.

For action

What mistakes were made in handling this post? What advice would you give to this headteacher and the personnel subcommittee?

The point on a scale at which you are prepared to appoint a suitable candidate can make a considerable difference to the field, and nowadays you have much more flexibility than in the past. This might incline you towards 'golden hallos', particularly in shortage subjects. This is why you have to start by working out what you can afford and how important this particular package is to the school. Do look at the long-term implications of the package, however, not just what it will cost this year. Indeed, in a climate of rising costs and inadequate funding, when schools are having to make staff redundant, the very idea of 'golden hallos' could raise a wry smile. A very real management issue for heads and governors is how to balance the need to attract quality staff in essential and shortage areas while shedding surplus staff elsewhere. Figures 6.1 and 6.2 illustrate how to present your staffing plan in diagrammatic form.

CASE STUDY 6.5 FOR ACTION

Your school is well down all the league tables; even in its own local area it is hardly a market leader. It has its full complement of social and other problems and is seriously undersubscribed. Write an advertisement for the post of head of English for which a good field is essential to your plans for revitalizing the school.

Moving the school forward – creating an effective staffing structure

A new headteacher should produce an ideal staffing structure, which will be implemented over time. This should be costed and referred to as staff leave. Although a big task initially, it does make it easier when vacancies arise, because much of the negotiations with governors and costing have already been carried out. Agreement then only has to be sought for new roles. And this is likely to be infrequent.

CASE STUDY 6.6 FOR ACTION

Figure 6.1 shows the staff structure when you took up your appointment as headteacher. Figure 6.2 shows the staffing structure that you aim to move towards over time.

For action

Prepare a presentation for the governors in which you explain your aims for future staffing. How can you achieve your aims?

Timing

The closing date for application is fixed before any advertisement goes out; indeed, usually it is all worked back from the date of the interview, so that the necessary personnel can attend. Normally you will want a maximum of 14 days between closing date and the interview, otherwise you may lose your best candidates to another post. Provide the candidates invited to interview with a programme of the day's activities and the functions of the selection panel. The letter of invitation should also set out what will be expected of the candidates.

SHORT-LISTING

The selection panel will need a basic core of information – the job description, person specification, procedures being applied and anything else to enable fair selection. Each member of the panel should have a list of the

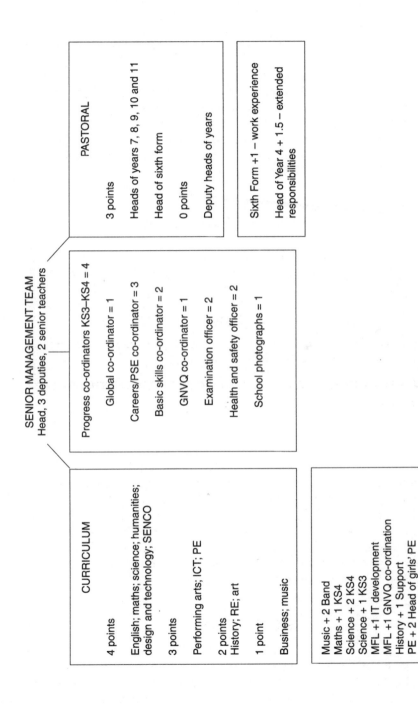

SENIOR MANAGEMENT TEAM
Head, 3 deputies, 2 senior teachers

CURRICULUM

4 points

English; maths; science; humanities;
design and technology; SENCO

3 points

Performing arts; ICT; PE

2 points
History; RE; art

1 point

Business; music

Music + 2 Band
Maths + 1 KS4
Science + 2 KS4
Science + 1 KS3
MFL +1 IT development
MFL +1 GNVQ co-ordination
History + 1 Support
PE + 2 Head of girls' PE

PASTORAL

3 points

Heads of years 7, 8, 9, 10 and 11

Head of sixth form

0 points

Deputy heads of years

Sixth Form +1 – work experience

Head of Year 4 + 1.5 – extended
responsibilities

Progress co-ordinators KS3–KS4 = 4

Global co-ordinator = 1

Careers/PSE co-ordinator = 3

Basic skills co-ordinator = 2

GNVQ co-ordinator = 1

Examination officer = 2

Health and safety officer = 2

School photographs = 1

Figure 6.1 *Staff structure on appointment as headteacher*

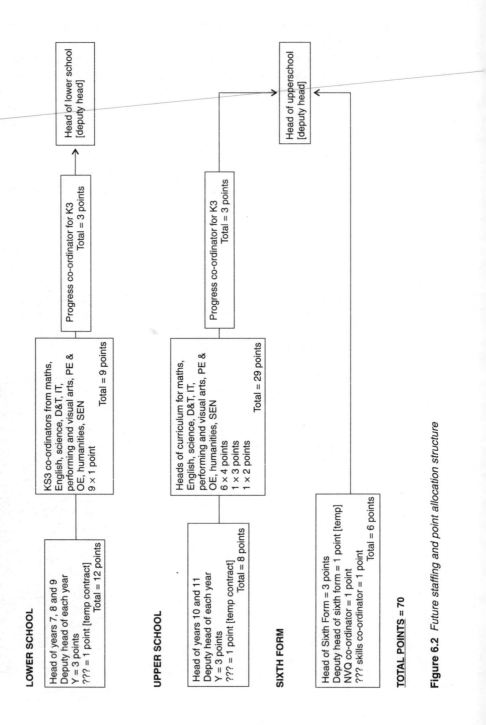

LOWER SCHOOL

Head of years 7, 8 and 9
Deputy head of each year
Y = 3 points
??? = 1 point [temp contract]
Total = 12 points

KS3 co-ordinators from maths,
English, science, D&T, IT,
performing and visual arts, PE &
OE, humanities, SEN
9 × 1 point
Total = 9 points

Progress co-ordinator for K3
Total = 3 points

Head of lower school
[deputy head]

UPPER SCHOOL

Head of years 10 and 11
Deputy head of each year
Y = 3 points
??? = 1 point [temp contract]
Total = 8 points

Heads of curriculum for maths,
English, science, D&T, IT,
performing and visual arts, PE &
OE, humanities, SEN
6 × 4 points
1 × 3 points
1 × 2 points
Total = 29 points

Progress co-ordinator for K3
Total = 3 points

Head of upperschool
[deputy head]

SIXTH FORM

Head of Sixth Form = 3 points
Deputy head of sixth form = 1 point [temp]
NVQ co-ordinator = 1 point
??? skills co-ordinator = 1 point
Total = 6 points

TOTAL POINTS = 70

Figure 6.2 *Future staffing and point allocation structure*

applicants and should have received a copy of the application forms before the short-listing session.

Don't forget that the chief education officer (CEO) or his or her representative has a right to attend meetings of the selection panel for teaching staff. The panel is required to consider any advice given by the attending officer. This is an advantage for you, as the LEA officer is usually experienced in selection procedures, could warn you of possible pitfalls and help you gently nudge governors who stray from the agreed criteria. It is a sensible move to record who is present, what advice is offered and, if it is not taken, why you have set it aside, because if the panel decides to ignore the advice and the case comes to tribunal, to have any chance at all you must be able to justify the decision.

The way a candidate has filled in the application form could make an initial good or bad impression on the panel members. They will need to balance this initial impression by using the criteria they have developed to help them analyse the data in the application forms. Indeed your most difficult task could be to persuade the panel to apply the criteria rather than rely on gut reactions at both the short-listing and the interview stages of the selection process. For this reason it is a good idea to use an evaluation grid, which helps keep the process methodical and objective and is a protection for you if trouble develops later on.

CASE STUDY 6.7 FOR ACTION

The selection panel at Bestwick Park High School is considering the applications for the post of second deputy head. The job description (see Case Study 6.11) makes it clear that it is a pastoral post. Both the existing senior teachers have applied. Neither is considered suitable, one because he has done little work in the pastoral side of the school and is generally regarded as having little to offer, and the other because she has a tendency to be both aggressive and rigid, and the head wants to restructure the pastoral system and improve contact with parents.

For action

Should either or both senior teachers be interviewed on tactical grounds? If the panel decide that it is more honest to remove them at this stage, because they have no hope of being appointed and not to do so would prevent better candidates from being interviewed, how should they go about it?

Take up references

References are a problem area. When you should take up references and how far they should influence the selection of a candidate are issues you will have to resolve quite early in the selection process. References have been discredited for a number of reasons:

❑ Often they tell you as much about the writer as about the candidate!
❑ They can create an impression of the candidate that could influence the short-listing or selection.
❑ Ethnic minority groups have felt disadvantaged by the reference process.
❑ A small number of LEAs will not use references at all because they do not consider them to be sufficiently objective.

Some heads or selection panels prefer to take up references on all or the most promising candidates as soon as the application forms are received, which can speed up the process of making an appointment. Most LEAs, however, recommend that references are taken up after short-listing, and that they should act as confirmation at interview stage, rather than form a part of the selection procedure. This makes it difficult for a disappointed candidate to be able to claim that an adverse reference prejudiced his or her chances. For the same reason LEAs discourage telephone references, although this is sometimes the only way to obtain a reference in time. Occasionally a post is offered 'subject to satisfactory references' if there has not been time for references to arrive before interviews.

Interpreting the reference should be approached with caution. References normally only contain positive statements, but they can nevertheless damn with faint praise or somehow manage to create a negative impression, so treat them with extreme care. They can sometimes sound a warning bell that things are not quite right and this can be extremely useful. For example, if they fail to match the candidate's application form in some important areas, say by not mentioning activities or qualities that the candidate has highlighted, you will begin to wonder about what the candidate has actually achieved. Similarly the choice of referee indicates something about the candidate, either because of the quality of referee the candidate has to offer or because, for example, the applicant has omitted to give his or her present headteacher as one of the referees and inevitably you will wonder 'Why not?' You will want at least two references so that you can check whether they convey the same impression of the candidate. The reference is useful in that you can tick off the good points against the criteria you have established.

Should you visit the candidates?

Visiting candidates in their own schools to help you gain an impression of them is nowadays discouraged for several reasons:

❑ You are unlikely to be able to visit all the candidates – visiting some, but not all, is unfair.
❑ Not all schools will want you to come – this may not be the candidate's fault.
❑ Watching the candidate teach in one school will not tell you how he or she will fit into a different institution.
❑ This kind of visit depends on one person's impression and feedback. If it influenced the decision, it could be questioned later on.
❑ What do you do if the candidate hasn't told his current school about the application?

Candidates' visits to the school

You will have to decide your policy about allowing candidates to visit the school before the formal interviews. At one time this was very popular, but unless all candidates have the same opportunity and can all take advantage of it, it discriminates against those who live a long way away. It is probably wiser to send short-listed candidates some additional information and take a full day for the interviews.

ON THE DAY

A well-organized day is a priority. It is nerve-racking enough for candidates to spend a day in an unfamiliar school and go through a formal interview. You do not want to make the experience either painful or unpleasant, nor do you want them to dine out on horror tales about your school. You will want to give any visitors, whether you appoint them to your staff or not, the best possible impression of the school. Making a group of candidates feel that this is a school that they would like to join is an important public relations exercise.

The day's programme should include an opportunity to tour the school and meet appropriate people for long enough for the candidates to gain an impression of the ethos of the school and the department. A good lunch in pleasant conditions is always appreciated. It needs to be made clear whether it is part of the interviewing process or not, as sometimes it is used for staff to get a feel of the candidates and, for senior posts such as deputyships, the candidates are made to play musical chairs, changing places for different courses. If it is not part of the selection process, it is only fair to tell the candidates that over lunch they do not need to 'perform'. Serving alcohol can also be an unfair test, particularly if only some candidates have already had their formal interview and some have not.

Most schools appoint staff using a formal interview as the main selection test, but often there are additional tests. A linguist, for example, will be expected to demonstrate his or her competence in the language(s). Quite frequently nowadays for senior posts such as deputyships, there will be a task such as working out a curriculum notation or suggesting strategies to deal with some current problem or initiative that the school is undertaking. The usefulness of such tests can depend on how well the task is set and whether the selection panel have given enough thought to what they want to get out of it. Sometimes the candidates are asked to take part in a group discussion, to see how they interact or what ideas they have to offer. The problem with this device is that it is so artificial it can fail to do justice to some good candidates. Psychometric tests, administered by outside agencies, are regularly used as a part of the process of short-listing for senior posts. As long as these tests are not the only method of selection they can be useful, but be wary of governors who place total faith in them. You should also perhaps bear in mind that some candidates may have done these tests, which will affect both their speed and the general tenor of their answers.

At the interview

The areas that you want to explore at interview, the interview questions and how they are to be asked should all be worked out well before the interview and the panel clearly briefed about the procedure. The questions should be structured so that each candidate is treated fairly and given the opportunity to do himself or herself justice. This does not necessarily mean that they must all be asked the same questions. Although a few LEAs still insist on this, it could actually penalize some candidates and could be challenged at tribunal as unfair practice. It is more important that each interview should have the same shape and include questions of the same level of difficulty. A solution to what remains a thorny issue could be to have mainly the same questions but a few specific questions slotted in for each individual. Candidates are usually interviewed in alphabetical order and, if some other procedure is adopted, the candidates should be told what it is and why it is being used. The length of the interview varies with the seniority of the post, but is likely to be a minimum of 20–30 minutes.

How to structure an interview

At the start of the interview the chairperson should introduce the panel members and make some attempt to put the candidate at ease. 'Icebreakers' or warm-up questions should be used early on. These require the candidates to talk about themselves in a descriptive way, and you could ask them to explain their current job title or to talk about the stages in their career. This question is an opportunity to see how well they can categorize.

The interview is the candidates' opportunity to talk, so make sure that they are given sufficient time to answer and that there are enough questions of a variety of types for you to get a rounded view of how the candidates perform. Although most of the time you will need to use open questions in order to get the candidates to express their opinions, sometimes you will want to focus in on a specific point and so use funnel questions. You may also use funnel questions to push candidates into a more precise answer, if they have been too vague. Avoid 'Do you agree?' because it pre-empts a real choice – candidates will think that they have to agree. At a senior level it may be a test of whether candidates are too ready to agree with what they think your view is, but beware how you use it.

Some questions should test what candidates think is important (eg attitude to a current initiative, or their priorities over the next three years if appointed head of department), while others should test what they know (eg about recent developments in their subject or current educational issues).

You will wish to know how they would tackle a problem, and you could approach this by asking them how they would deal with a particular situation or introduce a specific initiative. You may want to know how they view themselves and approach this through questions such as what they see as their strengths or weaknesses, or how they see their career developing. In some interviews it is important that candidates demonstrate a positive attitude to a particular issue (eg multi-cultural education or equal opportunities) and you will test this through such questions as 'How do you ensure equal opportunities in your department?'

It is your responsibility to see that the panel get a full picture of candidates and if an answer isn't clear to them, try to help the candidates clarify what they mean, either through a supplementary question or by explaining a technical answer to the panel.

The answers to questions like these will give the panel an indication of candidates' knowledge, what vision they have, how practical they seem to be and whether they can make points cogently and concisely.

AFTER THE INTERVIEW

Making the appointment

Some candidates are good at interviews; others may perform in the job better than they interview. This is why you should work from an interview summary for each candidate. It should be set alongside the person specification at the end of all the interviews. The interview summary is also a precaution against trouble if for some reason the appointment is questioned. When all the interviews have taken place, the adviser or consultant sums up the interviews, indicating the strengths and weaknesses of each candidate in order to focus the discussion and help the panel reach its decision. The officer or consultant does not have a vote, but can offer advice to the panel. Normally the weakest candidates are quickly eliminated and then the evidence about the remaining candidates is reviewed. This usually settles the matter, but sometimes there is a lot of discussion at this stage and the panel begin to argue about the merits of the candidates. The consultant or the head will have to make sure that this discussion does not reflect personal prejudices, but keeps to the criteria. Eventually a decision is reached, the officer or consultant fetches the candidate who has been chosen and the chairperson makes a verbal offer of the post. The unsuccessful candidates are usually offered a debriefing by the adviser, who bases his or her comments on the interview summary.

If the interview is for a headteacher or deputy headteacher post, the decision will have to be referred to the whole governing body for ratification. This means that a mechanism has to be set up to call the governing body together as quickly as possible, usually on the same day, so that a substantive offer can be made. It is possible for them to reject the choice, although this does not often happen.

Accepting the post

If the candidate accepts the post, that constitutes a contract, although as yet there is nothing in writing. Successful candidates often worry about the lack of proof that they have the post, and you should try to reassure them by explaining the procedure. Normally the head writes to the successful candidate within a few days, as often it takes some weeks before the legal documentation arrives from the education office.

Candidates may ask for time to consider because of other interviews. It has not been the practice in education to allow this, but if it has been difficult to recruit for a particular post, you have to wait for the person to make his or her mind up.

Another problem is the candidate who verbally accepts the post, and then accepts another job with better incentives. This is illegal, as a verbal contract has been made. In this situation, if you are an LEA school, the LEA is your best source of advice about the legal position, but it still leaves you with a problem – you are short of a member of staff and may have to start proceedings all over again.

CASE STUDY 6.8 FOR REFLECTION

I had a candidate turn down the post three weeks after the appointment and after the closing date for staff resignations, so reappointment was very difficult. Since she did not have a job and was not a member of a union, in practice there was very little I could do.

Headteacher commenting on an unsuccessful appointment

Not appointing

Sometimes there is no agreement or all the candidates are felt to lack the necessary qualities, in which case no appointment is made and the post is readvertised. If this occurs, the panel should be clearly advised as to whether this is such a shortage subject that readvertisement may not bring a better field. It is in this kind of situation that the adviser's or consultant's knowledge of the market-place should carry weight. Readvertising is expensive and may not be productive. On the other hand, no appointment is better than the wrong appointment.

If a disagreement occurs – advice for officers and advisers

A written record should be sent immediately to the governors in the event of a disagreement. This may be needed if subsequently the head or deputy appointed proves to be incompetent and the governors decide to sack him or her. The LEA will then need to prove that its advice was not heeded and that therefore the school should bear the cost of any redundancy and/or tribunal.

This record should be used alongside the interview summary form used by advisory staff. This records comments made on the people interviewed and should also include the notes on debriefing. An exemplar is given as Case Study 6.14.

Associate staff

Appointing associate staff differs from appointing teachers in some important respects. The CEO must be consulted before advertising a post that is for more than 16 hours a week, and the LEA can veto the appointment on the same grounds as for other staff in the school. There are, however, no attendance or advice rights. The Education Act is not specific about the precise method to be adopted, so you could in theory proceed on your own, but it is advisable to bring in representatives from the department concerned and some representation from the governors, though with associate staff appointments it can sometimes be difficult to get governors to give the time, as they tend to leave it to you. The recommendation for the appointment must include details of the hours to be worked, the grade (one of the existing LEA grades) and, if any discretion exists, the recommended salary.

EXEMPLAR MATERIAL

The case study material below follows through the appointment of a deputy head at Bestwick Park High School and provides exemplars of the kind of documents that you would need to write. They are for reflection.

The appointment of a deputy head at Bestwick Park High School

The vacancy for a headteacher or deputy headteacher must be advertised nationally throughout England and Wales.

CASE STUDY 6.9 FOR ACTION

The advertisement

Besthampton LEA
Bestwick Park High School, Bestwick Park Avenue, Besthampton PJL 134
Tel: Besthampton 2468. Roll 1,030; 150 pupils in the post-16 phase
Current Group 6 for deputy headteachers. Spine points 26–32

Headteacher Mrs B Gatlin, MA

Required from September

A suitably experienced and committed teacher to join the senior management team of this popular and well-resourced suburban comprehensive school as the second deputy head. Initially principal responsibilities will include co-ordination of pastoral care and some general administration, but there will be scope at a later date for the successful candidate to negotiate changes in role and task.

Application forms and further details of the post may be obtained from the headteacher at the school and should be returned there within a fortnight of the appearance of this advertisement.

Besthampton is an equal opportunities employer.

For reflection

What would a prospective applicant learn from this advertisement? Is it likely to attract candidates? What do you think should feature in an advertisement for a deputy head post?

CASE STUDY 6.10

General information about the school

A pack of information about the school and a job description are usually sent out to prospective candidates. It varies whether the person specification is also sent.

Bestwick Park High School

Bestwick Park High School was formed by the amalgamation of Besthampton Grammar School with the nearby secondary modern school, Park High School. It is an all-ability 11–18 mixed school, which takes a five form entry of 150 pupils. The school is popular and oversubscribed. It attracts pupils from the neighbouring villages as well as from Besthampton itself.

There are 1,030 pupils in the school with 52.6 full-time equivalent teaching staff. The clerical and technical assistance from 14 associate staff is very good indeed. Visiting music teachers set high standards in a wide range of instruments and contribute to the two school orchestras and to senior and junior choirs. 'Foodfair' provides refreshments for sale at break and a comprehensive lunch menu, including a health-food bar. Vegetarian food is always available and every effort is made to cater for special diets. Our excellent facilities are also a catering centre for the local meals on wheels service.

Our well-maintained buildings are set within 14 acres of pleasant grounds. These include eight laboratories, three art/pottery rooms, a well-equipped technology suite, two gymnasia, a lecture theatre, a dark room with excellent facilities, a recording studio, drama studios and a very well-stocked library. As well as two modern computer rooms, a network of computers is available throughout the school. The latest commercial and educational software is used and IT is employed very widely across the curriculum. There are online facilities and electronic mail links the school with schools abroad, including one in Moscow. There is a lively and active music department with its own suite and practice rooms, which provides opportunities for specialist tuition in piano, guitar, all orchestral instruments and solo singing.

The five forms in each year are of mixed ability. In year 7 the work is differentiated according to need to ensure continued progression. Groups for mathematics are set by ability during the first term. The National Curriculum is integrated into the programme for years 7–9 and the school places an emphasis on active learning. Special provision is made for individual learning needs; enrichment and extension are provided for those who are very able, and specific support, as appropriate, for others, both in and out of lessons. Besthampton Achievement Project courses are offered in most subjects.

A common course continues for all students in years 8 and 9, and a second modern language is introduced for most students. Students are taught in sets in some subjects, eg mathematics, modern languages, science and PE, which means that they are taught with others at the level that is suited to their ability and most likely to bring out the best in them.

Year 10 students study a common core of subjects in addition to some guided choices. The aim is to give a balanced programme over the two years leading to Key Stage 4. As well as departmental assessments, profiling is used throughout the school, leading to a record of achievement.

There is a large, popular and well-established sixth form. We are able to offer a very wide range of subjects at this level. Following detailed consultation the school aims to provide the most appropriate course for each student. There are 22 A level courses offered, as well as GNVQ in business and finance, and health and social care, together with a range of complementary courses. Sixth formers also have the opportunity to participate in a range of extra-curricular activities such as Young Enterprise and community service. Additionally a work-shadowing programme for all year 12 students is followed in all Besthampton schools during the last two weeks of the summer term.

There are numerous after-school or lunchtime clubs and societies. At present some 90 pupils participate in the Duke of Edinburgh Award Scheme at bronze, silver or gold level. Outside speakers and visits play a vital role in the life of the school and our pupils visit organizations of all kinds to attend lectures, exhibitions, discussions, etc.

Pastoral care is co-ordinated by one of the deputy headteachers. Each year is managed by a year head. The role of form tutor is regarded as crucial in pastoral care.

The Parent Teacher Association is very supportive and active, arranging many fund-raising and social events. They also take an active interest in the educational life of the school.

In-service training is considered to be very important and we encourage all members of staff to become involved both through school-focused initiatives and through attendance at county or other external courses. Staff development is managed by a staff development committee and co-ordinated by one of the deputy heads.

The headteacher is assisted by two deputy heads and three senior teachers, who work closely together as a management team. At present this team meets twice a week and collaborates with staff through whole staff consultative meetings, heads of faculty, heads of department, departmental, heads of year and tutor meetings. Recently the school has been reorganized into faculties and there are now six faculties: mathematics, English, science and technology, modern languages, humanities and expressive arts. The 18 governors meet termly. They take an active interest in the school, attending working parties and social functions, and there are five governors' subcommittees: curriculum, finance, personnel, buildings and marketing.

We believe in consultative management and are working towards collective management. Bestwick Park High School is proud to be an Investors in People organization.

CASE STUDY 6.11

Bestwick Park High School – job description

Post: second deputy head. **Salary scale**: Group 5. **Spinal point**:

Organizational relationship

The post holder will be directly responsible to the headteacher.

Service relationship

The post holder will be a member of the senior management team.

Purpose

As deputy head the post holder is a member of the senior management team. In that capacity he or she will contribute to:

❏ the formulation of the school's overall aims and objectives;
❏ determining and maintaining norms of behaviour and discipline for the pupils;
❏ the motivation of pupils and staff by personal influence and concern for human needs.

Duties

❏ to develop and implement a pastoral system that meets the needs of the school;
❏ the oversight and co-ordination of the work of the year heads and their teams;
❏ overall responsibility for the PSHE programme;
❏ overall responsibility for community links;
❏ responsibility for leading the development of a new school record of achievement;
❏ liaison with external agencies such as EWOs, social services, etc;
❏ to deputize for the headteacher as required;
❏ to undertake such duties as may be assigned to the post holder by the head from time to time.

CASE STUDY 6.12

Bestwick Park High School – person specification

Job title: Deputy headteacher, secondary comprehensive school

Category	Essential	Desirable
Qualification		
Academic	Good degree	Further relevant qualifications and /or in-service training

Professional	Qualified teacher status	
Experience		
Teaching	Secondary school teaching across the age and ability range	Experience in more than one school/LEA
Curriculum	Familiarity and involvement with new curriculum initiatives. Experience of leading curriculum development	
Management	Successful experience as a middle manager	Variety of middle management experience
Community	Evidence of commitment to community and parental involvement	
Extra-curricular		Evidence of involvement in/leadership of extra-curricular activities throughout career

Skills and abilities

To provide effective leadership
Ability to communicate with different audiences, eg parents, staff, etc

Ability to formulate, implement and evaluate short- and long-term objectives for school development

Ability to set and manage a budget

A thorough grasp of current educational issues

CASE STUDY 6.13

Letter of invitation

The letter of invitation sets out what will be expected of the candidate, and the day's programme of events. It also lists the interviewing panel. This panel will be larger than the short-listing committee and contains a mixture of governors. Although the governors are responsible for the appointment of a deputy headteacher, it is usual for the headteacher to be a member of the interviewing panel. The governors must also allow the CEO or his or her representative to attend and must consider any advice given, whether or not they have asked for such advice.

Dear Mr Farr,

I am pleased to invite you for interview for the post of second deputy head at Bestwick Park High School.

You are asked to arrive at the school at 9.15 on Thursday, 19 November. Parking will be reserved next to the front door of the school.

The programme for the day will be as follows:

9.15–9.45 Introductory session with the headteacher – all candidates

9.45–10.15 Tours of the school

10.15–10.30 Coffee with the senior staff

10.30–12.00 Carousel of individual interviews (about 15 minutes each interview): 1) with the headteacher and chair of governors; and 2) with the attached adviser and the divisional education officer

12.00–1.00 Lunch with the governors and senior staff

1.0 Formal interviews (a list of the interviewing panel is attached)

Please will you telephone the school to confirm your acceptance of the interview. I enclose an expenses form and a map of the immediate area for your assistance.

I look forward to seeing you on 19 November.

Yours sincerely,

Brenda Gatlin (Headteacher)

Interviewing panel for deputy headship on Thursday, 19 November

Mrs C Jervis, Chair of Governors

Dr P Pryce
Mrs S Briggs, County Council Representatives

Mr P Blaze

Mrs M Rolls
Mrs N Lees, Parent Governors

Mr J Locke
Mr F Perry, Co-opted Representatives

Mrs B Gatlin, Headteacher

Mrs L Castle, Attached Adviser

Mrs M Warden, Divisional Education Officer

CASE STUDY 6.14

The interview summary is an insurance against trouble later if for some reason the appointment is questioned.

Interview summary

Name of candidate ....

School ....

Post ....

This form should be used alongside the person specification.

Essential characteristics	positive evidence	negative evidence
To be decided before interview	During interview/ application	Forms/ references/ informal interviews

Desirable characteristics

To be decided before
interview

Record of advice given by the Chief Education Officer or his/her representative

Record of advice given to candidates on debriefing

This form should be used alongside the form already devised by the advisory staff, which records comments made on the people interviewed for
further reference for short-listing purposes. It should include notes on the
debriefing.

CASE STUDY 6.15 FOR REFLECTION/REVISION

A checklist for making an appointment

Vacancy occurs

Head advises – Governing body makes informed decision– LEA advises

Fill vacancy –   No – Reallocate any responsibilities internally
                   Yes – Meeting of selection panel

Task of the selection panel is to:

❑   finalize dates for short-listing and interviews;
❑   draw up a job description for the post;
❑   draw up a person specification;
❑   agree selection criteria;
❑   review school details and agree info package;
❑   agree advert and placement;
❑   agree format and procedure for interview.

For head/deputy? Yes

❑   Advertise nationally
❑   Send information to applicants
❑   Short-listing meeting
❑   References
❑   Interviews
❑   Debriefing for unsuccessful candidates
❑   File interview records
❑   For deputies – report back to full governing body for endorsement
❑   Confirmation to candidate of appointment
❑   Instruct LEA to appoint
❑   Contract issued

7

MANAGING PERFORMANCE

YOUR ROLE IN MANAGING PERFORMANCE

One of your principal responsibilities is to ensure quality teaching and to enable this the staff have to perform well. This chapter looks at how you carry out this important aspect of your role and concentrates on the difficult task of trying to deal with the problem of poor performance.

The obvious first port of call in considering staff performance is appraisal (now in place throughout the British system of education), which looks at the objectives and performance of individual members of staff. Where it is working effectively in schools, it makes an important contribution to assessing performance, but there are problems connected with centring quality assurance on appraisal alone. Appraisal has largely been seen as a developmental tool, rather than one targeting assessment, and as a management tool it is still in its infancy. Moreover, there is still a problem in finding the right balance between the needs of individuals and the needs of the institution. Appraisal does not always lead to an accurate diagnosis of problems because it is all too easy to buck the system. This is discussed more fully later in the chapter, but many problems combine to make it a less than ideal mechanism for monitoring performance.

Managing staff who are not performing well takes considerable time and effort. The process can also be stressful for headteachers, who have to ensure problems are handled in a manner that both complies with employment law and is seen to be fair. So how do you go about managing performance? Obviously you need to get an indication of how staff actually teach and this is likely to involve a programme of lesson observation.

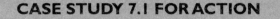

CASE STUDY 7.I FOR ACTION

In my previous school I visited at least one classroom every day.
I intend to maintain that habit as headteacher here.

Recently promoted headteacher
addressing his first staff meeting

For action

❏ How realistic is this new headteacher?
❏ Where do you as headteacher fit into a programme of lesson observation?
❏ What should you expect to know about how the staff are performing?
❏ What impact do you think his statement is likely to have on his staff?
(The previous head kept well away from their classrooms.)
❏ What are the management issues implicit in this case study?

Monitoring performance is a management function, of which appraisal (if it is working well) and visiting lessons are tools. You cannot, however, manage it all yourself. Sampling is obviously more realistic than trying to see everybody on a regular basis. It allows you to keep your finger on things without overcommitting yourself. However, your heads of department or faculty are the key personnel in this activity and it is they who to a large extent have to keep you informed about how things are going. The appraisal, observation or a letter from a parent should not be the first indication you receive if things are not going well. The middle manager should have a good working knowledge of the level of experience and expertise in his or her department and a finger on how things are going. If you receive a letter from a parent about a particular teacher, you need the head of department to be able to tell you about the content of that teacher's work, for example along the following lines:

❏ We planned this set of lessons together and we are all teaching the same.
❏ I regularly sample the books of each year group and the content has been covered.
❏ I visited one of Mr X's lessons last week and he was getting things right on that occasion.
❏ I checked a sample of his exam marking (or reports etc) and it is OK.

It is also part of middle managers' responsibility to keep the SMT informed if they have concerns about the performance of a member of staff in their section.

This means that you have to train your managers up in some of the necessary skills. Case Study 7.2 is an example of the well-intentioned but unsuccessful monitoring that is still occurring in many schools, which does not provide you with the evidence you need.

CASE STUDY 7.2 FOR ACTION

Monitoring lessons

Bestwick Park High School – lesson monitoring form

Teacher: G Vicars   **Date**: 19/3/2000   **Teaching group**: 7B
Number present: 29
Content/title of lesson: Peasant life in the Middle Ages

Table 7.1

Criteria based on Ofsted	Comments	Advice
General classroom organizational strategies	Well-organized classroom Lesson prepared	
Teacher sets high expectations/challenges pupils	Pupils challenged to complete set task	
Provides a range of teaching/learning styles	Lesson predominantly teacher-led	
Time and resources used effectivly	Generally yes	
Effective use of homework	Yes	
Equality of access and opportunity	Generally yes	Aim to use more illustrations to focus on peasant housing
Departmental assessment policy followed	Yes	
SEN provision/differentiation within the lesson	Aware of special needs and some help given	
Manages the students well and achieves high standards of discipline	Poor behaviour challenged, some pupils unsettled	Use rewards – praise. Challenge those who could manage more
Curricular objectives match needs of the pupils	Workheet prepared for SEN group	

Agreed negotiated comments/proposals for future action

A sound lesson. Teacher generally in control and pupils achieved set task. Aim for a more flexible style in Q and A sessions and perhaps introduce some pair work. Use more illustrations to focus activities. Use departmental resources to provide more specialist materials for the special needs pupils.

In-service: Arrange observation of subject specialists in the department.

Signed: J Davis, Head of Humanities

For action

❑ Summarize the main weaknesses of this lesson
❑ This monitoring document will not help the teacher move forward – why not?
❑ How can you, or your senior manager in charge of staff development, help your middle managers carry out this important aspect of their role more effectively?

The observation programme will give you and your middle managers the opportunity to observe good practice and, in areas where weaknesses are observed or new techniques need to be strengthened or developed, it will help to provide targets for development. The vast majority of teaching in schools would be adjudged satisfactory, but what happens if it is not?

POOR PERFORMANCE

In any organization you will meet with a range of expertise and some of the staff will emerge as poor performers. How do you recognize and deal with poor quality performance? Indeed what precisely is meant by poor performance? There is no simple definition, but it may help clarify things if you ask yourself 'Is this member of staff performing his or her job to a generally acceptable standard over the most important areas of the job?' This will apply to any member of the organization but, as Chapter 12 has been specifically devoted to managing associate staff, this chapter will concentrate on poor performance in the classroom. When we begin to look at what constitutes effective teaching and, conversely, what is poor practice, an obvious starting-point is Ofsted guidelines.

CASE STUDY 7.3 FOR REFLECTION

Ofsted framework for inspection: quality of teaching

Where teaching is good pupils acquire knowledge, skills and understanding progressively and at a good pace. The lessons have clear aims and purposes. They cater appropriately for the learning of pupils of different abilities and interests and ensure the participation of all. The teaching methods suit the topic or subject as well as the pupils; the conduct of the lesson signals high expectations of all pupils and sets high but attainable challenges. There is regular feedback, which helps pupils make progress, both through thoughtful marking and discussion of work with pupils. Relationships are positive and promote pupils' motivation. National Curriculum Attainment Targets and Programmes of Study are fully taken into account. Where appropriate, homework, which extends or complements the work done in the lessons, is set regularly.

Teaching is unsatisfactory where pupils fail to achieve standards commensurate with their potential. The teaching is ill prepared or unclear. Pupils are unable to see the point of what they are asked to do. They are not appropriately challenged, nor are they helped to form a useful assessment of their level of attainment and of what needs to be improved. Specific learning needs of individuals in the class are not recognized sufficiently. Relationships are insecure and inhibit learning.

As you become familiar with it, you will begin to appreciate that most of the attributes of good and bad teaching have been set out in the two paragraphs above. But Ofsted language is not user-friendly and the following list should further clarify poor-quality teaching. Poor performance is typified by:

❑ failure to maintain discipline – poor class control;
❑ failure to demonstrate mastery of subject matter;
❑ failure to impart subject matter effectively;
❑ failure to form a working relationship with pupils;
❑ failure to accept teaching advice from superiors or colleagues;
❑ failure to produce desired results – class scores poorer results than peer groups.

Research suggests that it normally manifests itself as a series of recurring incidents rather than a one-off crisis, and that the crisis, when it comes, is the result of mounting tension and escalating problems, ie the final failure rather than the first failure. Usually the poor performer will exhibit more than one of the listed weaknesses and they will be or become interrelated. Let us illustrate this with a case study that describes what it could be like.

CASE STUDY 7.4 FOR ACTION

Mrs A

Mrs A left the staffroom slightly after the bell, as she usually did these days. The majority of the class was already in the room when she arrived, and most of the remainder trickled in over the next few minutes. She waited for them before starting, and then had some difficulty in getting silence. When she eventually began the lesson, someone said 'We can't start yet. Tim isn't here.' Mrs A's question as to why not produced complete silence. The class's attitude suggested they might know or suspect where Tim was, but were not going to say. Mrs A urgently needed to teach a new topic before the examinations, so she gave up on Tim's whereabouts and started the lesson. The information was in a video programme. Neither Mrs A nor the video succeeded in capturing the class's attention. There was a lot of talking (which she did not try to stop), pupils rustled papers, some chewed steadily, several quietly got on with work for other lessons and one, hidden from Mrs A, listened to his personal stereo. A few pupils did try to watch the video, but found difficulty in taking notes; the programme was punctuated with their questions to one another about what they had seen. Mrs A sat at her desk finishing off some marking while the video ran for 20 minutes. She did once attempt to reprimand a pupil who talked too loudly to her neighbour, but the pupil concerned answered back and Mrs A backed off. Another pupil asked the girl to be quiet, so that they could listen, and the girl acquiesced. At the end one pupil asked a question about something she had not understood in the video, but Mrs A said it was her own fault for not watching properly and went on to the next stage of the lesson, which was giving the class notes about what they had watched. She tried to get silence, but then gave up and simply started the dictation. Her voice was monotonous, but quite audible if the pupils listened. Nevertheless, this part of the lesson was punctuated by comments such as 'What did she say?' and 'What's she on about now?' and pupils loudly rephrased the notes. This created more confusion and held up proceedings, so Mrs A had not finished when the bell went. She tried to set some homework, a follow-up exercise from the textbook, but no one was listening to her. The pupils left without waiting to be dismissed. Mrs A gathered up her things and headed back to the staffroom. Another lesson was over.

This case study, which is further developed later in this chapter, describes poor practice rather than complete incompetence, but the scenario includes a lot of the classic features of teacher failure:

❏ Weak discipline – not complete breakdown because both sides backed off from confrontation, but silence and a good working atmosphere were never established.

❏ A lot of time was wasted, particularly at the beginning of the lesson. The teacher was late and so were the pupils.

❏ The class didn't really understand what they were doing or why, and they certainly could not guess what the learning outcome of this lesson was meant to be.

❏ There were few attempts to interact with the class. The only direct question was administrative and provoked a hostile reaction.

❏ Bright pupils were not challenged, and there was no differentiation – the lesson was targeted to the whole class.

❏ Weaker pupils received no support. An attempt by a pupil to clarify a point was put down.

❏ Pupils resorted to explaining the topic to one another, which added to the indiscipline and general confusion.

❏ The teacher did not scan the class or patrol it, so pupils used the opportunity to do other work.

❏ At no time was a pupil addressed by name – did she actually know their names?

❏ Timing was poor – she was having difficulty completing the syllabus.

❏ She was unlikely to receive any homework – no one wrote the instructions down.

❏ There was a basic lack of respect – no working relationship had been established with the teaching group.

For action

You are the new headteacher of Bestwick Park High School. You are very aware of the Ofsted guidelines on satisfactory and unsatisfactory lessons.

As part of your preparations for a forthcoming inspection you visit the lessons of the faculty in which Mrs A teaches and observe a lesson much like the one described above. In what respects do Mrs A's lessons fall short of the guidelines? It is clear that chaotic lessons are a regular occurrence for this teacher. What should you do about Mrs A?

Patchy performance can also constitute a problem, either through uneven overall performance or because one aspect of the teacher's performance is less good than others, as the following case study illustrates.

CASE STUDY 7.5 FOR ACTION

Kevin was a very unassuming young man, and when he was appointed to the modern languages department at Bestwick Park High School, he failed to establish his authority with his classes, particularly some of the junior groups. Very quickly discipline problems began to emerge, and Kevin developed a reputation as a poor teacher with control problems. As a result of colleagues' remonstrances and some parental complaints, a support teacher was put in to help Kevin. When the support teacher went to see the head because she said things were actually getting worse, the head sent the deputy in charge of staff development to observe a couple of lessons and report back. The deputy (Mike Wade) found, to his surprise, that Kevin's reputation as a poor teacher was undeserved. He found that Kevin had one specific problem: his poor class control prevented him from getting started. In the Year 8 lesson that Mike observed, the pupils behaved themselves and Kevin was able to teach them. He explained clearly, questioned sensitively, made ideas clear to the pupils and listened attentively to their ideas and suggestions. Mike felt Kevin had a lot to offer pupils, but how was it to be achieved?

For action

You are the headteacher – how as a manager can you salvage Kevin?

CAUSES OF POOR PERFORMANCE

In order to tackle the problem of how to manage staff who are not performing well, we need to understand the causes, ie what lies at the root of poor performance. Obviously we have to be careful about stereotyping and need to appreciate that poor performance is rarely the result of one factor alone. When a teacher is experiencing difficulties in his or her classroom, the unsatisfactory performance may arise for a number of reasons:

❑ the employee – the most common cause;
❑ organizational factors connected with the job;
❑ the way in which the employee has been managed;
❑ external factors;
❑ a combination of factors.

In the majority of cases the problem arises from the employee's lack of skill as a teacher. This could mean crucially that the teacher lacks the intellectual ability needed to establish subject credibility. The most damning statement about a teacher I have heard recently is: 'What this teacher knows about his subject could be put on the back of a postage stamp . . . and would not fill it.' Not surprisingly this teacher had difficulty in maintaining his authority. He was all too obviously barely one step ahead of the pupils, could not answer any of their questions and very quickly lost their respect.

Another manifestation of lack of skill is when the teacher lacks the ability to impart information effectively ('Mr X's explanations are very confusing. They make matters worse rather than better, so everyone just talks and no one listens') or when the teacher uses methods that fail to engage the interest of the group ('Mr Y's lessons are so dull. All we ever do is write notes from his dictation').

Sometimes, however, the poor performance arises from the teacher's lack of motivation. It is important to distinguish 'can't' from 'won't' when evaluating and dealing with unsatisfactory performance. Case Study 7.6 illustrates this aspect of poor performance.

CASE STUDY 7.6 FOR ACTION

Mrs Carmichael

You have been in post as headteacher of a junior and infant school for two terms and have recently heard that your school will receive an Ofsted inspection during the next school year. Comments from parents that 'it depends whose class your child is in' signal that all is not well on the teaching front, so as part of your Ofsted preparation you undertake a programme of lesson observations.

As a result of the observations you are seriously worried about the performance of one of your year 6 class teachers, Mrs Carmichael. Her lesson plans are sketchy. Her subject knowledge at Key Stage 2 is satisfactory, but her treatment of the subject is both superficial and dull. There are missed opportunities in lessons, and the skills used do not match the list of what is required for geography at levels 3 and 4. Her preferred teaching method is question and answer, which she describes as discussion. You observe very little real discussion, because the questions, which are mainly closed and factual, do not enable reflection, but reinforce prior knowledge or require pupils to guess the answer. The pupils seem interested in the topic and willing to offer suggestions, though there are a lot of wrong answers. In correcting their mistakes, Mrs Carmichael tends to disparage them. The noise level in lessons is rather high and any interruption provides an excuse for many of the pupils to come off task. Mrs Carmichael sometimes has to struggle to pull things together. This all has an adverse effect on the flow of lessons and pupils' progress during them.

It is not only the interruptions, however, which affect the pace of lessons – all the pupils work slowly. During a written activity, following a question-and-answer session, you notice that three quite able boys, seated together at a table near the front, are working at the pace of far less able pupils and that none of the class has completed the task, although it is both short and undemanding. When you ask a pupil why he is not trying to work out the answer, he says 'If I wait, she will tell us the answer', and sure enough she does. Homework is completing the written task. In discussion later, Mrs Carmichael tells you firmly that she does not believe in differentiation other than by outcome. She argues that it is wrong to show up children by setting the less able infantile tasks.

For action/discussion

Compare this lesson with Ofsted criteria for good practice – what are the main weaknesses? As headteacher, what strategies should you employ in both the short term and the long term to help Mrs Carmichael improve her performance?

Mrs Carmichael is also the subject co-ordinator for the humanities area. Subject documentation lacks detail, the list of resources is short and subject coverage, mainly through topic work, is unevenly divided between years 3–4 and 5–6. There is clearly no monitoring of the subject or the teaching. You anticipate problems with the inspector responsible for humanities. Your conversation with Mrs Carmichael indicates that she considers all the problems to be someone else's fault. She is very disparaging and quite sarcastic about other people's efforts and clearly reluctant to undertake any of the work that could actually improve her subject.

For action

Where does Mrs Carmichael fit into Bramson's seven categories of difficult people (described in Chapter 8)? What strategies should you use to deal with her?

It could also be useful to compare Case Study 7.6 with Case Study 8.2, which describes Fred. Both teachers are clearly 'won'ts' rather than 'can'ts' and are also very difficult to manage.

Lack of effort and poor motivation are among the contributors to poor performance. This is particularly true of some mature teachers who have been in the profession for a long time. Lack of ability is involuntary; lack of effort is not, and where it occurs, it raises the question of why this particular teacher has stopped trying. In the cases of Mrs Carmichael and Fred, there is no indication of what turned these once good teachers into poor performers or poor managers. Case Study 7.7, however, suggests why the performance of the teacher concerned deteriorated over a period of time.

CASE STUDY 7.7 FOR ACTION

James – an example of poor management accentuating poor performance

James has been teaching for 15 years, most of the time at his present school. His performance never has been world-shattering. His subject knowledge is good, though recently he has made less effort to keep up to date. He lacks charisma, pupils find his lessons dull and almost from the beginning the head of department had to be careful what groups she gave him, as his discipline was weak and confrontations could occur. She worked round James, although he seems unaware that he has had a protected timetable. His four children are now reaching adolescence and financial pressure has made him ambitious for promotion. He has been on a couple of counselling and pastoral courses, and he applies for year-head posts whenever they come up, but his poor personal discipline and general lack of organization mean that his applications are never seriously considered. Debriefing is always kind, but the rejections mount up. When he applied for a head of department post in another school in the borough, he did not even get an interview. On the surface nothing has changed. He is still the life and soul of the staff social committee and his lessons are much as before, but his timekeeping is deteriorating, he does as little marking as possible and he dodges duties if he thinks he can get away with it. At his last appraisal interview, however, he said that, although he is reasonably satisfied with things as they are, he sometimes feels very depressed that he is always passed over for promotion.

For action

What are the causes of James's increasingly poor performance and how should the headteacher respond?

No effort has ever been made to improve James's performance, and now it is deteriorating noticeably. It is the almost classic scenario of poor management of an employee. His head of department could be classified as an 'avoider': she worked around the problem rather than confronting it. We do not know whether this was from misplaced kindness or from a reluctance to tackle a difficult situation, but it has had an effect on James. (Observation of James's lessons could have been reported very similarly to the example given as Case Study 7.4.) External factors also played their part – the cost of raising his family motivated James to seek promotion. Once again poor management strategies shielded him from any realistic appraisal of his performance or hopes but, as rejection followed rejection, he became depressed and demotivated. Once again his managers, at either department or SMT level, did nothing to help and his performance has begun to deteriorate. If remedial action isn't taken quickly, he could easily become a failing teacher.

How an employee is managed can have a considerable effect on motivation and effort. Case Study 8.2 describes Fred – a very difficult head of faculty. The abrasive management style used by Fred, especially combined with his effective blocking tactics, would have deterred all but the most determined innovators. Similarly, lack of resources or attention over a long period can affect performance. Failure to provide support or praise good practice can also affect a teacher's attitude adversely. This is explored much more fully in Chapter 5. Here a cameo indicates how a teacher can feel.

CASE STUDY 7.8 FOR REFLECTION

'It didn't seem worth making the effort as you would only rubbish anything that I did. Even when I was second class, you made me feel fourth class' (snippet from a teacher's appraisal interview). She is responding to the head of department's criticism that she no longer volunteered for her share of the department's responsibilities and that she grumbled when asked to contribute to curriculum development. False praise for mediocre or weak performances such as James's, however, is as bad as failing to give praise for good practice.

External factors can also affect teachers' performance in the classroom or how they carry out their responsibilities.

CASE STUDY 7.9 FOR ACTION

Alex

The deputy head in charge of staffing matters has come to you. He went into the staffroom early this morning and, for the second time this week, he found the head of Spanish sitting there with his head in his hands. He looked totally exhausted and admitted that he had not been sleeping well. He is in his early 30s, married with a young family and a heavy mortgage. When the deputy probed a bit further, he discovered that Alex was teaching Spanish at the local college three evenings a week and carrying out a whole range of paid building and repair work locally whenever he could get a commission. It was no wonder, said the deputy, that he looked tired out at 8 in the morning. You are particularly concerned because there are a couple of letters in your file about Spanish homework not being set or marked, and about the quality of the teaching. You are also aware that Alex has almost stopped mixing with the rest of the staff and seems irritable when approached.

For action

What should you do about Alex?

Compare Case Study 7.9 with this comment made recently by a headteacher. 'My staff are busy finding ways to meet their families' needs by increasing their earnings from non-school sources with the result that they perform the basic jobs and then firmly turn their attention to an impressive array of part-time jobs.'

As a headteacher, you will find that from time to time a number of external factors affect performance adversely in either the short or the long term. These include:

❑ health problems or illness;
❑ marital difficulties or breakdown;
❑ financial problems;
❑ journey to work;
❑ family problems – elderly parents or difficulties with the children.

Often there are several problems at the same time, eg financial and family. How do you ensure performance in these circumstances?

IDENTIFYING POOR PERFORMANCE

How do you find out how a teacher is performing? Initially you may think that the answer to this lies in teacher appraisal, but this is rarely the first indicator of poor practice in the classroom, although it may reinforce what is already known. This is because the teacher gets some choice in what is observed, so it is easy to hide problems (especially as the teacher is likely to prepare better than usual and the pupils may behave better than usual). Feedback about a teacher's performance actually reaches you regularly from a whole variety of other sources.

Feedback will come from lesson observation, complaints from pupils, parents or other teachers and from results. Dealing with complaints can take up a lot of your time. It is unlikely that the lesson observation used in Case Study 7.4 is really the first indication the headteacher will have had that Mrs A is experiencing difficulties.

Teachers will quickly pick up vibes about one another, but tend to keep quiet about a colleague's problems. They are most likely to want action taken about Mrs A if her indiscipline has an effect on their own classes – either because they are nearby and the noise from Mrs A's class makes it difficult for their classes to work, or because the pupils arrive from Mrs A's lessons so high that it is difficult to teach them. It is much more likely that sooner or later a deputation of pupils will arrive to complain about Mrs A and express their fears that they cannot achieve good results in the subject because of what they consider to be her poor teaching.

The most common source of information, however, is parental complaint. It has been suggested that the frequency of complaints about teachers is linked to the social class of the clientele, but most schools all too frequently receive phone calls, letters and visits about the performance of a member of staff or about how a pupil has been treated.

Telephone complaints are seen as less effective than writing or coming in person, although sometimes they are used if the matter is urgent. Most letters of complaint are addressed to the headteacher, as aiming at the top is seen as more likely to get action than writing to the teacher concerned (who may simply suppress the letter) or to a middle manager with limited powers.

A typical letter of complaint is shown as Case Study 7.10: it expresses dissatisfaction, offers a reason and requests immediate or future relief.

CASE STUDY 7.10 FOR ACTION

Letter of complaint about Mrs A

Dear Mrs Gatlin,

I feel impelled to write to you because Andrea is making so little progress this term in Mrs A's group. I have talked to her about this and I have also talked to her friends who are in the same group and they all say that the lessons are confusing both because other pupils are not attending and are talking and because Mrs A's explanations are so difficult to follow. To make matters worse, when Andrea asked Mrs A to explain some things more clearly, Mrs A told her not to be so rude and that she should have listened in the first place. Andrea says that she has given up trying to ask questions and cannot make sense of the lessons. Homework does not appear to be set regularly and when it is Andrea finds it difficult because she does not understand the concepts on which it is based. My sister who teaches this subject in another borough tried to give Andrea some help during the last half-term and commented that the group appears to be considerably behind the group she teaches. Andrea is doing very well indeed in her other academic subjects, but her lack of success in this subject in her GCSE year is influencing her choice of A levels and we are particularly disappointed about this. Some of Andrea's friends are in Miss X's group, where they are making very satisfactory progress. Indeed her friends in this teaching group have been trying to explain the work to Andrea. We should therefore be grateful if you would arrange to have Andrea transferred to Miss X's group forthwith.

Looking forward to hearing from you in the very near future.

Yours sincerely,

Mary Blane

For action

As headteacher, how should you respond to this letter and what action should you take about Mrs A? Bear in mind that you will be deluged with similar requests if you transfer Andrea. What do you do if the option blocks don't fit and you can't transfer Andrea?

A regular surgery for parents will certainly produce examples of parents who are dissatisfied with the performance of a particular teacher, because this is an easy form of direct access to the headteacher. Otherwise the parents will ring or write for an appointment. Sometimes they go straight to a parent governor in order to ensure that the complaint is heard or because you have not acted fast enough or reacted in the way that they want.

CASE STUDY 7.11 FOR ACTION

Under the old head we stopped complaining because she just denied that there was a problem and suppressed the complaints. She was a very authoritative person and you didn't dare challenge her judgement. But the problem didn't go away: it was suppressed and, if anything, as time passed we felt that it had got worse. Then she retired and you were appointed. With a new headteacher we thought it was worth trying again as our younger daughter has now reached year 10 and is suffering from Mrs A's teaching, so we came to your surgery. It is more than six months now, and you haven't sorted it out either. Mrs A's still there teaching appallingly, yet you are trying to tell us that everything is OK because the volume of letters is dying down. Of course it is: this is because the parents can see that you haven't done anything, so they have stopped writing because it is a waste of time, as we are not getting any results. Mrs A's teaching hasn't improved, but the parents have given up!

An angry parent at the headteacher's surgery –
it is clearly not her first visit about this problem

For action

You are the headteacher – how should you respond to the parent? What should you do about Mrs A?

Parental complaints are the most powerful pressure on you to do something about a weak member of staff. Obviously a chronic complainer carries less weight than the parent who usually supports the school, but comes in desperation about a particular issue. The volume of complaints about a particular teacher will affect your attitude and your reaction, as will persistence on the part of the parents.

DEALING WITH POOR PERFORMANCE

There are three main types of response to poor performance:

1. tolerance/avoiding the issue;
2. salvage attempts – trying to improve performance;
3. induced exits and/or dismissal.

TOLERANCE/AVOIDING THE ISSUE

This is an all-too-frequent response. Managers are often reluctant to confront incompetent performance or hope that over time a teacher's difficulties will go away, or perhaps that the teacher will go away. Case Study 7.7 about James is a classic example of misplaced tolerance. The problem of his poor class control is not confronted in the early stages of his career and he is allowed to think that his performance is no worse than anyone else's and he is giving satisfaction. Often the problem is compounded because appraisal and other forms of teacher evaluation put a good face on what is happening and either focus on soft targets, so avoiding the problem, or fudge the issue through adopting a form of words that does not really indicate to the teacher that his or her performance is not up to standard. Case Study 7.2 was a typical example of misplaced kindness in feedback from lesson monitoring. The teacher concerned would not be able to develop his skills unless his head of department was honest with him about his performance in the classroom.

CASE STUDY 7.12 FOR ACTION

Exemplar of an evaluation report

Mrs A is to be commended for volunteering to be part of the team for this new initiative. She has worked hard to prepare the syllabus and although there have been some teething troubles, mainly concerned with interpreting the instructions from the board, I am sure that these will soon be ironed out and the course will prove successful.

This could be interpreted as:

- ❏ Mrs A is teaching a course for which she is not trained.
- ❏ She does not know what she is doing.
- ❏ She is one lesson ahead of the pupils.
- ❏ There have already been all kinds of problems.
- ❏ Let us hope for a miracle.
- ❏ Maybe she will leave.

For action

What advice should you as the headteacher give to this head of department?

Poor performance is tolerated for a variety of reasons:

- ❏ misplaced kindness (to whom?);
- ❏ reluctance to face possible conflict;
- ❏ lack of relevant management skills;
- ❏ possible cost in time and effort;
- ❏ knowledge of how difficult it is to get someone out;
- ❏ problems of competency procedures.

Reluctance to confront the problem usually means that nothing is done and over time the situation gets worse. Avoiding the problem takes other forms besides pretending it isn't there. It often includes damage limitation. Mrs A can't be allowed to teach A-level classes because the volume of dissatisfaction will be too great to suppress, so what shall we do with her? The head of department then sits down and identifies the classes where it is considered that she will do the least damage and she is allocated to teach them. In the USA teachers can be transferred within a region from school to school to mask their difficulties or to non-teaching duties. In California, for example, some teachers who were not succeeding in the classroom were reassigned to work in the museum or the curriculum centre, to drive the school bus or, in one case, to become a member of the building and maintenance team. We do not have escape hatches of this sort, and it is largely untrue that the incompetent are promoted out of teaching.

SALVAGE ATTEMPTS

CASE STUDY 7.13 FOR ACTION

Mrs A

There was yet another letter about Mrs A in the day's postbag, very much along the lines of Mrs Blane's letter in Case Study 7.10. This one, however, accused Mrs A of incompetence in the classroom and, among other things, claimed that the teacher was destroying the pupil's enthusiasm for the subject, which last year, when she had been taught by Miss X, had been her favourite subject. The letter requested a change of group for the child or a change of teacher for the group, and that in the interests of the pupils the school 'did something' about this teacher.

You take this letter to the deputy in charge of staff development, with the comment that this is the third of its kind this term and that 'we really must do something', but you know that he will have already tried everything that you can think of to help this member of staff. This includes checking the subject content, which the head of department has assured him is no different from what is being taught to the other classes and is monitored regularly.

You have checked Mrs A's results against those achieved by other teachers in the department, and her results stand up. What is more, the take-up rate for A level of her group is no lower than for the other groups and this does not change from year to year. When you say this to any of the parents who complain, you are told that the pupils only pass because everyone in Mrs A's group goes for private tuition and you cannot disprove this.

The deputy head has worked closely with the subject head of department to try to develop Mrs A. You have both observed lessons on several occasions and feel that, although she may be pedantic and uninspiring, she is actually sound. Although her control is weak, she is delivering the required content. She finds it difficult to cover the syllabus to time because of her control problems and has difficulty in enforcing homework, but technically she is accurate and she has thought about what she has to teach. She is terribly dull and you can understand why the pupils tend to turn off, but she was prepared to listen when the head of department tackled her about the problem and they have worked together to try to increase the variety in her lessons. The trouble is that, if anything, this made matters worse because the change in style did not come naturally to her and tended to make her nervous so that she sounded tense and snappy. The deputy's observations indicate that she does not refuse to answer questions but that she lacks flexibility and is put off by questions. This makes her seem aggressive or negative when a pupil interrupts her exposition to backtrack on something, and you feel that worrying about this and the other associated problems has made her even more uptight about her teaching than she was originally.

You are sorry for Mrs A, but you consider that the real problem lies in her inability to establish a good working relationship with her classes. They don't like her and this leads them to question her subject credibility. She has developed a not totally deserved reputation as a poor teacher and pupils try to avoid being placed in her group and complain if they are in a set taught by her. This has been going on ever since she was appointed.

For action

❏ What are your strategies in both the short term and the long term?
❏ What can you do about this kind of ongoing problem?
❏ What should the school do?
❏ How much does your role as headteacher mean you will consider this problem differently from the deputy in charge of staff development?

The legacy of avoidance and tolerance of poor performance makes it very hard not only to confront the problem when it will no longer remain buried but also to remedy it. The head of department and the deputy in charge of staff development have tried a number of strategies to help Mrs A. These include:

❏ a pep talk about the need to improve her image as a teacher;
❏ getting the poor performer to watch a good performer;
❏ giving the poor performer a lot of advice about 'how to do it better';
❏ spending more time planning the lesson activities;
❏ frequent observations to see if progress has been made;
❏ checking the exercise books and homework done by her pupils;
❏ sending her on courses to update her knowledge or practice;
❏ holding department Inset sessions;
❏ behaviour modification;
❏ team teaching;

❑ sending her to assertiveness training or interpersonal skills or class control workshops;

❑ monitoring results across the sets.

These strategies do not seem to have brought about either an immediate or a wholesale improvement. From the sound of things, Mrs A is marginally worse than before the salvage operation started. Why is this? First, it has been established in US studies of teacher incompetence that remedial action is more likely to succeed with *beginner* teachers and even then the success rate is low. Mrs A, for example, is set in her ways and changing her approach will be difficult for her. This helps to explain why her performance is worse using methods with which she is insecure. It may seem abrupt and very hard on a teacher who has believed himself or herself satisfactory (or at least no worse than others) suddenly to be labelled as the weak link in the department chain.

In the past praise was given too easily; now the manager is extremely wary of praising anything at all lest it impede competency proceedings, yet praise and encouragement are very important to motivating someone to try to perform well.

Sometimes the problem is incorrectly assessed and the wrong kind of support is given. In Case Study 7.5 about Kevin, the problem is class control, yet the remedy is to provide a support teacher to help Kevin with teaching techniques and methods. It doesn't help because it is unnecessary, and Kevin struggles on with no support for class control until the problem is reassessed by the deputy head. Improvement, when it occurs at all, is likely to be in small rather than large steps – parental expectations will be very high that you can 'do something about Mrs A's teaching'. They will not be easily satisfied and this will put even more pressure on the teacher.

Failing teachers are rarely if ever changed from ugly ducklings into swans, but more perhaps could be achieved. The sections that follow make some suggestions as to how you could improve your management of teachers who experience difficulties.

Diagnosis

Apart from catching the problem early, correctly diagnosing it could help you find appropriate solutions. You must be rigorous about collecting evidence because, to address the problem, you need hard data, ie precise information about how the lesson was conducted, rather than soft data, such as intuitions or opinions. Case Study 7.5, Kevin, showed us how easy it can be to misinterpret a situation because no one has really bothered to investigate properly. You must review the file on the failing teacher very carefully and focus your observations or other evidence collection precisely. You will need to give instances of the specific difficulty, when you became aware of it and what action was taken.

You also need to be precise about the nature of the difficulty. Is it lateness, absenteeism, discipline, lack of content, appropriateness of content or what? It is important to try to work out how far the causes lie within the individual, how far they arise from the job or its context and to what extent they are external in origin. The ongoing case study about Mrs A's problems in the classroom indicates how difficult it can be to sort out which of the associated problems is actually the *key* difficulty. Some problems are temporary and, once they are over, performance should revert to normal. Many of the external factors could be eased through stress management or appropriate counselling. This is another reason why correct identification of where the difficulty lies is so important. Three kinds of information help in diagnosing whether the origins of the trouble are internal, ie within the teacher, or external. They are all concerned with observation:

1. *Distinctiveness*: how does this teacher's performance in this topic compare to how he or she teaches other topics or year groups? If other tasks are done better, then either performance is patchy or the cause is likely to be external.
2. *Consistency*: how does performance change with time? If the pattern repeats itself over and over again, the problem is likely to be internal.
3. *Consensus*: how does this teacher compare to others teaching the same topic? If his or her performance is similar to that of other teachers carrying out the same task, then an external attribution is likely.

Appraisal has helped some middle managers to develop their observation skills, but this is still an area where schools would benefit enormously from training up their managers, as lesson observation is still all too often much too general. An example of focusing observation so as to set targets against which you can monitor improvement is given in Case Study 7.14.

CASE STUDY 7.14 FOR REFLECTION

From a discussion between the head of department and Mrs A

As how much work is actually done in your lessons featured in several of the letters we have received, it might be a good idea if my lesson observation focused on how much material is covered in the time.

After the observation

I noticed, for example, that a lot of pupils sat for several minutes at the beginning of the lesson while they waited for other pupils to arrive. During that time no one started work. You would gain at least five minutes per lesson if you set an activity during that time. You could set a short revision exercise to test whether the last lesson was fully understood. This would help the pupils with revision. Sometimes you could set a short activity as a lead into the lesson. It is important that you make it clear that the exercise or activity counts as part of the lesson's work and that those who arrive late make up this task, otherwise pupils will see this part of the lesson as a punishment rather than as a learning opportunity.

The observation focused on one aspect of a lesson – how much content there was or material covered within a 40-minute session. Gaps were observed and suggestions made as to how to get more work done.

Confronting the problem

Where poor performance has been diagnosed it is essential to involve the teacher concerned. How you go about this is as crucial to whether you can help the teacher improve as is providing the right support structures. Dealing with a complaint by making an appointment with the teacher, confronting him or her with the letter and going through it point by point is almost as bad as raising the complaint at a departmental meeting. A strong daily relationship within the department in which openness and a willingness to give and receive feedback about performance are well established makes it much easier to tackle difficulties where they occur. Nevertheless holding a disciplinary or investigative interview with a colleague is never easy and is likely to be extremely stressful for both sides. Almost certainly you will meet with a defensive reaction first because the teacher experiencing the difficulties has probably tried to hide them for as long as possible. The denial stage is usually followed by cover stories, the attempt to blame someone else (usually naughty pupils) and finally an attempt to allocate the problem to external causes ('no one can teach under these conditions').

Stewart and Stewart (1983) suggest an agenda for this kind of discussion session, which you may find useful as a basic framework around which to structure the meeting. You must first agree standards and that there is perceived to be a gap. You then need to agree the size of the gap, who takes responsibility for it, what actions are needed to reduce it and the time frame.

Stewart and Stewart also make some useful suggestions about possible approaches to this interview:

❏ Make it as easy as possible for the person to do what you want – do not let it degenerate into a battle.
❏ Handle the problem not the person. This is a classic counselling technique and a very good one. It enables you to adopt a problem-solving approach and takes some of the heat out of the debate. It also makes it easier to suggest changes to behaviour. If the session is perceived as a personal attack, you are unlikely to get a positive outcome and the teacher will become both more defensive and aggressive or depressed.
❏ Find the knot that is easiest to undo and begin there. Time management or lesson organization, for example, is easier to tackle and improve than is the failure to establish a good working relationship. Real lack of the talent to teach children is virtually insoluble, however hard you try, and it may be better to face this.
❏ Try to give the teacher some hope. Encouragement will help a teacher try to persevere, even if things are very difficult. Yet you must not lie to the teacher – false hope is not doing him or her a service, and you have the problem that any praise you give the teacher could be used in evidence against you later on if the teacher's competency reaches tribunal.

INDUCED EXITS

'We don't dismiss a teacher. We never have and we never will. We try to encourage teachers to leave, we don't kill them' (quoted in Bridges, 1992).

Dismissal is the harshest solution to teacher incompetence and the most infrequently used, but sometimes as a manager you have to face the fact that, whatever you do, the teacher experiencing difficulty is never going to improve – so what do you do? Basically there are two routes to follow: competency procedures or induced exits.

To prove a teacher incompetent can be very difficult, especially if the issue was dodged initially and the teacher can produce positive appraisal statements, or criticisms were not documented until late in the day. From the evidence provided in this chapter it would be difficult, for example, to *prove* that Mrs A is an incompetent teacher. Indeed your own monitoring of the situation would provide support for Mrs A's case if she had to appeal against dismissal on competency grounds:

❏ She is teaching the National Curriculum and other required content.
❏ She attempts to set homework.
❏ She does prepare and has made an effort.
❏ She listened to the advice and tried to follow it.
❏ She started as part-time and the school asked her to increase her commitment to full-time teaching.
❏ Her pupils' results are as good as those of other members of the department.
❏ The school drafted her on to teams running difficult new curriculum initiatives in the course of which the team experienced teething troubles delivering the project. Difficulties here would count as external factors connected with the job.
❏ Although Andrea, the pupil mentioned in Case Study 7.10, was deterred from doing the subject at A level, other pupils taught by Mrs A were not, and the take-up rate at A level from her classes was as good as from the other sets.

Although it could be shown that she is not regarded as a good teacher and has some weaknesses, particularly in the area of class control, this is not enough in itself. Thus if competency goes to tribunal on an insufficient basis, it could fail. Tribunals are expensive and, win or lose, generate bad publicity for the school. For this reason in the past it was infrequently used. As one headteacher said, 'I will not carry a case to this stage unless I am sure that I can win.' Generally, although the number of competency cases is on the increase, it is still the case that, whenever possible, headteachers look for other ways to edge a failing teacher out. In Mrs A's case the most likely route would be to see whether she can be persuaded to take some form of early retirement. This is only a viable option if the teacher can afford it, as good early retirement packages are not currently available.

Having to face the fact that a member of staff experiencing difficulties has come to the end of the road, will not improve and 'should go before she is pushed' is difficult enough. Usually all your instincts are to go on trying to work towards improvement well past the time when you really believe matters will improve. It is your job to decide when that is no

CASE STUDY 7.15 FOR ACTION

I've got to tell her to go

I know that I have to talk to her about considering early retirement, because that is a much better option for her than being forced out and having to go through capability proceedings, but I just don't know how to handle it. How should I broach the subject? Just how do you go about telling a failing member of staff that it is better that she should go before she is pushed?

From a conversation between Mrs A's head of department and the deputy head responsible for staff development

For action

❑ What are the issues raised in this case study?
❑ What advice should the deputy head give the head of department and on what grounds?
❑ What support should be provided for Mrs A and for the head of department?
❑ How do you as headteacher prepare your deputy and the middle managers concerned so that they can manage difficult issues of this kind?
❑ What is your role as headteacher in dealing with this situation?

longer cost-effective. Having to confront the member of staff with the unpleasant fact that he or she is regarded as a failing teacher and that capability proceedings are being contemplated is even harder and managing someone through an induced exit can be extremely stressful for both sides. It is an emotional ordeal fraught with difficulties.

In the USA some principals have been trained to use a form of counselling called 'prospective counselling' to help them deal with staff in difficulties. It has been appropriated from medical counselling, where it is used to help patients who have decided to undergo major surgery. This training involves the manager in experiencing the unpleasant consequences in advance, usually via a role-play or simulation, and helps him or her to make plans for dealing more effectively with the situation when it actually occurs. Although this does not seem to be available here at present, at least it is worth your while giving a lot of time and thought to how the employee is likely to react and what strategies you could adopt given different possible reactions.

To manage the situation effectively, however, you will need not only all your counselling and assertiveness skills, but also a lot of determination and perseverance when things get nasty. Success or failure in this arena can also depend on your ability to be an effective negotiator.

'You need a strong ego and the conviction that the knot should be cut and that what you are doing is in everyone's best interests. I have been called inhuman, a Hitler, and have got used to staff claiming that I am the problem, not the teacher whose retirement I am negotiating' (from a discussion at a headteacher conference about managing induced exits).

CASE STUDY 7.16 FOR ACTION

I don't see why we are having this discussion. I don't believe I can be all that bad. Early retirement doesn't make sense for me at the moment. What would I do at home? Besides I can't afford it without substantial enhancement and I am advised that this is unlikely.

Mrs A

For action

Exploratory conversations with Mrs A do not seem to be going according to plan.

What strategy should the headteacher adopt now? What advice would you give this headteacher and why?

Very often a combination of strategies is employed to 'persuade' a teacher to resign or to take early retirement. Of these strategies, pressure – either direct or indirect – is the one most regularly used. It provides managers with a weapon to make a failing teacher think very seriously about whether he or she wants to continue.

Using *direct* pressure means that you confront the teacher directly with his or her inadequacies and will be extremely hurtful for the teacher concerned. Applying *indirect* pressure involves changing the teacher's working conditions in such a way that he or she becomes reluctant to continue under those circumstances. You need always to walk warily enough to avoid any suggestion of harassment.

Another strategy is negotiation, either directly with the teacher or through the union representative. A request for early retirement can sometimes be negotiated in this way. Early retirement schemes offer a way out for hard-pressed headteachers with too many undevelopable ageing teachers, particularly if they are linked to inducements. LEAs, however, are no longer providing funding for such schemes and it can be difficult for an individual school to fund a package that might persuade a teacher to go early.

Nevertheless, induced exits through resignation or early retirement with enhancement provide a teacher experiencing difficulty with an opportunity to go gracefully. Beware, though, that it is not seen by others as the rewarding of failure, because this could demotivate your best teachers. You will also need to take into account fair treatment of the person making the exit, the state of your finances and any criteria the governors may have developed for this contingency.

Capability procedures

As it has become easier and speedier to remove a member of staff on competency grounds, and headteachers and governing bodies have seen others succeed, the number of cases being brought has increased significantly. Most of these cases do not go through to the end, as the teacher resigns before a verdict is reached.

To satisfy an industrial tribunal following dismissal, the employer must prove that:

❑ dismissal was based on a fair and thorough investigation;
❑ correct procedures were observed and proceedings were conducted in accordance with natural justice;
❑ the decision was a reasonable one given all the circumstances.

The three rules of natural justice are:

1. The employee must know the full case against him or her.
2. The employee or employee's representative must be given an opportunity to explain or defend himself or herself.
3. Those conducting the hearing must be impartial. The person hearing the case must be unbiased. Bias is defined as holding an adverse view or prejudging the issue. Impartiality must be demonstrated.

Dismissal for poor performance may be because either the employee is incapable of performing his or her duties or the employee, although possessing the necessary skills and abilities, fails to exercise them. (The above is based on Drummond, 1990.)

Incapability means that training, exhortation or encouragement would not enable the employee to do the job. The incapability would be either because of incompetence or ill health. The teacher experiencing difficulties would have to be given at least one warning by the manager, which clearly defined the difficulties, provided with training and given prolonged support before incapability proceedings could be put in process. The targets set and any action plans should always have a timescale and a review period. The review period can be extended if necessary, but if there is still no improvement, then you proceed to disciplinary or other action. Everything done must be confirmed in writing to the employee. The procedure is summarized in the following checklist.

A checklist for handling incapability

Formal procedures – who does what?

❑   first written warning – headteacher;
❑   second / final written warning – headteacher;
❑   dismissal by a disciplinary panel of governors;
❑   appeal – governors' appeals committee, comprised of different governors from the disciplinary panel.

What should be included in the written warning?

❑   performance standards and the gaps between performance and standards explained;
❑   period of assessment appropriate to circumstances and details of how this has been or will be carried out;
❑   what support has been or will be given;
❑   the next stage of the procedure explained.

Employee's rights – ignore these at your peril

❑   to prior acknowledgement of complaint;
❑   to state his or her case at the hearing;
❑   to question witnesses;
❑   to be represented by a representative of his or her choice;
❑   to be treated reasonably.

If incapability is due to ill health, the position is different from incompetence. Dismissal is acceptable if there is no possibility of a teacher's health improving sufficiently for him or her to continue in the post. Dismissal in these circumstances is not regarded as a disciplinary matter and is usually approached sympathetically in consultation with the teacher.

CASE STUDY 7.17 FOR ACTION

In the end Mrs A could not afford to seek early retirement and the school decided not to risk capability proceedings. As headteacher how do you manage the ongoing problem of Mrs A? Her presence is like a red rag to a bull for a minority of vociferous parents, who argue that you should remove her from teaching their offspring. The department finds having to provide ongoing support a strain, and the whole affair is demoralizing for all concerned. How do you manage this extremely difficult problem?

For action

What advice can you give this headteacher and where can he or she get support?

CASE STUDY 7.18 FOR ACTION

Gordon

Gordon was scanning the *TES* when you passed through the staffroom. You heartily wish he could get promoted, but you know how unlikely this is. He has been applying for posts unsuccessfully for years now, and his hopes remain undiminished in spite of numerous rejections. He also applies for every opening within the school, regardless of whether he has the relevant abilities or experience and now this has gone beyond a joke. He does not seem to mind these disappointments. He works exceedingly hard and is on a lot of working groups, especially the ones you can volunteer for, but he is a man of minutiae, not a fount of ideas, and he can bog down any meeting he attends in a morass of detail. He is a year head, but his punitive attitude to the pastoral system is such that pupils prefer not to seek his support and staff avoid involving him if at all possible. You would like him out of the pastoral system, as his relentless tenacity makes him appear unsympathetic and provokes a constant stream of letters from angry or irritated parents. He has no place in your long-term plans for the school. He already applies for every possible in-service training course and his training record fills pages of Inset file, but training seems to make little difference to his performance and you feel that sending him on yet more courses will not substantially improve his prospects.

For action

You are the new headteacher of Bestwick Park High School. What should you do about Gordon?

CASE STUDY 7.19 FOR ACTION

Pete

Part 1

Pete had been an outstanding PE specialist in his day, and for many years was a first-rate head of department. By the time you take up your post as headteacher, the PE department is no longer one of the school's market leaders. Although the department is competently organized and competes successfully in local competitions, particularly in football, Pete's own PE specialism, the range of activities is limited and very traditional. Pete is very reluctant to think about any changes to the existing curriculum and especially hostile to the idea of including dance. Unusually for a PE specialist, he has not developed any other strings to his bow; he has not built up his expertise in a subsidiary subject or a management area. You are aware that there are some good young teachers in the department – indeed this is one reason why the department is successful abroad – but Pete's opposition to change blocks development opportunities for these teachers. One of them is a dance specialist. She introduced a dance course in her last school that was highly praised by Ofsted. She has come to see you because she is keen to start a similar course in your school. You believe that another of the younger teachers is very talented and has the potential to be a good head of PE, and you do not want to lose him. You believe the school would benefit from moving to a shadow system, but do not see Pete in the role as head of faculty.

For action

What options are open to you as headteacher?

Part 2

As an Ofsted inspection was expected shortly, you decided to wait, because you expected Ofsted to be critical of the leadership of the department. This could provide you with a lever with which to move Pete from his post. At the feedback to the department, however, although there is mention of the limited range of activities, the leadership and management of the department are highly commended. Afterwards, you challenge the inspector to defend this grade and he explains that, although the department is very traditional and would benefit from developing the range of sports offered, it is actually very well led and managed (according to the Ofsted criteria).

For action

How can you move forward from this situation?

8

MANAGING CONFLICT

Every so often you will find that you have to resolve conflict between individuals or groups of staff. The case study below explores the kind of dispute that sometimes arises in a school, when one of the parties to the dispute is a member of the senior management team.

A CONFLICT SITUATION

CASE STUDY 8.1 FOR ACTION

Chloe, an excitable but respected member of staff, has arrived in your office. It is the day before the end of term, and she is in tears. She declares that Sonia, the new deputy head, is always shouting at her and has made her look foolish in front of the pupils. Although she acknowledges that everyone is tired at this time in the term, she says she will resign if Sonia shouts at her again.

Sonia was internally promoted to the post only six months ago, but has a great deal to contend with. The other deputy, George, has been absent for much of that time, having a serious operation from which he is still convalescing. Sonia is extremely conscientious, works to all hours and finds it difficult to delegate. She likes things to be done her way, and is suspicious of Chloe's more intuitive approach and flow of helpful suggestions, which tend to lead to major upheavals. Although she accepts that Chloe is a hard worker, she deplores the outbursts that seem to be a component part of all Chloe's activities. Chloe, in turn, never makes any allowance for the difficulties of Sonia's position, or appreciates that her own interventions do not always seem to others as altruistic as they seem to her. Relations between the two members of staff have never been good, and seem to have deteriorated with Sonia's promotion. Recently there have been a number of clashes between them, mainly connected with cover and communications, and now, just before the end of term, matters have come to a head.

For action

You are Erica, the headteacher. How should you deal with this sensitive problem in which your deputy is one of the parties to the dispute?

For reflection

The problem outlined above is an extreme example of the kinds of personality clash that can occur in any organization: conflict has built up between two members of staff until, just as term is ending, it has emerged as a public clash, and now one of the combatants has asked the headteacher to intervene. Obviously so violent a breakdown in the relationship between the two members of staff cannot be allowed to continue, and it is important to minimize the effects of the confrontation as fast as possible.

Erica needs to start by breaking the problem down into short-term and long-term issues. In the short term she needs to resolve the public row between two members of staff, where a middle manager has complained about how she is treated by the deputy and has threatened to resign.

What should Erica do about Chloe's threat to resign? She should be aware of whether Chloe has threatened resignation before (and if so how regularly). This is quite likely because Chloe is clearly well known for her outbursts. This incident is certainly unfortunate, but it may be less significant than if there was an explosion of a normally calm and stable member of staff. This prior knowledge should influence how Erica deals with the situation. Chloe has appealed for help and clearly needs to vent her feelings somewhere, and Erica's full attention and sympathetic ear will probably relieve the immediate tension.

Erica also needs to see Sonia, because she has not heard Sonia's side of the story. It is important to get the two of them to make it up, at least on the surface, as soon as possible. As the senior manager, Sonia will lose most face, which is another argument for a speedy resolution of the problem. It would also help to retrieve the situation if Sonia took the initiative and made some gesture towards reconciling herself to Chloe.

On the other hand, Erica could play it down and see what effect a cooling-off period has. It is not impossible that, with the time to reflect, Chloe might regret having involved the headteacher, or she might wish to withdraw the complaint – after all it has been heard. Certainly it would be better if the two were able to sort it out for themselves than for the head to act as arbitrator. If Erica chooses to take this path, however, she must ensure that Chloe, and possibly other staff, do not perceive her as inactive and doing nothing about the problem, or interpret it as 'the management always sticking together'.

Once Erica has dealt with the short-term issues, there remains a much more complex problem to resolve. A personality conflict between two forceful members of staff is potentially very damaging for a school – factions could form from the supporters of each side (arguments were already occurring in front of pupils and could involve pupils), and if the conflict were allowed to continue, the quality of the education provided for pupils could be adversely affected. It is an essential function of management to create a harmonious working atmosphere in which the talents of a diverse group of people, each with different skills, abilities and personality, can complement one another and contribute to the effective running of the school. However, in this school, harmony was breaking down.

To deal with the situation in the long term, Erica must first analyse the underlying issues inherent in the problem. This analysis will involve diagnosing the problem, categorizing the symptoms, considering the viewpoints of the people concerned, suggesting possible causes and breaking the problem down into its component parts. The exercise is worth doing because it will indicate what the management issues are and so help to generate solutions.

Analysing the issues

Issues connected with Sonia

One issue is Sonia's approach to her role as a manager. Although we only know about the problem she is experiencing with one member of staff, there are indications that she seems to be preoccupied with the task to the detriment of her effectiveness in managing staff. She seems to be low on the interpersonal skills needed for the job. Her use of her position power as a deputy head in charge of the daily running of the school affects the way that she relates to staff. She seems to be using an authoritarian style, which has provoked Chloe's resentment.

The case study suggests that Sonia is having to work very hard and is under some stress. There are two reasons given for this: the long-term absence of the other deputy (was she doing both jobs?) and her own attitude to her role (unable to delegate and rigid in her approach).

There is probably also a confidence issue. Sonia was recently promoted and the description of her behaviour suggests that she is anxious to prove herself 'up to the job'. The promotion has probably had additional effects, making her reluctant to admit to even minor errors, and seeing Chloe's advice or interventions as unnecessary interference.

Issues connected with Chloe

The issues connected with Chloe are much more personal. Although only suggested by the case study, they emerge from speculating about Chloe's motives for her behaviour. The matter is clearly very important to Chloe and seems bound up with her own personality, self-image and how she thinks she is viewed by the establishment.

Chloe visibly dislikes Sonia's management style and is dissatisfied with how she is being treated by the deputy. The present quarrel could easily have its origins in Chloe's attitude to Sonia's recent promotion. Sonia's skills and abilities are very different from Chloe's, and the head clearly valued Sonia's abilities in making the appointment. Whether or not Chloe was actually passed over for promotion, the institution appointed someone for whom Chloe had neither liking nor sympathy, and she may have had difficulty in understanding and adjusting to the appointment. Chloe would not have supported Sonia for the post, but now has to live with her appointment. It is possible that Chloe sees Sonia as blocking her access to the head, ie if she has an idea, she now has to go to an unsympathetic deputy.

Chloe's visit to Erica indicates that she is very anxious to put her version of events, perhaps before anyone tells the head that there has been another outburst. This appeal could be as much a call for attention as a genuine complaint – Chloe wants to be noticed and valued for the good work she is doing. Whereas it is important to Sonia to prove that she can manage, Chloe is taking the opportunity to draw the head's attention to what she sees as Sonia's deficiencies and is implicitly criticizing her appointment as deputy head.

Issues connected with Erica

How did Erica manage the induction of her new deputy and what training or support was provided? The first year in a new post is usually hard, but internal promotion is particularly difficult to manage and can lead to all kinds of jealousies amongst the staff, if not handled sensitively. There are always plenty of people waiting for the mistakes and the opportunity to say, 'We always knew that she was not up to the job.' The incident involving Sonia and Chloe thus raises the question of whether enough support was provided for Sonia as a new senior manager.

Chloe's reaction to Sonia's appointment also raises issues about how Erica manages and motivates her staff.

Possible management approaches

Erica clearly needs to monitor her deputy more closely, so that situations such as the row with Chloe aren't allowed to develop, but she must not do this in a way that seems to undermine Sonia.

She has to make Sonia more aware of the other dimensions of her role as a manager, perhaps particularly her role as a manager and developer of personnel. She has to look for ways to provide Sonia with the support and encouragement to develop the confidence to manage more flexibly. Later (so that staff do not link it with this incident) she should provide Sonia with the opportunity for management training to develop her interpersonal skills, especially perhaps in dealing with difficult or intransigent staff.

She ought to lighten Sonia's workload, but she must approach this sensitively, as Sonia will interpret it as a judgement on how she has coped so far. If George, the other deputy, is going to be absent for the following term, then Erica should make more equitable arrangements for his responsibilities so that they are shared among the management team or someone is given an acting responsibility. It would be wise to ask Sonia which tasks she would like to keep. Sonia will probably argue that she can manage, but she shouldn't be allowed to prevail, as lightening her task and cutting down the number of hours she has to work should eliminate a lot of errors and generally help her relationships with staff.

Chloe's need to be noticed could be met by a job appraisal interview delivered by Erica in person. This would serve the purpose of providing Chloe with the attention and encouragement she needs and the reassurance that she is a valued member of the community; it would also give Erica the opportunity to address the issue of the effect on the school of Chloe's all too frequent outbursts. Erica may have to approach this issue through Chloe's own promotion hopes – Chloe can hardly expect promotion if she is likely to have violent altercations with the staff she has to manage.

THE CYCLE OF CONFLICT

If conflicts are not resolved they are likely to escalate, moving from minor disagreements to major battles. Such conflicts often start with a disagreement over some substantive issue – perhaps each party wants more of a limited resource, or has a different and incompatible view of how to deal with a particular problem. Whatever the issue, the parties differ and take a position of 'either/or', which means 'Either we do it the right (my) way or the wrong (your) way' and 'The more I get my way, the less you get your way.' Such an interaction is usually fairly unpleasant for both parties and even more unpleasant for the rest of the staff, who can get drawn into the conflict as each side seeks supporters.

As the conflict escalates, the parties develop negative feelings towards each other. This mutual dislike may eventually turn to loathing, especially when the conflict is compounded by a second argument developing over another issue – the parties are likely instinctively to disagree with anything that the other supports. At the same time they are likely to avoid each other. They may have to attend a lot of the same meetings, but they will not voluntarily seek to create situations in which they have to work in association. This serves to minimize the immediate feelings of frustration and impotence of one to the other, and it helps them to create a stereotype of their opponent either as someone generally undesirable who will take advantage of others, or as someone totally unreasonable. It does not matter who lost or won the first round, the so-called 'winner' is just as likely to dislike, avoid and expect a fight as is the 'loser'. This tendency repeats itself over and over again in an ever-increasing cycle of animosity and fear, until finally it comes to a head, possibly over a less important conflict than the original disagreement, and it is for this reason that, as the headteacher, you will from time to time find yourself dealing with violent disagreements between staff over what seem to you to be trivial issues.

Case Study 8.1 had many of the features described in the classic cycle of conflict, but unusually one of the combatants was a member of the SMT.

This needs particularly sensitive handling, but all conflicts will make considerable demands on your ability to manage people. If disagreements between members of staff such as those described above are not to affect the well-being of your school, you need to become the kind of headteacher who is able to resolve conflict and reconcile the warring parties. Although it may not come naturally to you, you can learn to manage conflict constructively.

STYLES OF CONFLICT MANAGEMENT

Different people use different strategies in managing conflict. These methods are usually learnt in childhood and become habits. We use them automatically, without thinking. We are often not aware of how we act in quarrels; we just do what comes naturally. But we do have a pattern of how we deal with conflicts with other people and, because it was learnt, we can always change and improve it by learning new and more useful ways of dealing with the conflicts. The first direct steps to managing conflict successfully should be a review of one's own typical style. There are five main styles or possible approaches, as illustrated in Figure 8.1.

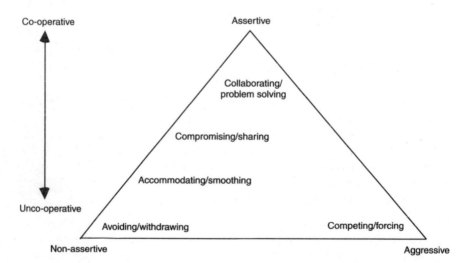

Figure 8.1 *Styles of conflict management*

Competing/forcing

Competing is aggressive and unco-operative. If you use this approach, you will try to overpower those involved by forcing them to accept your solution to the conflict. Your goals will be more important to you than personal relationships or the needs of others and you tend to assume that conflicts are settled by one person winning and the other losing. You want to be the winner because it will give you a feeling of pride and achievement; losing would give you a sense of weakness and failure. Your methods will include attack, use of power or position and intimidating the opposition. It is useful:

❑   when quick, decisive action is needed, eg in emergencies;
❑   where important but unpopular courses of action need implementing;
❑   on issues vital to institutional welfare, when you know that you are right;
❑   to protect yourself from people who will take advantage of soft or non-competitive behaviour.

This approach is typified by such statements as:

❑   I'm not prepared to change my position.
❑   I want to make my position quite clear.
❑   My view is the most logical.
❑   If you don't agree to do this, I'll. . .
❑   I know best; you had better. . .'
❑   Do as you are told.

Accommodating/smoothing

Accommodating behaviour is unassertive and co-operative. It involves making concessions to avoid conflict. You might adopt this approach when it is important that nothing rocks the boat, ie when a period of stability is essential. A subset of this approach is smoothing – 'Let's put this aside and agree to disagree for now. . .' A smoothed-over conflict has a disturbing habit of resurging, but it can be useful if it allows you to deal with other more urgent issues. It is also useful:

❑   when you realize that you are wrong;
❑   when the issue is more important to the other person than to you;
❑   to build up credit for later use;
❑   when you are outmatched or losing;

❑ when the preservation of harmony or avoidance of disruption is especially important;
❑ to allow people to make mistakes.

This approach is typified by such statements as:

❑ I concede that point.
❑ I agree with you there.
❑ I will do as you think best.
❑ What is your preferred outcome?
❑ You have convinced me.
❑ I'm glad we agree on that.

Avoiding/withdrawing

Avoiding behaviour is unassertive and unco-operative. You tend to feel helpless, that you can't resolve the issue and you shy away from dealing with it. Sometimes this is because you know you will not be supported by the staff, governors or LEA, eg if you have had trouble in the past and not succeeded (war-weary syndrome – you can't face any more conflict). You may adopt this approach because relationships are so important to you that you are not prepared to endanger them and you do not think that any conflict or clash of interests is worth the uproar. Sometimes this strategy will include passing the buck, eg to governors, so that someone else has to deal with the problem. Deputy heads avoid by referring the matter to the headteacher. It is useful:

❑ when an issue is trivial, of only passing importance, or when more important issues are pressing;
❑ when you see little chance of satisfying your concerns;
❑ when the potential damage of confronting the conflict outweighs the benefits of resolution;
❑ when you need time – to think, to let people cool down, to gather information, to discuss the issue with others;
❑ when others can resolve the issue more effectively;
❑ when the issue seems symptomatic of another, more basic, issue.

This approach is typified by such statements as:

❑ I can't take the responsibility for this decision.
❑ I'd prefer not to discuss it now.
❑ That's outside my brief.
❑ I won't be drawn on that.
❑ Let's talk about that later.

Compromising/sharing

Compromising behaviour is assertive and co-operative, and falls on the middle ground between competing and accommodating. If you adopt this approach, you are seeking a workable solution and are prepared to give up part of your goals in order to persuade the others involved in the conflict to give up part of their goals. Compromising involves bargaining: you offer some concessions provided that they offer some; for this reason you will sometimes see this approach to handling conflict described as bargaining. You are seeking a solution in which all parties can be seen to have achieved some points and no one loses too much face. It is useful:

❑   to provide the parties to a conflict with partial satisfaction or to achieve temporary settlements to complex issues;
❑   when goals are moderately important, but not worth the effort of more assertive modes;
❑   when two opponents with equal power are committed to mutually exclusive goals;
❑   to arrive at expedient solutions under time pressure;
❑   as a back-up mode when collaboration or competition fails.

This approach is typified by such statements as:

❑   I'll give you. . . if you'll give me. . .
❑   Let's find a quick solution.
❑   I suggest that we meet half-way.
❑   Let's split the difference.
❑   I'm prepared to. . . if you. . .

Collaborating/problem solving

Collaborating behaviour is assertive and co-operative – the opposite of avoiding. You will tend to view conflict as a problem to be solved, as in Case Study 8.1, and you will want to achieve a solution that will resolve the conflict in both the short term and the long term. You are not frightened of conflict, but regard it as a challenge. You will want to confront the problem in order to clear the air and begin to work towards a solution that can be mutually acceptable. You value both relationships and goals and will be prepared to work with both parties, perhaps initially individually and then together, in order to clarify the issues and work out how to rebuild the relationships. It is useful:

❑   to find a solution when both sets of concerns are too important to be compromised;

❑ when the objective is to test your own assumptions, understand the views of others and learn;
❑ to gain commitment by incorporating others' concerns into a decision;
❑ to merge insights into a problem from different perspectives.

This approach is typified by such statements as:

❑ How can we solve this?
❑ Let's work together on this.
❑ Where do we differ?
❑ What is mutually acceptable?
❑ Let's investigate the problem.

How do you find out what your dominant style is?

You may have recognized yourself instantly in the descriptions given above, but if not there are tests available commercially to help you work out your natural or dominant style. They normally involve answering a series of questions designed to see whether you are relationships- or goal-centred (people or task) and to which of the five categories you are most inclined. You may score quite highly in more than one category, as you often have to adopt the most effective approach to deal with a particular situation. In that case look for which column is the longest. If you are feeling brave ask some staff to assess you and compare their results with your own score. They may perceive you very differently – you may think you are a collaborator, but they may think of you as an avoider!

Not surprisingly the most common styles involve fighting and avoiding, as these represent the reflexive, built-in fight or flight response to a threat. Bargaining is the next most frequent approach used, with smoothing and problem solving by far the least used of the five. The most effective approach to managing conflict is, however, usually the collaborative or problem-solving approach. Success depends largely on your ability to handle this kind of situation and on your interpersonal skills.

Key interpersonal skills for managing conflict

Active and attentive listening are key techniques when the combatants are telling their stories. You need to both get the story straight and demonstrate that you are prepared to give your full attention to those involved. Attending behaviour gives important clues to the individual who has sought your help: an open posture indicates that you are willing to hear what he or she has to say, regular eye contact indicates that you are paying attention and verbal signs signal that you are following the story and willing to hear more. Similarly, nodding from time to time encourages the speaker to continue. Active listening, ie repeating what the speaker has said and restating it in your own words, is also important because it helps to clarify what is meant and helps to correct misunderstandings.

Sensitive use of questioning also plays a major part in handling conflict. You need to get the balance of open to closed questions right in order to elicit the most information. More open questions can appear to be counter-arguments denying the validity of the other person's viewpoint, and closed questions will simply elicit 'yes' or 'no'. Sometimes an appropriately focused 'in-between' question can move forward the sharing of information, which may generate ideas for problem solving. An example of this kind of question could be 'What common interests do we share in solving this problem?' Often you will want to probe into a situation. You can do this verbally with a follow-up question such as 'Then what happened?' or non-verbally by raising your eyebrows. A very good probe is an expectant pause (but you have to resist the impulse to jump in and fill the silence) because it can often extract more information than a direct question.

DEVELOPING YOUR CONFLICT MANAGEMENT SKILLS

It has repeatedly been observed that interpersonal skills seem to be the hardest to use effectively just when they are needed most and, indeed, when involved in conflict, people often seem to abandon them altogether. For example, instead of active and attentive behaviour, they use the opposite behaviours – closed posture, lack of eye contact or dead silence. This seems to occur because the body's response to a conflict situation is to manufacture large quantities of adrenalin, which raise blood sugar levels in preparation for fight or flight. Restating another person's feelings is also difficult in a conflict situation because conflict seems to cause people to focus on their *own* emotions and to ignore or deny someone else's. The problem is connected with the fact that conflict makes people behave aggressively and, whether you are personally involved or attempting to mediate, the aggression makes you feel threatened. It is thus physiologically difficult to confront conflict in ways that are productive. So what can you do either to improve your skills in handling conflict or to ensure that you do not lose them at a crucial moment? One way is to learn the interpersonal conflict management skills so well that they become almost reflexive, 'conditioned responses' to conflict situations. The most useful strategy, however, is to use a structured step-by-step framework for dealing with the conflict.

A structured approach

This approach assumes that the situation is a problem to be solved rather than a battle to be won or a danger zone to be avoided. If you get used to using the format and practise frequently it becomes second nature. Automatically you will begin to think 'Where have I reached in the cycle?' and be able to stay on track when it seems to be getting difficult. You will begin to recognize the tactics that the various parties are using as tactics rather than becoming drawn into the contentious areas of the dispute. Remember that when we reviewed the various approaches to managing conflict we commented that the problem-solving approach is the least used, yet it is the most effective. It will take you a while to master the technique. It will not come overnight, nor by magic, but like most other management skills it can be learnt and improved.

Using a structured approach enables you to present the issue far less emotionally than might otherwise have been the case. You turn it into a problem on which you can collaborate in attempting to solve it. It contains an appeal for assistance to both the parties: 'Can we agree to work together to try to sort this situation out?' This avoids the accusations or threats with which the incident will have started. Case Study 8.1 showed how the approach brought together the interpersonal skills, attention and listening the parties required, and the detachment necessary to make the problem more manageable.

What are the steps that you have to take in order to use this approach?

Provide an opportunity for the combatants to talk to you individually

This is when you have to demonstrate your listening skills. You have to draw the people out, get them to tell you what the problem is and how they feel about it. However busy you are, you must never hurry this stage.

Clarify and define the issue

This is when you have to get each person to make a clear statement of what they see as the cause of the conflict and precisely what they are arguing about. If it is difficult for you to understand what it is all about, or it takes a while to work through the emotions and accusations and arrive at the underlying issues, go on probing. You do this either by restating what you think is the problem and asking if you have interpreted it correctly or by asking for further explanation or more detail until you have got it perfectly clear. Some conflicts are caused by differences in perception, rather than any real difference of interest or opinion and you may be able to sort it out simply by clarifying things.

Explore possible solutions

This could mean brainstorming ideas or bargaining for concessions. You will have to establish under what conditions both parties will be satisfied. It is their problem, and only indirectly yours in that it affects the smooth running of the school, so you should beware of *providing* the solutions, otherwise they will be regarded as imposed and not owned by the parties involved, and the conflict could re-emerge. If this does happen there is likely to be the added complication that they will blame you. So you have to work slowly and carefully towards an acceptable solution by getting them to generate the ideas and discuss them. In Case Study 8.1 the issues were separated out into short term and long term – taking this approach will also affect the solutions suggested.

Decide which is the preferred solution

Each person will have to decide which of the possible options is best alternative. If you haven't handled the early stages too well, this could provoke some selfish responses, but collaboration should have set in and, if the preferred solution is itself open to modification at any stage, you are well on your way to reaching agreement. Sometimes you will have to do some persuading – if this occurs try to avoid things becoming personal again. Discuss the implications of the preferred solution so that everybody knows what it entails.

Create an action plan

It is important to clarify what has been agreed and what is to happen next. The best way to do this is by creating an action plan and if possible setting a review date because this helps the parties to be clear about what they are going to do, how they are going to do it and by when.

For action

Case Study 8.1 described a conflict between the school's deputy head and one of the teachers. The problem-solving approach was adopted but the problem was not completely resolved. You are Erica, the headteacher. Draft an action plan for resolving this conflict.

MANAGING DIFFICULT PEOPLE

As well as managing conflict you have to manage some difficult staff. Case Study 8.2 provides an almost classic example of a difficult member of staff, whose own performance made it difficult for others to give of their best.

CASE STUDY 8.2 FOR ACTION

Fred had been head of faculty for as long as anyone could remember. He had survived many changes in the educational system, didn't like current developments and didn't think any initiative was worth bothering about. He did the absolute minimum; it was a job and no more. He had no ambition, no desire for early retirement and no notion whatsoever of his role as a developer. He had very little interest in any of the projects initiated by members of the faculty, and even less in helping or supporting his team when problems occurred. Indeed, he tended to be very unsympathetic and sarcastic in his dealings with other members of staff. He could be very difficult and aggressive, and on occasion his bad language could empty the staffroom. Anyone allocated to Fred for appraisal had subsequently requested a change of appraiser, and students could not be allocated to this faculty. His attitude engendered considerable frustration within the faculty, as many of the staff would like to have seen it play a more active role in school affairs. Anyone of ability tended to seek promotion elsewhere, and of course Fred's longevity blocked promotion opportunities for others.

You have been putting off dealing with the problem of Fred, whom you consider to be undevelopable. But now there has been a deputation from the faculty and the deputy head in charge of staff development insists that some action should be taken. What do you do about Fred, whose poor performance is affecting how other people do their jobs and whose aggressive behaviour is affecting the whole staff?

Bramson (1981) has identified seven stereotypes of difficult people, as detailed in the following sections.

Hostile aggressives

They are the bullies, often very aggressive and confrontational. Fred fits into this category absolutely. They can be very destructive of people and ideas. Their sarcasm and cutting remarks can also adversely affect the morale and performance of other staff.

Complainers

Nothing is ever right for these members of staff and they never do anything to help solve a problem. Their constant whingeing can be wearing for everybody, and some of it can rub off, affecting the attitude of other staff. The problem for you as a manager is that these people have an unerring talent for putting their finger on real difficulties. You ignore these at your peril, even though you can't always see when they have identified a major flaw in a scheme. Whether they feel powerless or simply don't like taking responsibility themselves is difficult to tell, but they can be extremely irritating.

Silent unresponsives

Putting over a scheme to a group of silent unresponsive staff is every headteacher's nightmare and can be a very depressing experience. They are clearly not enthused by your scheme, but won't tell you why and won't enter into any kind of dialogue; indeed they won't communicate at all beyond the occasional monosyllable. What is really infuriating for you as a manager is that you don't know precisely what it is that they don't like, but their non-co-operation speaks volumes. You will never makes these staff even part owners of their own development.

Super agreeables

These members of staff are OK to be with at the time, when to all intents and purposes everything is fine, and they seem to be totally in support of anything and everything you want to do. Then you wait for them to carry out the things that they have agreed so readily to do. You can wait a very long time, because these members of staff fail to deliver. Avoidance of conflict is more important to them than doing the job, and getting these horses to water can cause you a lot of hassle.

Negatives

These members of staff will happily rubbish any and every scheme you put up. Basically they are anti the organization, the rest of the staff, you, the education system and anything else you care to name. Opposition is their blanket reaction to any change or new idea, especially anything that could mean more work for them. It usually takes the form of: 'I can't see why we should want to do that', 'It can't possibly work!', 'The pupils won't do that', 'We'll only get a lot of letters of complaint from parents' or 'We've done it before and it didn't work then!' What makes it worse is that negatives never resist the opportunity to say 'I told you so!' if things do go wrong. Their negative reaction is a classic blocking manoeuvre, not reasoned but intuitive. Sometimes negativism is the result of burn-out; more often, for whatever reason, the negativist feels defeated and does not want to be involved in any more change. The reason can be more personal: the negativist may have been passed over for promotion and is resentful of you or the school or both and will determinedly make it difficult for the management to make changes to the system.

Know-it-alls

We have all suffered from people who are absolutely sure they are right and insist on doing it their way. Some know-it-alls have genuine expertise, which if used well can benefit the organization, so you can't simply turn down their offers of assistance – however infuriating you find their attitude. In their arrogance and self-confidence, however, they erode and pre-empt others and you have to watch teams being taken over by this kind of know-it-all, as they threaten other staff and can make them feel inadequate. As a senior manager you will have to monitor this very carefully, as it could damage an important initiative. Other know-it-alls are in a different category altogether. They are the phoneys who claim to know everything, but everything they touch is a disaster. They can be relied upon to make a difficult situation worse. You have to learn which know-it-all is which and work out appropriate strategies for each.

Indecisives

These staff 'witter on' for ever but never make any progress because they hate making decisions. Getting these horses to water can be very difficult indeed. They seem to hope that if they can put off the decision long enough, the whole thing will go away. You have to watch them very carefully or in spite of hours spent talking about a project or problem nothing will ever get done. Sometimes indecisiveness is linked to a desire to please everyone, but it can be infuriating for colleagues. Another facet of indecisiveness is avoiding taking responsibility and you will find that problems are constantly referred back to you or a policy produced by a group led by someone of this type will make you responsible for everything. This kind of buck passing can leave you with an impossible workload and a staff who are unable and unwilling to think for themselves.

To this list I would also add *minimalists*. They exist in all organizations and have got doing as little as possible down to a fine art. They can seem to be very busy, but their output is low. They go on about how hard they are working and may even believe it, but they are making work expand to fit the time allowed rather than seeking projects. It is difficult to get much work out of these people, who will usually protest that they are fully committed already and can't undertake any more.

Some people have more than one of these characteristics at the same time and this makes them even more difficult to deal with. Fred in Case Study 8.2 is an example: he is a hostile aggressive, a negativist and a minimalist. His rudeness and bad language are bullying tactics designed to ensure he gets his own way. He rubbishes every new initiative both to avoid work and to make things difficult for others in the organization. He knows absolutely how little work he can get away with and operates within this framework.

How then do you deal with difficult people?

Listening and counselling

Some difficult people have become difficult because things have gone wrong in the past and the situation may be retrievable. Chloe, described in Case Study 8.1, must have been difficult to deal with both because she all too frequently had emotional outbursts and because she felt threatened and ignored. Such people respond to genuine attention and to deal with them you will need your listening and counselling skills. Using the problem-solving approach described earlier will allow you to detach problems from personalities and this can enable you to move forward.

Deflecting aggression

With others, such as the hostile aggressives like Fred who are using bullying tactics, you cannot be seen to allow them to win, as they are testing your authority – very like when pupils misbehave to see what their teacher will do. Fred, for example, cannot be allowed to go on insulting and swearing at his colleagues. The interview in which you insist that he controls his language could become very unpleasant indeed, so it must

The aim is to diffuse aggression in the other person

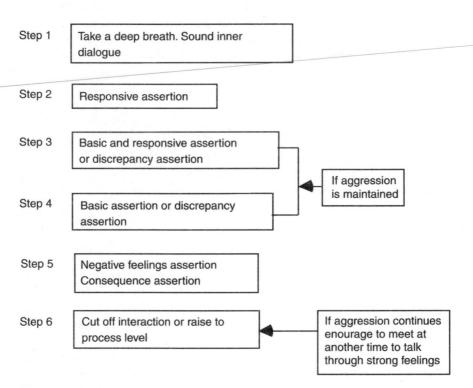

Figure 8.2 *Guidelines for handling aggression*

Key:
Basic: a straightforward statement that stands up for your rights by making clear your feelings/opinions. *Responsive:* you try to find out where the other person stands. *Empathic:* includes some element of empathy. *Discrepancy:* you point out the difference between what has previously been agreed and what is actually happening. *Negative feelings:* you draw attention to the undesirable effect the aggressive behaviour is having on you. *Consequence:* you inform the other person of the consequences of continued aggression, and also provide a let-out so he or she can change the behaviour (Back and Back with Bates, 1982).

not be allowed to get personal and you will certainly need all your skill in handling aggression. Dealing with aggressive people can be very difficult and some guidelines for diffusing aggression could prove useful. I am grateful to Rod Young of SIMS Management Services for providing the guidelines for handling aggression that follow.

Demonstrating assertiveness

You will need to show assertiveness because you must not allow the aggressive teacher to see that he or she has got to you, and your ability to take charge of the situation is central to your success in dealing with difficult people. What exactly is assertiveness and how can you be assertive when dealing with someone like Fred, whose rudeness gives him the initiative?

Assertive behaviour is interpersonal behaviour based on honesty. It is demonstrated by clear statements of needs, opinions and feelings, directly stated, without apology. It is balanced by sensitivity to and respect for the rights of others. It involves demonstrating that you do understand the other person's position, stating your own views and feelings on the matter under discussion calmly and clearly and making it quite clear to the other person what you want to happen or be the outcome of the situation. Don't sound apologetic because it allows the aggressive person to take the initiative.

In dealing with Fred you have to show that you are not intimidated by his bullying or his bad language, which are not going to deter you from your purpose. You also need to show Fred that you are in control, eg by turning his time tactics on him, eg 'I need to be away by 5 o'clock, so there is no point wasting time abusing the system. If you have serious criticisms of the new scheme, I am prepared to hear them.'

Combining empathy with firmness is another useful assertiveness technique, eg 'I appreciate that you don't like the new procedure, Fred, but it has been agreed by the staff and now that it is in place I'd like you to see that your department follows the new practice.' This kind of statement contains an element of empathy, but goes on firmly to insist that he conforms to current organizational practice. Sometimes you have to repeat the statement or put emphasis on what you want in order to get an aggressive person to listen.

Sometimes it is helpful to offer an alternative to the unacceptable behaviour. 'Fred, I was unhappy about how you expressed yourself. Abuse is never productive. I understand you don't like what is happening, but it would be much more helpful if you tell me why you feel as you do. Making personal comments helps neither of us sort the problem out.'

Drawing attention to how *you* feel, rather than concentrating on how he feels, is an assertiveness technique that you might find helpful with a difficult member of staff, eg 'Fred, it is unpleasant and unfair to go on at me like this' or 'I really don't enjoy having to talk to you like this, but when a senior member of staff behaves in this way, it has an adverse effect on the rest of the organization and it makes things much more difficult for me.'

This technique is also useful with those staff who don't deliver the goods such as the super agreeables:

> Because you haven't completed the task, it means that I shall have to do the job myself and will now have to do the work over the weekend to get it done on time. I feel annoyed about this as I had planned to do several other jobs this weekend and now they will have to be postponed. Next time I should be grateful if you only promise what you are sure that you can deliver. I am very disappointed about what has happened.

This makes it very clear indeed what the effect of the super agreeables' inactivity has been. Peer pressure could also be employed. For example, in dealing with Fred, if a staff committee exists it could censure or put pressure on Fred, whose use of the staffroom could be made conditional upon 'good behaviour'.

It can be helpful to make clear to the person the consequences of non-co-operation. It also gives that person a let-out, ie the opportunity to change his or her behaviour. Say, for example, that one of the technicians persistently took home equipment but never bothered with the proper procedure to do this. He took no notice of the head of department's remonstrance and was rude to her. She has come to you. The technician maintains that it is all very stupid. He doesn't see why he should bother with all this red tape and is generally difficult. In the end you have to be spell out the consequences of defiance. 'If it occurs again, I am left with no alternative but to proceed to the formal disciplinary procedure. I'd prefer not to.' Disciplinary procedure (dealt with in Chapter 7) should only be used as a last resort.

9

MANAGING THE PARTNERSHIP WITH GOVERNORS – 1

Governors govern, heads manage

As a result of the Education Reform Act of 1988, governors are much more important to the running of a school. Their vastly enhanced responsibilities include deciding budget priorities, determining staffing complements and gradings, selecting staff at all levels and making decisions about staff discipline and dismissal.

The powers of the governing body have also expanded. LMS, open enrolment, the National Curriculum, etc have placed emphasis on the role of the governors in determining the future direction of the school. It has become fashionable to use business terms to describe the working relationship between governors and the headteacher. Indeed, one CEO wrote to governors recently saying 'It may be helpful if you see your role as that of a non-directive director, who sets the direction that a school should take' and this kind of terminology has generally been adopted. The word 'direct' is the key to the governors' new role – the governors' concern should be with policy and determining priorities, not intervention in the daily management of the school. This kind of comparison also fails to take into account your role as chief professional and educator; Case Study 9.1 perhaps puts this in perspective.

CASE STUDY 9.1 FOR REFLECTION

Main roles of the governing body – DfEE advice

To provide a strategic view

❑ The governing body should focus on where it can add most value – that is in helping to decide the school's strategy for improvement.

❏ It should help to set and keep under review the broad framework within which the headteacher and the staff should run the school.
❏ The governing body should focus on the key issues of raising standards of achievement, establishing high expectations and promoting effective teaching and learning.

To act as a critical friend

❏ Its role is to provide the headteacher and staff with support, advice and information, drawing on its members' knowledge and experience.
❏ It is responsible for monitoring and evaluating the school's effectiveness, asking challenging questions and pressing for improvement.
❏ It is a critical friend because it exists to promote the interests of the school and its pupils.

To ensure accountability

❏ It is responsible for ensuring good quality education in the school.
❏ The headteacher and staff report to the governing body on the school's performance.
❏ It should not rubber-stamp every decision of the headteacher – it has a right to discuss, question and refine proposals.
❏ It should, however, always respect the professional roles of the headteacher and the staff and their responsibility for the management of the school.
❏ It is answerable for its actions and for the school's performance to the parents and the wider local community.

The changes in education have affected the traditional pattern of powers and responsibilities, and have altered the whole relationship between the headteacher and the governors. The days when governors nodded when the headteacher spoke are long gone. As the head, you have lost some powers that you wielded in the past, including much of your power to determine the school curriculum, but this is not because curricular responsibility now resides with governors (which technically it did in the past) but because central government, through its directives, has taken control of much of the curriculum and left you with only the fine tuning. Where governors have gained additional powers and responsibilities is in the areas of finance and personnel, although even here (for maintained schools) the LEA retains last-resort responsibilities, a factor that has led to some tensions between governing bodies and LEAs.

Some governing bodies exercise their powers widely, but most remain content to take the advice of professionals in the field. The fact that the CEO quoted above felt that he needed to put out advice in the vein that he did indicates that some governing bodies must have flexed their muscles. There have been some clashes between headteachers and either a group of governors or the whole governing body, which have received considerable attention from the media and led to demands, including some from influential bodies such as NAHT, that the powers of governors be more clearly defined or severely restricted.

The change in power and responsibilities led to a growing awareness that a new relationship was needed between governors on the one hand and headteachers and the senior management team on the other. The relationship is intended to be a working partnership. It usually takes time in any organization for new partners to learn to work with one another and in some schools there has been a steep learning curve. It has not proved easy for a working partnership to develop and there have been some hiccups.

CASE STUDY 9.2 FOR ACTION

Compare the two quotations that follow and comment on what they tell you about the nature of the relationship established between governors and headteachers:

1. 'The art of working together may be delicate but it can also be fruitful.'
2. 'The governors are happy to exercise power, but far less happy to take responsibility when things go wrong.'

Your predecessor may have been resistant to change, clinging to his or her residual powers and reluctant to implement the new arrangements fully. If this is the case, often the governors see the change of personnel as an opportunity to alter the balance of power. At other times, a basic lack of respect or trust on one side or the other has made an effective working partnership difficult to establish. One of the main reasons for this is uncertainty about the nature of the partnership and the precise role each of the partners should play. Indeed, a question frequently asked by new governors is: 'Who does what?' It is not only new governors, however, who have difficulties with role definition and establishing where the boundaries should lie, and although the legislation has been in place for several years, there are still issues about 'who does what'.

As a new headteacher, it is very important for you to be able to form a good working relationship with the governors. Each side should understand its own role and responsibilities and those of its partner, and be prepared both to undertake its own responsibilities and to stay within the boundaries of its authority. The next section suggests how the division of responsibilities might work in a number of the key areas connected with the running of a school. Bear in mind, however, that even a definitive list of who does what will not do more than paper over the cracks in a poor relationship. Mutual respect for each other's role must be established.

ROLES AND RESPONSIBILITIES – WHO DOES WHAT?

In broad terms, the headteacher has responsibility for day-to-day decisions about the management and curriculum of the school and *the governors have a strategic overview*. To make this work in practice, however, the full governing body should agree the general framework of activities.

Planning and policy making

The governing body has the responsibility for planning and policy making and for producing the school's management/development plan, which is officially the governing body's development plan. The governors take decisions, they determine the aims, ethos and priorities of the school, but much of the nitty-gritty work of formulating the development plan is likely to be done in practice by you and your SMT.

Curriculum

It is the governors' responsibility to determine curricular policy in consultation with the headteacher. In practice this is restricted by central government directives (such as the National Curriculum) and by the LEA's curriculum statements. The latter may be modified with the LEA's approval. The governors are also required to have policies on a number of specific areas of the curriculum or aspects of education such as sex education, religious education, health education or drugs, and the governors are held responsible for the delivery of the curriculum. The head or SMT will supply the information and advice or, indeed, the first draft of the school curriculum plan, for discussion and subsequent approval by the governing body. As headteacher, however, you are responsible for the detailed *implementation* of the curriculum.

Staffing establishment

The governors are responsible for determining school staffing levels. As headteacher, you will draw up the initial staffing plan based on the school's needs and the overall development plan. This is because this task needs detailed professional knowledge. It requires a good understanding of the existing structure, a finger on the pulse of likely resignations and skill in assessing how to match the staff to the future curriculum needs of the school in both the short and the long term. (An exemplar of a staffing structure is included in Chapter 6.) The governors, however, either as the full governing body or as a staffing subcommittee, are responsible for the major decisions about staffing, for example what the staffing complement should be, or what proportion of the overall budget should be devoted to staffing, or whether to use any surplus for staffing or spend it on other areas. Their decisions must be informed and largely based on the information you supply through the staffing analysis and proposed plan, and this illustrates the nature of the partnership and just how closely you have to work together.

Appointments

The governors now have the responsibility for managing appointments. Although in maintained schools the LEA remains the ultimate employer, drawing up advertisements, drafting job descriptions and person specifications and criteria for short-listing have become the task of the governors. Ensuring that the governors work within the rules is your responsibility, and this means in practice that you do a lot of the initial drafting, offer professional advice and guide the governors through the procedures, avoiding possible pitfalls. A full discussion of how to manage staff selection can be found in Chapter 6.

Salary issues

The governors' personnel responsibilities include determining salary levels for all members of staff. Confronting salary issues can be a minefield.

Governors have to master the terms of whatever the current pay award is and work out how to apply them and what changes in their procedures this will entail. Often headteachers have to act as interpreters for a new scheme whose implications they have barely had time to analyse and assess themselves. The governors have had to develop a pay policy. This should be in place, but you will have to assess how adequate it is and advise them of any necessary changes. Getting the pay policy right is one of your most important tasks, as the criteria provide the governors with their best defence against criticisms of their individual decisions. Drafting a pay policy is described in Chapter 10, where an exemplar is provided.

Personnel issues

The governors deal with personnel issues, but the day-to-day management of the staff is very much your responsibility as headteacher, and it is only the complex problems that you should refer to them. The governing body could be described as the adjudicator between the headteacher and the staff on personnel issues. This enhanced responsibility for personnel requires considerable expertise and has involved the governors in having to learn about grievance procedures, disciplinary issues and redundancy, and has made courses on personnel issues the most oversubscribed area of governor training. The position of staff governors on committees dealing with personnel matters is sensitive, but essentially they are expected to fulfil their role as governors, and they are only instructed to withdraw if their own or relatives' employment or prospective promotion is to be discussed, or where they have a greater interest in the matter under discussion than other teachers at the school would have. Personnel issues are discussed in detail in Chapters 7 and 10.

Finance

The governors are responsible for approving and monitoring the budget. The finance subcommittee tends to be the most popular governors' subcommittee, probably because it is thought to be the powerhouse. Through its discussions and recommendations, the finance committee will have influenced what goes into the budget plan both before and after the drafting stage. The financial plan should be an integral plan of the overall school development plan, and getting this right necessitates very close liaison between you and the finance subcommittee. Once the budget is approved, the daily management of the money must be your responsibility. The governors do have a duty to monitor financial management, and the finance subcommittee will expect the senior management team to report back regularly to them, while in turn they will have to report back to the full governing body.

Charging/premises

It is the governors' responsibility to determine the policy for charging for school activities and the use of the premises outside school hours. The headteacher implements the policies, oversees site inspections and reports to the governors.

Marketing

The marketing plan is usually drawn up by a governors' subcommittee or staff working party, which produces ideas for the governors' approval. It is rarely the work of the headteacher. Implementing the plan is your responsibility, though you may choose to delegate many of the proposals to individuals or groups.

Resources

Here you would expect to act as adviser to the governors on policy, because they are dependent on your professional expertise. But you also need their advice about how to get some of the resources you want. Usually the governors will work through a resources subgroup, whose task will be to assess what the needs are over a period of time, but it is for the governing body to decide the priorities and allocations and for you to apply them.

Discipline

The 1988 Education Reform Act makes the governors responsible for producing a written statement of general principle for pupil discipline, of which you as headteacher must take account. You are, however, responsible for the maintenance of order and good behaviour on a day-to-day basis – making the school rules, deciding how they should be enforced and dealing with individual cases.

When serious indiscipline occurs, it is the head who excludes a pupil. Because exclusion carries a financial penalty, it is imperative that documentation is fully in place. The head must inform the governors and, if it is a maintained school, the LEA must be informed – there are clear procedures, which must be followed. The parents have the right to make representation to the LEA or to the governors and need to know what their rights are. (The prospectus informs parents how to go about this.) It is the duty of the governing body to consider and respond to representations and complaints and to hear appeals. The headteacher is not usually a member of a governors' subcommittee formed to hear representations or appeals.

Responsibilities in respect of information

Schedule 3 of the Education Reform Act 1988 established the flow of necessary information from the governing body on the exercise of its responsibilities. The governors have to supply the LEA, the Secretary of State, the DfEE, parents and teachers with any information requested of them.

These are some of the main areas about which they have to provide information and for which they are accountable:

❑ an annual return to the LEA about the curriculum in the current year;
❑ an annual return to the LEA about pupils for whom the National Curriculum has been disapplied or modified;
❑ an annual report for parents;
❑ an annual general meeting for parents to which all parents are invited;
❑ responsibility for ensuring that all policies and procedures relating to employment have been fully communicated to staff.

Although they have the responsibility to provide the information, the governors are dependent on you and the senior management team for analysing or supplying their data.

The above listing of the governors' responsibilities indicates the magnitude of the task that they now have. They decide direction, determine priorities and allocate resources. In reality the governors have been empowered with responsibility for all the really important decisions (except those reserved by the DfEE) and, in spite of LMS, your power as headteacher has been reduced.

Although it is much rarer now for governing bodies to rubber-stamp the head's proposals, they would be very foolish to disregard them altogether. As neither professionals nor full-timers, they are dependent upon you and your SMT to interpret legislation and guide them through a lot of complex or detailed information, and most of the time this will make them anxious to listen to your advice and be guided by you. They will be keen to do whatever is felt to be in the best interests of the school. Individual prejudices can cause hiccups, but governors have power as a group, not as individuals, and the common sense of the group usually prevails and improves the quality of decisions, especially as each decision has to be explained and justified. As headteacher, you can exercise your option to become a governor, which most heads do. Even if you do not become a member of the governing body, you can still exert influence through drafts and briefings, so most of the time you can still expect to get what you want.

Where the adjustment has come is in the *relationship* – there need to be give and take, trust and common sense if the partnership is to work.

> There is evidence that many headteachers are struggling with the new relationship. Many only seek approval when the decision is irrevocable. Some wonder how the motley crew, who sit round the table once a term or more, can ever be shaped into a decision-making team and hope that if they keep calm, the politicians too will eventually see that it is impossible. Most, if they are honest, yearn for the days when the governors came to the school's big events, made encouraging but futile noises about the school's achievements and occasionally stood by them when a difficult decision had to be defended.

This extract from a contribution by Joan Sallis at a governors' training session indicates that not all headteachers have really come to terms with the changed relationship. Neither of course have all the governors. The extract below is from the BBC's governors' training project, *Working Partnerships*, and sums up the current position rather well. You may find it useful when there comes a need to remind the governors what their role should be.

> The role of a school governor is to:
> ❏ support the school, but not uncritically;
> ❏ explain its policies to parents and the community, but not blindly;
> ❏ watch its standards, but with care, humility and with an open mind;
> ❏ oversee its policies and its use of resources, but not in tiresome detail.
>
> These responsibilities should be carried out as a governing body and they should be carried out with the knowledge and understanding of the school.

Making a success of the partnership is yet another test of your management skills, but it is a crucial one. If you try to pretend that the legislation of the 1980s hasn't happened and that the governors' power has not increased, sooner or later you will find yourself on the road to a confrontation.

MAKING THE PARTNERSHIP WORK – SOME GUIDELINES

❏ Make the framework of responsibilities clear to each side – try to avoid boundary disputes.
❏ Think positively and constructively about the relationship and work at developing it.
❏ Utilize the strengths that governors can bring to the school – they should complement your professional skills.
❏ Provide full information – don't hide things, share disasters as well as triumphs.
❏ Involve the governors in the life of the school – the more that they are involved, the more they will understand.

If you follow these guidelines towards building a good working relationship with the governors, confidence and trust should develop on both sides, and your governing body should become an asset and an important source of support for you. The case studies that follow explore the kind of situations that might arise and suggest ways to make the partnership between the governors and the senior management team work effectively.

THE PARTNERSHIP IN PRACTICE

CASE STUDY 9.3 FOR ACTION

Moving the governors forward – a strawberries and cream approach

There had been an Ofsted inspection shortly before I took up my post as headteacher. The governors were upset and hurt by the criticisms made by the inspection team, and found it difficult to believe anything serious could be wrong with the school. They knew attainment was low, but they said firmly that this was because of the catchment area of the school. Not surprisingly, the report was very critical of the governors, regarding their role as underdeveloped. The governors thought this was extremely unfair, as they felt they always supported the school strongly, attending its concerts and fêtes as well as the termly governors' meetings.

They wanted to hold a strawberry tea for the first governors' meeting that I was due to attend. I said 'No, thank you' to this. There were some major items on the agenda, and I preferred a strictly business meeting. I told them we needed to spend most of the meeting reviewing our response to the Ofsted report. This was urgent because, as far as I could see, very little had been done to address the issues raised in the inspection report.

The majority of governors greeted my report, which was structured in terms of targets resulting from the Ofsted criticisms, with incomprehension. My predecessor's reports had been couched in terms of the activities undertaken by the school, with no analysis or anything strategic. Nevertheless I had not appreciated the full extent of the governors' lack of education in carrying out their responsibilities.

By the end of the first meeting, I was beginning to grasp that they did not understand at all what work they were expected to do. For a start, they simply listened to my report without asking any questions. I listed tasks that needed to be undertaken by governors and waited for volunteers. Nothing happened. They seemed to expect that I would take care of everything and that their role was to approve my proposals and actions. A minority appeared to believe that if I asked them to undertake a task, I was abdicating my own responsibility as headteacher.

It was obvious that I had a major task ahead of me in terms of governor education. I was not only going to have to tell them that I did expect real work, but I was also going to have to tell them how to do it and monitor their performance to ensure that the tasks were actually completed. I had to show that I could give leadership to the team of governors. We were clearly not yet functioning as a team, and trust and understanding had not built up.

I started by presenting them with a much fuller picture of what was happening in the school than my predecessor had given them, and I did it in terms of objectives and targets rather than description. I made sure that they were fully informed of all the problems we faced and their implications, and that they understood what was involved in the decision-making process.

At first they felt threatened by the amount of information and some of the technical language used. They had been so protected by my predecessor that there was also some resentment of the change in expectations that immediately followed my appointment and of the fact that subcommittees were expected to meet regularly and report before each full governors' meeting. I involved them firmly in every decision being made, made sure they took appropriate responsibilities for agenda items and checked progress regularly. As time went on they began to realize that I expected them to offer firm proposals about which option we should choose and to support it with reasons.

I encouraged them to come into school more, so that it was not only the concerts and prize-givings they attended. I targeted these visits carefully so that it was a learning experience for the governors and enhanced their understanding of what good teaching was about. This impacted gradually on their ability to handle appointments as they became clearer about what kind of teachers we needed, and it became easier to persuade them to apply the agreed criteria rather than try to base appointments on a gut reaction to the candidate.

I made sure that they knew about the area governor-training programme and how to take advantage of it. Relating the issue of training to a value-for-money approach made sense to the business governors. I always invited the governors to whole staff Inset sessions and a few began to attend. This had a knock-on effect on their understanding of some of the issues we had to address and the development of their own working relationship with staff. Over time an increasing number of governors took up the opportunity for training in areas that interested them or were important for the school's development. After a while, the business governors began to offer training opportunities or facilities from which both staff and governors could benefit.

A few of the governors began to skip the meetings now that they were so much more businesslike than in the past. I did not pressurize them to come, but I kept a record of their attendance in case they wished to stand as governors next time. In fact, when their term of office came to an end, these governors simply stood down and it was never an issue. The majority, however, began to improve their practice and a few became real assets. A few governors had felt kept out by my predecessor, and had found the way meetings were run extremely frustrating. These governors were the first to come on board. Those who were involved in business or were accountants quickly grasped the financial planning implications and began to offer constructive advice.

I had audited the governors' expertise in terms both of their professional qualifications and of their known strengths or interests. I tried to build on these whenever the opportunity arose and to structure subcommittees appropriately. I also looked for areas of expertise amongst the parents and community so that when the opportunity presented itself we would be able to choose from stronger candidates than in the past.

It took time – more than a year. I have been here three years now and I am only beginning to feel that we are a 'performing' team. The governors are certainly better informed and have a much greater understanding of how a school has to be run.

For action/discussion

What are the issues raised by this case study? What strategies did this headteacher adopt to deal with the problem and how successful were they?

Case Study 9.8 provides guidelines for evaluating the governors' performance. Test it by evaluating where the governing body stood at the beginning and end of this case study. (The case study uses team-building terminology; for further information, see Trethowan, 1985.)

CASE STUDY 9.4 FOR ACTION

I am aware that there isn't time for us all to become experts in every aspect of school life and that some areas are so hedged about with legislation that it is genuinely difficult for governors to have more than a very general overview, but I am beginning to feel strongly that we should be more involved and be given more information. We just seem to be there to rubber-stamp things. At the last governors' meeting we were given the health and safety policy to approve. It was actually drawn up by a senior teacher who is in charge of health and safety in the school. When I got home I read the policy and realized that there were a lot of references to LEA memoranda about reporting of accidents, letting of kitchens and suchlike. I'm a fairly new governor, but I've been on the governing body long enough to know that I've never seen any of these documents. It seems to me that the school is operating a policy of 'Keep your fingers crossed and leave it to the headteacher.' How are we meant to take responsibility for what we haven't seen?

From part of a conversation at a governors' conference

For action/discussion

❏ What does this extract tell you about the relationship between the governors and the headteacher in this school?
❏ What is the main difference between Case Studies 9.3 and 9.4?
❏ What role are the governors taking?
❏ What advice would you give this headteacher and on what grounds?

CASE STUDY 9.5 FOR ACTION

The induction of new governors should include the following:

❏ briefing material – about the functions and responsibilities of the governors;
❏ briefing material – about the school;
❏ a copy of the most recent Ofsted report and the school's response (action plan);
❏ the opportunity to spend time in the school;
❏ time to talk to the headteacher – before and after the first meeting;
❏ information about the area governor-training programme;
❏ the opportunity to observe some of the subcommittees at work;
❏ linking each new governor with a mentor on the governing body.

For action

❏ Plan the induction programme for a governor who is elected during the four-year cycle. Are there important differences in managing the induction of a group of governors from that of an individual?
❏ Some governors have expressed interest in spending more time in school. What are your priorities in planning a programme for them?

CASE STUDY 9.6 FOR ACTION

The gap between policy and practice

At the annual governors' meeting for parents, the governors found themselves facing criticisms from a small but vociferous group of Asian parents, who asked what the governors were doing about the racism occurring in the school. The chair of governors was nonplussed, as no racist incidents had been reported to him. He asked the speaker to elaborate and the parents described name calling and harassment of girls wearing Muslim dress to school by a group of Year 10 boys. The parents wanted to know how this fitted in with the equal opportunities policy statement recently distributed to parents by the governors. The governors found it difficult to answer the questions, but pledged themselves to look into the problem and take appropriate action. The following morning an irate chair of governors sought an appointment with the headteacher to discuss the problem.

For action

❏ What are the issues raised by this case study?
❏ What should the respective roles of the headteacher and the chair of governors be in dealing with this matter?
❏ What advice would you give this headteacher and why?

The chair of governors, having pledged himself to look into the matter, has to find out whether the criticism that racism is occurring in the school is justified and, if it proves to be true, how serious it is. He will have to report his findings to the whole governing body, and they will then have to meet to consider the problem and decide what strategies to adopt.

Where does the headteacher fit into all this? The complaint has not been made to the head, but to the governors, so the headteacher cannot act without reference to them and must take direction from them. It is, however, the head, as the person on the job, who will have to undertake the initial investigation, but the governors, through the chair, will need to monitor the situation closely.

It is clearly not enough for the governors simply to have all the necessary policy statements; they have to see that they are implemented. The headteacher is directly responsible for implementing the policy. It is his or her task to establish and maintain a multicultural ethos and equal opportunities for all members of the organization. He or she is also responsible for the good order and discipline of the school. If the school's hidden curriculum and actual practice differ substantially from its published aims, then the headteacher and the governors will have to face the fact that a serious problem exists and that corrective action is needed. Both parties, the governors and the headteacher, have a responsibility in the matter and, if the situation is to be put right, they have to work together to find solutions.

If the accusations turn out to be true, there are a number of issues to address:

❑   what to do about the pupils responsible;
❑   how to improve pupils' attitudes;
❑   how to help the pupils cope with harassment if it occurs;
❑   how to make staff more aware of and more active in dealing with such incidents;
❑   how to ensure that name calling and teasing are recognized as racist and not regarded as trivial.

In many ways the problem is one of awareness. Both the headteacher and the governors seem to have been unaware that a problem existed, and the staff seem unaware of what constitutes racism. Awareness training that centres on recognition of different categories of racist behaviour and suggests some partial responses will probably be beneficial for both staff and governors, and running the sessions as joint Inset open to both staff and governors will demonstrate that it is not only the staff who need this training. A governors' working group, which includes staff representation, could be given a brief that includes organizing the necessary training, exploring ways in which to support the victims and deal with the perpetrators and continuing to monitor the situation. Recording each incident that occurs and acting to check all cases of possible racism will deter some pupils from the more overt racist bullying. It will take longer to deal with latent racism. The curriculum and materials used in the school will need to be checked for racism as, although most textbooks have changed with the times, some old books are still in use. Addressing the issue through the personal, social and health education (PSHE) curriculum is a more obvious longer-term solution, but it will only become effective once the teachers' awareness and understanding of the issue have improved, otherwise their teaching will lack credibility. The school's pupil council also needs to be involved. It will probably be a sensible move to make the governors' working group permanent, because of the need to monitor equal opportunities on a regular basis.

CASE STUDY 9.7 FOR ACTION

Making appointments

You are the headteacher of Bestwick Park High School. Your deputy is retiring this summer and you are hoping to appoint someone who enjoys managing change and development. You have drafted the job description and the person specification in consultation with the governors, and had thought they understood what you wanted. In addition, you have taken the CEO's advice about the procedure to follow, the criteria for selection and the wording of the advert. The advertisement duly appeared in the national press and, because Bestwick Park is a popular school, it attracted a good field. Now the time for short-listing had arrived. Faced with the pile of application forms, the appointments panel, a governors' subcommittee, seemed uninterested in the criteria that had been so carefully devised to provide a basis for the short-listing. What really worries you is that they seem oblivious, or in some cases actively hostile, to equal opportunities considerations, and inclined to rely on 'gut reactions' to applicants' letters and forms.

For action

What strategy should you adopt in this situation?

Normally a governor is one of the interviewing panel for teaching appointments. You like to vary the governor in order to build up expertise. At an interview for a second in the modern languages department, the governor is new to interviewing but has a business background. You brief him as fully as possible about what is required and he says that he understands. Nevertheless it soon becomes clear that the governor is taking a very different view of the candidates from you. His clear preference is for someone who you are sure will not integrate well into the department team or be able to deliver the attainment you need for the school to achieve its target and, most importantly, his answers to your questions do not indicate that he has the potential to develop.

For action

How do you prevent a major clash developing? How do you ensure that you get the best candidate for the post?

CASE STUDY 9.8 FOR ACTION

Evaluating the governors – exemplar

Bestwick Park High School – Governors' effectiveness questionnaire

Policies and priorities

1. Are the governors sufficiently involved in the school?
2. Do the governors help the school with daily tasks?
3. Do individual governors play an active part in specific areas of the school?
4. Are governors sufficiently informed about the school?
5. How often do the governors visit?

Relationships inside and outside school

1. How often do the governors meet the staff or pupils formally or informally?
2. Do the governors know whom to approach at the LEA for help and advice?

3. Has a 'link governor' been appointed and how much use is made of him or her?
4. Do the governors know the community the school serves?

Roles and relationships within the governing body

1. Do all the governors know one another?
2. Are new governors made to feel welcome?
3. Are the governors encouraged to take on responsibilities within the group?
4. Does the governing body regularly share ideas, skills and knowledge?

Meetings

1. Are the meetings interesting and stimulating?
2. Does everybody have a reasonable opportunity to say what he or she wants at meetings?
3. Are the meetings of reasonable length and frequent enough to cope with tasks effectively?
4. Do governors' meetings get things done?

For action/discussion

❏ What form of governor evaluation is operating in your school? Who organizes it? How is it reported?
❏ The DfEE booklet *Governing Bodies and Effective Schools* (1995) lists six features of effective governing bodies: working as a team, good relationship with the headteacher, effective time management, effective meetings, knowing the school and training and development. How far did the evaluation operated by Bestwick Park match the DfEE list? What other aspects of the governors' work would benefit from evaluation?

10

MANAGING THE PARTNERSHIP WITH GOVERNORS – 2

The spate of government legislation of the late 1980s and early 1990s greatly enhanced the powers of individual schools at the expense of LEAs in respect of resource allocation, salary and employment. These powers have not, however, been delegated to you as headteacher, but to the governing body of the school. The previous chapter sought to demonstrate how essential it is that you make the partnership with governors work because of the closeness of your linked roles. This chapter continues to develop the theme of your relationship with the governing body, explores the structures and mechanisms you will need to establish the policies, and offers some guidelines for dealing with some of the problems involved in managing resources and personnel.

CREATING THE STRUCTURES – GOVERNORS' COMMITTEES

One of the problems that the governors had to address was how to divide up the work. It is simply unrealistic for the whole governing body to deal with every task. The growth of the volume of work has led to a mushrooming of committees, but the two structures most regularly used are governors' working groups and subcommittees of the governing body.

A governors' working group or party is much less bureaucratic than a committee and does not need a formal agenda or minutes. Its advantage is in being a useful way of getting a group of governors and staff to work together. It lacks any real power because its recommendations have to be referred back to the whole governing body for discussion and ratification. This can be a major advantage for you because it prevents power being concentrated in a small group of governors. A subcommittee of the governing body is a formal organization, which must have a chairperson and vice-chair who must be governors (but not staff governors). Its membership and terms of reference are decided by the full governing body and it has to have the same procedural arrangements as the parent body, eg chairperson's casting vote and withdrawal criteria. These are designed to prevent ambiguity or overlap of functions between the various subcommittees. Subcommittees have much greater power than working groups because the decisions made here have the status of decisions of the full governing body, and are reported as information in the minutes of the governing body. They do, however, have to refer back the pay and conditions policy, where the regulations make it clear that it has to be formulated by the full governing body.

You may well have to advise the governors which structure they should adopt, although they may have very definite ideas. It makes a lot of sense, however, to use a mixed system. Where there is a clear task and it will hold things up to keep referring back to the whole governing body, then use a subcommittee. Where the issues are controversial, or there could be conflict between different committees, or where a clique could develop that might try to arrogate power properly belonging to the governors as a whole, then use a working group.

Foundation schools are bound by their instruments and articles of government, which usually require them to have committees on admissions, pupil discipline and staffing – to deal with matters related to staff discipline. Appeals committees are also required to handle complaints from parents and staff.

Each school makes its own decision about its preferred number of committees and their format. Each subgroup has to have both governors and teachers (most frequently members of the SMT), so there shouldn't be too many, as they will all have to have regular meetings. The most commonly used subcommittees, whether working parties or committees, are:

❏   finance;
❏   resources;
❏   buildings;
❏   curriculum;
❏   personnel;
❏   marketing/promoting the school;
❏   community.

There is obviously some overlap between these groups, which is another reason why it is important to establish clear terms of reference for each of them. Most schools find that they need five or six committees to manage their affairs – creating more is usually counterproductive. An appeals/grievances committee must be in place, however, and this must be formed from a distinctly different group of governors from those serving on the personnel committee.

CASE STUDY 10.1 FOR ACTION

Terms of reference for Bestwick Park High School finance subcommittee

❑   to advise the governing body on financial strategy and policy within the resources available;

❑   to receive, consider and present to the governing body annual estimates of the school's budget and annual turn-out budget;

❑   to keep under review the staffing establishment of the school and to recommend to the governing body and to the personnel subcommittee the financial limits for salaries and wages within the overall school budget;

❑   to receive regular reports on the school's income and expenditure, to set these against the annual budget and to report to the governing body on their findings;

❑   to provide the governing body with advice on resources and services to the school and in particular to undertake the setting up of contracts for services as required by the governing body;

❑   to review from time to time and update the governing body on the financial memorandum, DfEE and LEA circulars and other documents pertinent to financial matters.

For action

❑   Compare this subcommittee's terms of reference with those of the finance or finance and general purposes subcommittee of your own school. Do the terms of reference cover everything necessary for the committee to function effectively?

❑   Draft terms of reference for either the buildings group or the personnel subcommittee.

STATUTORY POLICIES

It has become essential for the governing body to have a clear set of policies on a range of educational issues. Many of these policies are now statutory, resulting from the Education Acts of 1986, 1988 and 1990. Others arise from issues confronting the school. How do you set about constructing the policy statements?

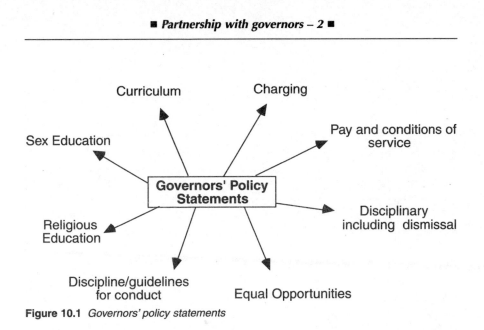

Figure 10.1 *Governors' policy statements*

Guidelines for constructing policy statements

Given the need for a range of policy statements (and some schools now have so many that they are producing them in booklet form), it makes sense to adopt an in-house approach towards them all. It also makes it easier for the governors to understand the methodology and what the person who has done the initial draft is trying to achieve.

1. Create a working group that includes both governors and professionals. Co-opt or seek advice from outside the school if you need particular expertise.
2. Define the terms of reference clearly so that the group understand the task, the deadlines, etc.
3. Set the objectives – this can be done either by the whole governing body, who will instruct the working group, or by the working party, which will have to start by determining the guiding principles and desired outcome.
4. Create a standard format or model for all your policy statements. This not only creates an in-house style, but also ensures you cover all the areas that should normally be included in a policy statement.

Some of the exemplar policies available are virtually pamphlets in themselves because of all the information they include, and have perhaps lost their way. If you group your policies into one handbook there is no need to keep repeating the background of the school as a preamble to every policy. A page at the beginning of the booklet can include any relevant information about the school.

A model policy statement

Aims

Keep the aims distinct from the objectives. Aims should be general; objectives are your achievable targets. Sometimes you will need to start the policy with a rationale section of what you believe or, as in the case of a school's pay policy, with some general principles.

Content

In the case of the school's curriculum policy, this section will explain the main features of the school's curriculum. In a specific area of the curriculum, eg citizenship or sex education, the policy statement will list the main curriculum areas through which the policy is delivered and describe what is covered. An exemplar is given below as Case Study 10.2.

Methodology

This section describes teaching methods or your general approach. It is most commonly used for policies dealing with aspects of the curriculum, but can also be used to spell out the steps you are going to take to enforce the policy. Sometimes it works better to combine content and methodology under the heading 'Delivery'.

Management

This section describes who is responsible and for what. As well as describing how the policy will be managed, this is the section where you include 'liaison with' and list the 'other relevant policies'.

Evaluation

This section spells out how the policy will be reviewed, how regularly and by whom, ie the evaluation procedure. Many policy statements are good on statements of intent, weaker on methods of delivery and there is a tendency to skip evaluation altogether, so this last section is a test not only of whether you have grasped the general principles of writing a policy, but of where you intend to apply it. (See Case Study 9.6, which described a governing body being taken to task for its failure to implement its anti-racist policy.)

The two case studies that follow provide exemplars of governors' policy statements, which you can test against your own policies and the model.

CASE STUDY 10.2 EXEMPLAR

Bestwick Park High School – multi-cultural/equal opportunities policy

Rationale

This policy statement defines multi-cultural in its widest sense, ie not only referring to colour or ethnicity, but including all the factors *influencing* culture, including gender, class, ethnicity, religion, where individuals live, etc. Therefore every classroom has a multi-cultural range of students, who bring to the school a selection of different cultural understandings, influencing how they learn and interpret the world.

Education for equality ensures that learners develop autonomy over their learning in a secure environment in which their understandings of the world are valued and used as a basis for learning.

Aim

Bestwick Park High School aims to provide access for all pupils to the full range of educational and personal development opportunities so that they reach their full potential physically, socially and academically. The school aims to provide for its pupils a curriculum and learning environment that values cultural diversity and builds on the experiences of all the members of the organization.

Objectives

❏ to develop a commitment to equality throughout the organization;
❏ to develop a curriculum that delivers our aim;
❏ to develop teaching methods and learning approaches that help us to create a learning environment that will promote equal opportunities;
❏ to provide the educational context that promotes awareness and positive attitudes.

Delivery

Curriculum

Both the content and the way it is presented can address issues of equality. All curriculum subjects can contribute, and the list that follows is intended merely to provide exemplars:

❏ *PSHE* – this subject has an obvious contribution to make through curriculum content (eg the syllabus contains a unit on stereotyping). In addition, discussions on issues relating to equal opportunities and prejudice raise awareness and help promote positive attitudes. The rationale of the PSHE programme is to support personal development and equip pupils with the means to challenge inequality, racism and prejudice wherever they find them.

❏ *History* – the syllabus includes units of world history, eg World War II, which encourage pupils to view events from a number of different perspectives. Through the study of the past, pupils can begin to understand inequality in society. Contributing units include:

– the Industrial Revolution (KS3) – 19th-century working and living conditions, working-class movements, and class, economic and political inequality;

– revolutions that reordered society, eg (KS3 and KS4) France 1789 or Russia 1917 – the inequitable distribution of power and wealth and the move towards democracy;

– suffragettes (KS3) and humanities GCSE – gender inequality;

– black or indigenous peoples of America – colour and inequality.

Evidence work helps our pupils recognize bias and appreciate the extent to which the cultural heritage or personal prejudice of a writer may influence his or her interpretation of events.

❏ **Science** - the science curriculum emphasizes that it is not neutral or value-free, but a cultural activity practised in a particular political/economic context. It endeavours to avoid tokenism and to give science a wide context. The science curriculum addresses racism through its discussion of pseudo-scientific genetic theories that divide humanity into distinct racial groups and justifies the doctrine of master and inferior races.

Teaching and learning

Pupils receive overt and covert messages from the way in which a class-room is organized and from their role in the classroom. A variety of teaching and learning strategies can be used to promote equal opportunities:

❑ to enable our pupils to interact in a variety of ways with the teacher and to reach their potential (see our special needs policy);
❑ the pupils' own experience is valued and built on;
❑ ideas and assumptions are challenged;
❑ teamwork and collaborative strategies are regularly employed;
❑ materials are regularly monitored and pupils made aware of the context of the material;
❑ displays represent social, linguistic and cultural diversity;
❑ resources are relevant, open and accessible, enabling pupils to negotiate and develop their own ideas and take some responsibility for their own learning;
❑ regular audits are carried out to check where we stand.

School policies and practice

A number of school policies contribute to equal opportunities, eg behaviour policy and code of conduct, anti-bullying policy, special needs policy and pastoral policy. These policies should ensure that the organization and its members will react to any incidents that occur and lead by example.

Some of our current initiatives will also contribute to equal opportunities, eg our monitoring programme will help us record what pupils achieve in terms of value added and will influence future planning, and the Investors in People initiative will contribute to the promotion of the school as one community.

We shall continue to take advantage of training opportunities that raise awareness or inculcate good practice. Appointments should follow good practice and equal opportunities procedures.

Management

The named person in respect of equal opportunities is Mr S Tucker, head of science. Heads of department are responsible for subject delivery. Year heads are responsible for pastoral aspects and for the PSHE programme. Staff development is co-ordinated by the deputy head. The ultimate responsibility for the school's policy rests with the governors.

Evaluation

Regular monitoring and sampling will be used to check the tone and language of our documents, how regularly incidents occur and how we react to them. Curriculum audits will be used to check where we stand in respect of content and methodology. Receiving the Investors in People accreditation will be a clear sign that we have made progress. Feedback will help us monitor awareness and perceptions.

CASE STUDY 10.3 FOR ACTION

Schools now have a much greater discretion in determining the pay of the staff they employ. They have had to draft a pay policy and to do this they have had to work out the criteria on which to base it. This case study follows through what happened at Bestwick Park High School. Although it centres on pay policy, it can be used to compare how to approach any new structure that the governors may need to put in place.

After receiving details of the recent pay awards and new structures, Miles Standish, the chair of governors, gave a summary of the main changes to the governors' meeting, having been briefed by Brenda Gatlin, the headteacher. The governors were concerned about the implications, and how to ensure that they treated people fairly and consistently. The head emphasized the possibility of facing trouble in the future if they did not draw up a pay policy that provided them with clear principles by which to operate.

The governors were quite experienced in drawing up policy statements and were happy to do this for pay, but some could see that the complexity of the new regulations and the sensitivity of this particular issue made drafting the policy and getting it accepted by the staff a particularly difficult undertaking. The meeting agreed to get staff views at an informal lunchtime session, as it was felt that teachers would find a policy more acceptable if they had had some input to it.

A working party of governors and staff was entrusted with the task of producing the first draft of the new pay policy. The governors set the group clear objectives. The policy should:

❑ help the school achieve its aims and objectives as set out in the school development plan;

❏   apply to all staff, not just the teaching staff;
❏   reward staff fairly and equitably;
❏   help motivate staff;
❏   enable staff to understand the basis of pay decisions;
❏   ensure that all decisions were fair and consistent.

The terms of reference also spelt out a number of factors or considerations the working party had to take into account. The policy would have to:

❏   be in line with the school development plan and the LEA's pay policy;
❏   take account of the school's budget proposals;
❏   take account of pupil number forecasts;
❏   take into account any national or local factors that could affect decisions or implementation of the policy;
❏   be consistent with the school's equal opportunities policy;
❏   be brief but sufficiently precise to meet the needs of the school;
❏   provide the opportunity to create a mix of annual and continuing payments, and keep a balance between allowances and discretionary scale points;
❏   ensure that proper relativities existed, eg between the pay levels of the head, the deputies and the other staff.

It was also decided that because a good working knowledge of the new pay regulations was essential, the first working session should be a training session for the working party to brief them fully about salary matters. The Besthampton governor training scheme provided someone who both briefed them about the regulations and took them through the LEA's own policy statement. They also looked at pay policies that the headteacher had borrowed from colleagues elsewhere.

Once the working party had grasped the implications of the new regulations and received feedback from the staff sessions, they moved on to determining the general principles of the policy, and deciding how it should operate. The area that provoked the most difficulty was in deciding what criteria to use. Finally, after a great deal of discussion, they decided to stick to the criteria listed in the pay and conditions document. Once general agreement had been reached, two members of the group volunteered to do the drafting, and the working party amended and agreed the draft before it went to the full governing body, where it was debated in detail and further amended. The governors had complied with the regulation that the pay policy had to be the work of the whole governing body. (The final text of the Bestwick Park pay policy is given below as Case Study 10.5.)

They sought the advice of the teacher governors as to how best to fulfil their duty to communicate the policy to the teachers and associate staff. It was decided that copies of the draft document should be displayed in the staffroom for 10 days, with personal copies made available on demand, and that the next long staff meeting should include the discussion of the draft as a major item. Members of the working party (where possible) and the chair of governors were to attend. This session led to some slight redrafting, after which the policy was finally adopted by the governing body.

For action

❏ What are the issues that arise from this case study?
❏ Why was the initial task entrusted to a working party and not delegated to a committee?
❏ How do the procedures adopted at Bestwick Park compare with those followed in your own school?
❏ How could they be improved?

CASE STUDY 10.4 FOR ACTION

Key issues to be considered in drafting a pay policy

❏ Have all of the employees who work in the school community been considered?
❏ Does it deal effectively with the most relevant issues such as recruitment, retention and motivation?
❏ Will it promote the staff's professional development?
❏ Is it compatible with the school development plan?
❏ Is it compatible with the school's budget arrangements?
❏ Has it taken due regard of all relevant legislation, eg equal opportunities?
❏ Does it consider all discretionary payments and any other pay-related elements that can give rise to costs within the school's budget?
❏ Does it ensure that appropriate differentials will be created and maintained between posts held within the school?
❏ Who is to manage and administer it?

❑ Does it determine the power of appointment for new and temporary staff to be delegated to the headteacher?

❑ What criteria does it establish for special payments such as relocation packages?

❑ Does it provide a practical appeals procedure?

❑ Is it clear how the policy will be disseminated both now and in the future, eg for new staff?

❑ Will it be reviewed annually and by whom?

CASE STUDY 10.5 EXEMPLAR

Bestwick Park High School pay policy

General principles

The governing body of Bestwick Park High School seeks to ensure that all teaching and associate staff are valued and receive proper recognition for their work and contribution to school life, and will endeavour within its budget to use the national pay scales and discretions available to it as the 'relevant body' to recruit, retain and motivate teachers of quality to ensure the best possible delivery of the curriculum.

Aims

1. to maintain and improve the quality of education provided for pupils in the school by having a pay policy that supports the school's mission statement and development plan;
2. to have a staffing structure related to the school's development plan;
3. to show all staff that the governing body is managing its pay policy in a fair and responsible way.

Management of the policy

The governing body has responsibility for establishing the school's pay policy and for seeing that it is followed. It considers and approves the overall pay structure for all staff. The governing body delegates authority to a personnel subcommittee to administer the pay policy on its behalf. The subcommittee will comprise the headteacher, vice-chair of governors and four other governors. It requires its members to treat information about an individual's earnings as confidential. Its responsibilities are exercised within the constraints of the school's delegated budget and in accordance with the school's financial plan.

A second subcommittee, for appeals and grievances, will comprise the chair of governors and five other governors.

The two subcommittees will be appointed annually by the full governing body. No governor may be a member of both the personnel and the appeals subcommittees.

Consultation

A representative group from the governing body will consult fully with members of staff when drawing up the pay policy and during each annual review of the policy, in line with best practice. Each member of staff and each governor will be given a copy of the pay policy. The governing body will also consult with the LEA where appropriate.

Equal opportunities and employment legislation

The governing body seeks to provide equal opportunities for all staff, in accordance with the school's equal opportunities policy and equal pay legislation.

Vacant posts

Full information relating to vacant posts, including those carrying additional points, whether permanent, temporary or acting, will be made known to staff in time for them to apply for posts for which their training and relevant experience are appropriate.

Job descriptions

The headteacher, on behalf of the governing body, will provide these for all staff when they are first appointed and at an annual review in consultation with staff in the summer term. Written statements of the terms and conditions of employment will be provided by the LEA.

Appraisal

The governing body will follow current national and LEA guidelines about how appraisal links to pay.

Job relativity

The governing body will seek to ensure that there is proper relativity between jobs within the school.

Records

Records of salary will be confidential to the individual concerned and the personnel subcommittee.

Grievance

If a member of staff has a grievance relating to his or her salary, he or she should follow the grievance procedure.

Associate staff

Pay and conditions

1. The governing body will work within the national and local structures agreed with the unions in accordance with the employer's contractual conditions of service. These are Besthampton Pay, national conditions for APT&C staff (protected), national conditions for manual workers and local amendments. The governing body delegates decisions on salaries, job descriptions and gradings to the personnel subcommittee.
2. The personnel subcommittee of the governing body will evaluate the range and grade of each post based on the requirements of the job description and personnel specification. These will be compiled from the LEA's model job descriptions, which have undergone job evaluation in accordance with the legal requirements.
3. The personnel subcommittee will grade all new appointments on either Besthampton Pay or the manual workers' pay scale. Employees who have not previously elected to transfer to Besthampton Pay will be protected on APT&C conditions until their post is evaluated and regraded or until they are contracted to a new post.

Manual workers

Once the personnel subcommittee has decided the grade of a manual post, the post holder is on a fixed wage, paid weekly, subject to a national pay award, whenever it occurs.

The site manager and assistant site manager's pay will include 15 per cent performance-related pay, and the governing body will withhold this element if specified performance is not attained. Performance-related pay is not paid during sickness absence.

Besthampton Pay

The personnel subcommittee will determine the starting salary within the range and will base this decision on the following criteria:

- ❏ level of experience;
- ❏ qualifications;
- ❏ added value to the school;
- ❏ level of training required to fulfil the needs of the post;
- ❏ present salary;
- ❏ protection in cases of redeployment;
- ❏ next incremental due date (if appointed between October and March this will be 18 months).

The minimum starting salary at age 21 is ISN 5.

The governing body can award merit or accelerated increments within the range at any time during the financial year. Criteria for this decision will be:

- ❏ achievement exceeding normal job requirements but at an equivalent level of responsibility;
- ❏ completion of key tasks to a degree that exceeds the line manager's recorded expectations;
- ❏ undertaking a specialized project at an equivalent level of responsibility to the post holder's current job description.

Annual increments are payable on 1 April each year subject to satisfactory performance. They are managed through the appraisal process.

Honoraria

The governing body will award an honorarium to an employee temporarily carrying out work of a higher level. This will be calculated on the difference between the post holder's substantive salary and the bottom ISN of the appropriate range for the new tasks or a minimum of one increment, whichever is the greater, pro rata for the number of hours worked and the period of time involved.

The personnel subcommittee will review job descriptions annually and will re-evaluate the grade if responsibility or accountability are increased, decreased or changed.

Teachers

1. The governing body will follow the requirements and guidelines of the current school teachers' pay and conditions document in exercising a pay policy for the teaching staff. The discretion allowed by this document and the accompanying circular will be used according to identified school needs and based on clearly laid-down criteria subject to annual review and available funding.
2. The personnel subcommittee together with the headteacher will review on an annual basis all teaching staff salaries and will make an assessment of each teacher's salary. An individual assessment report will be given to each teacher for implementation the following September. Any teacher who wishes to query his or her salary should raise the matter in the first instance with the headteacher. If the matter is not resolved, the grievance procedure should be invoked.
3. The headteacher may at any time during the year make recommendations to the governing body regarding changes to a teacher's pay and conditions in the light of unforeseen circumstances. The governing body delegates authority to the personnel subcommittee to give approval for changes required during the course of the school year.

Teachers on the common pay spine

1. *Qualifications* – the governing body, in line with the current school teachers' pay and conditions document, awards two points for a good honours degree (first class, upper- and lower-second class) or equivalent, or for a higher qualification. In some cases a teacher in post without such a qualification may subsequently so qualify and therefore become entitled to two points, unless that teacher already has the maximum of nine points allowed for experience and qualifications. These points once awarded are a permanent entitlement in any post.

2. *Experience*
   - Mandatory: the governing body will award one point for each year of recognized teaching service up to a maximum of nine (seven for those with two qualification points). A year of recognized service is one in which the teacher has taught for part of at least 26 weeks in the school year.
   - Discretionary: the governing body has determined the following number of points for directly relevant experience outside teaching: one-third for maternity/paternity (up to a maximum of two points); and one-half for particularly relevant experience (up to a maximum of five points). Mandatory and discretionary points once awarded remain a permanent entitlement for the teacher in any post.
3. *Responsibility* – the governing body will need to determine the number of posts with additional responsibilities and the corresponding number of points each will carry. Such additional responsibilities will need to be clearly defined and linked to job descriptions. Such posts could carry up to a maximum of five points. They may be either fixed-term or permanent, as determined by the governing body. The governing body will seek to ensure that similar responsibilities carry similar points.
4. *Excellence* – the governing body will need to review annually to determine whether to exercise its discretion to award points for excellence. These points may only be awarded on an annual basis. If the governing body decides to award such points, it is essential to agree clear and objective criteria before any awards are made. Further advice on this will be issued. If a teacher is to be put forward for advanced skills teacher status, proper procedures, as set out in DfEE guidance, must be followed.
5. *Recruitment and retention* – the governing body will need to determine whether or not it wishes to exercise discretion in awarding up to two points for recruitment and retention.
6. *Special needs*
   - Mandatory: the governing body will award a minimum of one point to teachers who wholly or mainly teach pupils with statements of special needs.
   - Discretionary: the governing body will use its discretion to award a second point to teachers who wholly or mainly teach pupils with statements of special educational needs.

7. *Frozen payments* – the governing body will exercise its discretion to preserve existing permanent discretionary scale points over and above the assimilated salary.

Heads and deputies

1. *General* – the governing body is aware that heads and deputies do not receive annual increments and they will therefore ensure that careful consideration is given to these salaries in the annual review. The following guidance from the school teachers' pay and conditions document will be followed and used when and if it is appropriate to do so: awards may be given on a temporary or permanent basis; it is in order to pay a higher salary than that falling within the normal range if that salary is considered inadequate.

2. *Criteria* – the criteria to be taken into account when reviewing the salaries of the head and deputies include the responsibility of the post, length of service, whether the post is difficult to fill and the overall performance by the head or the deputy, assessed by a defined procedure taking into account overall management objectives.

3. *Process* – the process for considering an award for the head or deputy will be as follows:

    —   The standing committee appointed by the full governing body to make recommendations on the pay of the school's head and deputy or deputies will, when considering the salary to be paid on the first appointment to the school, need to have regard in particular, but not exclusively, to the first three of the statutory criteria set out in the school teachers' pay and conditions document.

    —   Thereafter, the standing committee should establish an annual timetable for its work. This will be concerned particularly with the fourth of the statutory criteria to which the governing bodies are required to have regard. The timetable for reviewing this should include: 1) at the onset of the school year, setting the basis on which performance will be reviewed, including the personal and school-based objectives and some indication of the exceptional standards that need to be achieved to justify some progression up the pay spine; 2) during the school year, reviewing the progress towards meeting personal and school-based objectives, taking into account any new factors that may have arisen; 3) at the

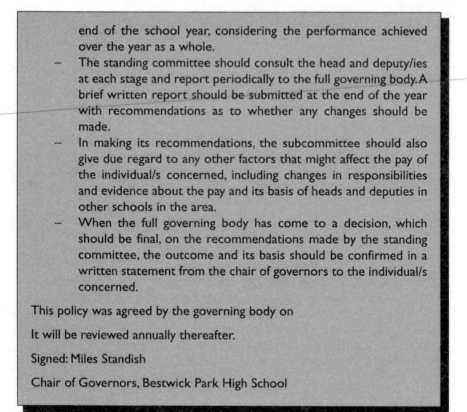

end of the school year, considering the performance achieved over the year as a whole.

— The standing committee should consult the head and deputy/ies at each stage and report periodically to the full governing body. A brief written report should be submitted at the end of the year with recommendations as to whether any changes should be made.

— In making its recommendations, the subcommittee should also give due regard to any other factors that might affect the pay of the individual/s concerned, including changes in responsibilities and evidence about the pay and its basis of heads and deputies in other schools in the area.

— When the full governing body has come to a decision, which should be final, on the recommendations made by the standing committee, the outcome and its basis should be confirmed in a written statement from the chair of governors to the individual/s concerned.

This policy was agreed by the governing body on

It will be reviewed annually thereafter.

Signed: Miles Standish

Chair of Governors, Bestwick Park High School

PERSONNEL ISSUES – MANAGING STAFF CUTS

The largest part of any school's budget is spent on staffing, and if the budget is tight, then invariably it is the money spent on staff that comes under scrutiny. Although there is evidence that schools look at non-teaching posts in the first instance, because such a large part of the staffing budget is spent on teachers, governing bodies may be forced to consider reducing the number of teachers that they employ. The case study that follows explores this scenario.

CASE STUDY 10.6 FOR ACTION

Managing staff cuts

On receipt of the budget figures for the following year, Mrs Gatlin phoned the chair of governors to inform him of the bad news. Miles Standish was furious: the governors had spent a lot of time ensuring the school budget was managed properly, but now felt let down by the LEA. However, the priority had to be coping with the immediate problem. They agreed that the first step was to get the bursar to do an analysis of the implications of the cuts, and that the finance subcommittee should make suggestions about the areas in which cuts might be made.

It was essential to follow procedures precisely, as failing to do so could be expensive. They would also need to act swiftly because there were only three dates in the financial year on which teachers could be dismissed on grounds of redundancy (31 August, 31 December and 30 April). Teachers had a statutory entitlement to one week's notice for each year of service up to a total of 12 years, so a teacher who had 12 years' experience, who was to be dismissed, needed to be given notice by 30 September. If the school failed to complete all the necessary steps in time to give proper notice, contractual and/or statutory, then the school would be liable for salary until 31 December, which would add to the budget problems. Mr Standish agreed to the head's proposals.

The finance committee meets

At the finance committee's meeting it became clear that trimming was not going to solve the problem. There had been too many lean years for them to have accumulated savings substantial enough to help them now, so they were left with the problem of staff cuts. They would need to reduce the complement by at least one, possibly two. They had to decide what staff cuts to make and how to approach the matter with staff. In view of the gravity of the situation and the need to ensure that procedures were followed absolutely, the finance committee referred the matter back to the whole governing body to decide how to proceed, and a special budget meeting was called.

The governors' meeting

The governors were appalled at the situation and some time was spent composing a letter to the LEA, suggesting that it improved its forward planning in future, and deploring the cuts. In considering the staff cuts they quickly realized that they could not simply ask the head to nominate a suitable member of staff and, although a few of the parent governors would clearly have liked to suggest one or two of the less popular and effective teachers, this approach was quickly squashed. They had to be seen to be fair. They decided to set up a governors' working party, to create a possible formula to use. This would mean additional meetings but, with such a sensitive issue, they had no choice.

The head asked for advice about how and when to broach the matter with the staff. It has always been her practice to be open with them, and she believed that to act otherwise in a matter that intimately concerned them would forfeit their good will. In addition, the staff governors would be put in a difficult position. There would in any case probably be rumours: the head had heard that Besthampton School, Bestwick Park's nearest rival, was in an even worse position. The contractual problems made it essential that people should be given notice within the time limit and could mean that more notices had to be issued than were eventually needed. On the other hand, she did not want to worry people unduly and be accused of scaremongering.

It was decided that the head should use the next weekly staff meeting to do an update on the school's budget position. Staff would be made aware that a serious problem existed, that a governors' group had been asked to look at ways in which cuts could be made and that this could lead to the issuing of redundancy notices. A longer staff meeting would be held after school in the following month when the position was clearer, and at that meeting the situation would be fully explained and discussed with staff. The governors asked Mrs Gatlin to produce a consultation paper for the staff meeting. One of the staff governors proposed that some governors should attend the staff meeting, and Mr Standish and Nandish Samani, one of the parent governors, were nominated to attend.

Informing the trade unions

Mrs Gatlin proposed seeing the union representatives at the same time as the issue was raised with the staff. This was in accordance both with the rules, which state that the recognized trade unions must be consulted at the earliest opportunity, and with her own wish to brief them and clarify the processes of consultation. She considered it important to co-operate with them as far as possible.

The working party meets to determine the criteria

At the meeting it quickly became clear that they could not simply apply industrial techniques (first in, last out) for handling redundancy in an educational institution. If different criteria were applied, however, the school could have to demonstrate why. Yvonne Perkins, the deputy head in charge of curriculum and timetabling, was especially horrified by the suggestion, which could wreck the development plan. They had recently made several appointments that would benefit the school in the long term, and didn't want to lose those staff.

Nandish Samani suggested seeking volunteers, as happened in his firm. This often meant that the management didn't have to nominate people for redundancy. There would probably be some staff who were near the end of their teaching careers, or who wanted to leave teaching. Another governor thought this an excellent suggestion as a starting-point, but that priorities would need to be established, as it could attract more volunteers than needed. There was concern that this method would mean losing staff from the subject areas where they couldn't afford it. Mark Tulley, the area officer, agreed this was a drawback of a voluntary system, but suggested they could save money by replacing an experienced, expensive teacher with a younger teacher not at the top of his or her scale, or with a newly qualified teacher.

He went through the factors they would have to consider. The criteria had to take account of the school's needs and priorities, and the specific skills, experience and potential of staff in managing and developing the curriculum and managing the school as a whole. They also had to take account of those on fixed-term and part-time contracts. He made it clear that cutting down a part-timer's hours could help, but that ending a fixed-term contract counted as dismissal and, if the reason for dismissal was really redundancy, then the governing body would have to follow proper procedures in accordance with employment legislation.

The discussion on the skills and expertise of the staff made the working party realize that staff had potential value as well as current value, and that suggesting teachers with qualifications in shortage subjects or who had been appointed specifically to play a major role in the school's future

SPECIFIC SKILLS AND EXPERIENCE							STAFF INITIALS						
MANAGING THE SCHOOL	a	b	a	b	a	b	a	b	a	b	a	b	a
Team leader													
Special needs coordinator													
Staff development/INSET													
Probationary support													
Middle school liaison													
Early years													
Management of SATs													
MANAGING AND DEVELOPING THE CURRICULUM													
Mathematics													
English													
Science													
Technology													
Humanities													
Art and Display													
Music													
PE													
RE													
ESL													
Assessment													

a = current   b = potential because of skills and experience

Figure 10.2 *Criteria matrix – reduction in staffing*

development for redundancy would be counter-productive. Qualifications and experience in National Curriculum core and foundation subjects, RE and special needs, or qualifications to teach a wide range of ages or to switch between subjects, all had a quantitative value. They therefore tried to establish criteria using the school's development plan, staffing and curriculum sections, as a starting-point. The area officer suggested that the group draw up a matrix to display how individual members of staff met the criteria (see Figure 10.2).

Using the matrix made it much clearer which posts and therefore which members of staff could be considered as surplus to requirements. The next step was to get the governors to agree to adopt the criteria matrix, and then to consult the unions and establish what their view was.

The staff meeting

At the staff meeting, the headteacher announced that she would see personally all members of staff who met the criteria in order to discuss the position and establish whether anyone wished to volunteer for redundancy. If there was more than one volunteer, the LEA would select the volunteer with the longest continuous service record.

Volunteers are interviewed

The staff to be interviewed were given the choice of having their union representative present at the meeting. Where the teacher chose this option, Brenda Gatlin asked Mark Tulley to be present too, so that both sides had an adviser. Most staff preferred a less formal session and the chance to talk privately to the headteacher. One teacher requesting an interview was Clive Draper, head of geography. He said he would like an opportunity for early retirement, preferably with a couple of years' enhancement. He was uncomfortable and pressurized with the endless stream of innovations, most of which he didn't approve of.

This request created a problem for Brenda, as geography was a National Curriculum foundation subject and had not been identified by the working group as surplus to requirements. Yet both the headteacher and the area officer could see advantages for the school in taking up his offer, particularly as within the humanities faculty there was a very promising candidate for the head of geography post and Clive could be replaced with a newly qualified teacher, which would save the school money. Brenda didn't want to reject Clive's offer out of hand. It gave them some flexibility, but meant that they required more than one person to go. She hoped Miss Cline, the head of classics, would want to go, as they didn't need a full-time classics teacher any more, let alone a head of department.

Ultimately three staff left as a result of the cuts: Clive Draper and Celia Cline were offered and took slightly enhanced early retirement, and Miss Rossiter, a part-time teacher in home economics, accepted redundancy. This enabled the headteacher to make an internal promotion to the vacant head of geography post, appoint a newly qualified teacher to the geography department and a part-timer to teach the few periods of classics, which was all the school required in this subject area.

Discussing the affair with Miles Standish before the final governors' meeting of the year, Brenda Gatlin said that she reckoned they had come out of it reasonably well. There had been remarkably little acrimony when it came to the point and, as a result of the cuts, the school's budget was in the black again. In the circumstances it was as much as could be hoped for, though they were all too aware that there was nothing left to trim anywhere the following year.

For action

❏ What are the main issues raised by this case study?
❏ Compare what happened here to the flow chart (Figure 10.3).
❏ What strategies were adopted in dealing with the problem? How effective are they likely to be in practice?
❏ How would you have dealt with the problem?
❏ Write your own checklist for handling staff cuts.

What can you learn from this case study?

You manage a budget but do not determine how much you will receive. You plan your budget as best you can, but definite information about your budget share often arrives well after the planning has been done and sometimes cuts are made at a very late stage. This case study explored the kind of problems you might have to face as a manager when things go wrong, and how you react to a financial crisis. Can you keep calm and cope in a crisis, can you think on your feet, can you get the best out of your partners (the governors) in this situation and can you manage the stress of making a long-serving colleague redundant?

Handling staff cuts is a delicate exercise. It indicates the kind of skills you need to manage today's schools – negotiation, communication and ability to manage public relations as well as the budgetary concerns around which the scenario revolves. It also involves managing decline. Unlike innovation, the most you can hope to achieve is to make the best of a bad job.

This kind of crisis puts the partnership with governors to a real test. This case study showed the partnership with governors operating effectively. It is when things go wrong that the partnership falls apart and individuals act unilaterally.

The case study also indicated how important it is to be aware of employment legislation such as Section 188 of the Trade Union and Labour Relations Consolidation Act 1992, which requires recognized TUs to be consulted at the earliest opportunity. Similarly, make sure your procedures are in line with the Education Reform Act of 1988 and any subsequent modification, or the governors may find themselves at the losing end of an industrial tribunal in which a protective award gives the trade unions a 28-day delay. European legislation also affects you and this urges you to undertake consultations, which should cover ways and means of avoiding collective redundancies or reducing the number of workers

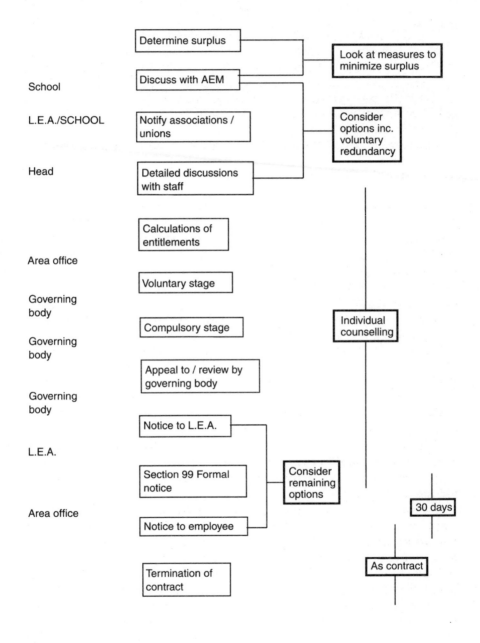

Figure 10.3 *A flow chart for managing staff cuts*

affected. Not only do you have to ensure that there is consultation, but you must make it meaningful. Remember, however, that consultation is not quite the same as negotiation.

Some hints for handling staff cuts

❑ Examine all available options first and be seen to do so.
❑ Work through the governing body – an issue of this sensitivity should not be managed just by the headteacher or by the chair of governors.
❑ You need to know the law – consult your LEA officer, or buy in consultancy. If necessary nominate one of the governors to acquire the necessary expertise on behalf of the group.
❑ Consult as soon as possible or beware of legal pitfalls.
❑ Make sure that the consultation is meaningful – if the unions suggest a different solution, be flexible enough to consider it.
❑ Establish clear criteria and be seen to apply them.
❑ Agree a timetable so that you are able to meet the deadlines for declaring people redundant.
❑ Be as open as possible – especially in informing staff about new developments. This is a very threatening situation for them and suspicions will be rife. It is a test of your public relations skills at all stages.

Making good use of your governors

Individual members of the governing body are given responsibilities. These vary according to need. After external funding had greatly increased Bestwick Park High School's supply of up-to-date technology, which created some issues about how ICT should be managed, the school decided to appoint an ICT governor. Case Study 10.7 is an extract from his role and duties.

CASE STUDY 10.7 FOR REFLECTION

Bestwick Park High School – the role and duties of the ICT governor

The ICT governor should:

- ❏ be a specialist in this area;
- ❏ take the lead role in the compilation and update of an IT strategy for the school in order to ensure that the school gets value for money from its financial dealings for ICT;
- ❏ evaluate what ICT hardware and software the school already has and what it does with it;
- ❏ find out how ICT currently fits into the teaching of the main curriculum subjects;
- ❏ check the most recent government information about requirements for ICT;
- ❏ look at and understand the differences between using ICT to administer and manage the school and the curriculum, and its use to support learning in the classroom;
- ❏ with the head and staff, develop a vision of where the school will be in one and three years' time;
- ❏ check what funding is in place to maintain the system and keep it up to date, and develop proposals for keeping the system up to date;
- ❏ liaise with the finance committee about the budgetary implications of your proposals;
- ❏ report back to the governing body at regular intervals so that this becomes a running record of your proposals and their progress.

11

MANAGING MEETINGS

We cannot run schools without meetings. They have several purposes:

❑ They enable us to share knowledge and information with colleagues.
❑ They enable us to identify problems, opinions or attitudes towards issues.
❑ They enable us to discuss issues and reach corporate decisions.

Organizationally they fulfil a useful function because:

❑ they help create cohesion by bringing staff together as a group;
❑ they allow people to air their feelings and views;
❑ they involve people in discussion and decision making.

As a senior manager you spend a lot of time managing meetings – either directly or indirectly – so it is important that you manage them effectively and that they achieve their objectives. Most schools work to a meetings cycle. Case Study 11.1 shows the calendar of staff meetings for one school over half a term.

CASE STUDY 11.1 FOR REFLECTION

Bestwick Park High School – spring term calendar of meetings

Wednesday 9 January	Staff meeting
Wednesday 16 January	Heads of faculty meeting
Wednesday 23 January	Heads of department meeting
Wednesday 30 January	Heads of year meeting
Wednesday 6 February	Year meetings
Wednesday 13 February	Staff meeting

As the headteacher you are responsible for managing three kinds of meeting:

1. those you chair – eg staff meetings or heads of faculty meetings;
2. those at which you represent the school, eg consortium meetings or area heads' meetings;
3. those you don't attend at all – ie meetings run by the school's middle managers.

MEETINGS THAT YOU CHAIR

Staff meetings

Handling the staff meeting successfully is a real test of a head or deputy's management skills. Whole staff meetings may take a number of forms:

❏ The traditional staff meeting held once or twice a term – it lasts an hour or an hour and a half and deals with general or miscellaneous issues.
❏ Information-giving sessions or 'briefings' – these are short, 10- to 15-minute sessions held daily or weekly, usually before school.
❏ Staff meetings held as Inset – often used to raise awareness on a particular current issue. The head acts as trainer or brings in an 'expert'.
❏ Staff meetings focused on a particular urgent issue – to sound out opinion or reach a decision. Often this kind of meeting has to be added on to the ordinary cycle.

Of these meetings, the traditional general staff meeting seems to present the most difficulty. Until recently there was very little research into how school meetings are run or how staff react to them. However, for their book, *The Reality of School Management*, Derek Torrington and Jane Weightman (1989b) and their research team carried out observations of a number of different kinds of school meetings and concluded that the whole staff meetings were 'the most difficult to manage and the least successful' of all the meetings that they observed.

> Staff members generally found general staff meetings unsatisfactory. This was largely due to the number of people present and consequent unwieldiness as a means of discussion or questioning for clarification. Many heads (who nearly always chair such meetings) obviously found the occasions difficult to handle and some regarded the process of such meetings as destructive of their authority. When observing general staff

meetings, we often found that there was poor preparation and preliminary information, so that the staff attended without any readiness for the
matters to be addressed and without any apparent will to make the
meeting succeed. The head then had to win them round and seldom
succeeded in overcoming the initial disadvantages.

Torrington and Weightman, 1989a (MOSS findings)

Why are staff meetings so difficult to manage?

The size of the meeting and the large number of people attending is an
important factor. The inevitable diversity of interests and variety of points
of view create a difficult management exercise.

The purpose of the meeting is not always clear to those who attend. Is it
meant to be an information-receiving session or a genuine discussion?

How regularly or infrequently the meetings are held can contribute to
the problem. If the interval between meetings has been too long, you end
up with a cluttered agenda of urgent items and no time to discuss them
properly. This can be frustrating for staff, who feel that they are not being
given a chance to say what they think. If the meetings occur too frequently,
staff will resent having to attend yet another meeting.

The MOSS findings indicated that staff meetings are not always well
prepared, all too often lacking an agenda or briefing papers.

The room used for the staff meeting or the way that it is arranged can
contribute to the problem of controlling the meeting. A staff meeting held
in a classroom with staff seated at desks creates a 'them and us' situation.
Staff may feel that they are being treated like pupils and resent it. Holding
the meeting in the staffroom reduces the formality, but can make the meeting difficult to control.

Some common problems with meetings can also affect staff meetings.
For example, there may be much discussion, but no decisions – issues are
aired, but not resolved; or there may be a lack of genuine consultation, in
which case the staff will feel that the decision preceded the consultation.

CASE STUDY 11.2 FOR ACTION

When the old head left, I expected things to become more democratic, not less, but when I looked at the meetings calendar for
the term, I realized that instead of having a full staff meeting in

each half-term, there was only one listed for the term. I know that the last staff meeting was quite fractious and gave the head a hard time, but surely he knows that we need to vent our feelings sometimes. I had heard quite a lot of muttering about the way things are going under the new regime, but now people are really suspicious.

For action

❑ When this new head found difficulty in dealing with a difficult staff meeting, his answer was to reduce the number of full staff meetings on the termly calendar. Comment on this strategy and what it indicates about this head's management style.

❑ What could be the justification for reducing the number of full staff meetings?

❑ What advice would you give this new headteacher?

❑ How can you improve your management of staff meetings?

The answer is not to abolish whole staff meetings but to improve how you manage them. Chairing a meeting of 50 or more people isn't at all easy. What you need to do is provide yourself with a supportive framework. Taking the advice offered below about presentation and venue could also help to make the meeting easier to control:

❑ Dealing with a diversity of views could be made easier if you prepare carefully. Sound out opinions in advance if a sensitive issue is to be discussed, and come to the meeting armed with answers to some of the questions that are likely to be raised. No one really expects you to have answers to everything, but if you have the relevant documents with you and have clearly done your homework, you will get a better reception than if you haven't.

❑ Build on the diversity – showing people that you value their contribution and are prepared to take on board a good suggestion can actually turn a difficult meeting.

❑ Headteachers tend to be the focal point of the whole meeting. It makes sound sense to share out the work so that the deputies introduce some of the items. It then becomes more of a team effort and provides good experience for the deputies.

❑ Don't forget that chairing skills can also be improved with training. A checklist for chairing meetings can be found later in this chapter.

❑　Always clarify the purpose, eg 'This meeting is to provide the staff with information about the latest developments in. . .' indicates that it is an information-giving session.

❑　Plan your meeting cycle so that the gap between meetings is neither too long nor too short. Once in each half-term is a common format, but is probably insufficient. Two per half-termly cycle should work, but if business mounts up, either issue an information bulletin or call an additional meeting. Whatever you do, don't go on adding items to an already overcrowded agenda or let the meeting run over time.

❑　Good preparation is an essential component of a successful staff meeting. The agenda should be published in advance so that the staff are not taken by surprise. Springing a change unannounced upon a large audience tends to provoke hostility. Briefing papers, if the issue is at all sensitive or complex, and appropriate staff asked in advance to lead the discussion can take the heat out of a difficult situation or help to focus the meeting.

❑　If part of the problem arises from the venue, change it. Try out different venues until you find the one that suits your style.

❑　An important part of your role as chairperson is to summarize the debate and clarify what the next step is to be. Decisions should be recorded in the minutes and be readily available to staff. Indecisive discussions are time-wasting and irritating, and will result in a hostile climate at the next meeting. Consultation must be real or it will be counterproductive.

❑　Make it a practice to evaluate the meeting. This means using a checklist of questions such as:
　–　What were my objectives for the meeting?
　–　Were all these objectives achieved? If not, what went wrong?
　–　At what point did things go wrong?
　–　What could I have done to prevent these difficulties?
　–　What have I learnt from this meeting that will influence how I organize staff meetings in the future?

CASE STUDY 11.3 FOR ACTION

The staff meeting was held in the staffroom, the staff sitting in easy chairs round small coffee tables. It commenced at 3.40, but a lot of staff had still not arrived. They trickled in over about 20 minutes, providing a constant interruption to the meeting, as they wandered over to the kitchenette to make themselves tea, and then took it back to their seats. The head chaired the meeting. There was no published agenda so no one knew how many items there would be, but minutes were taken by one of the business studies teachers. The head appeared ill at ease, tense and uncomfortable with the meeting. Even minor items seemed to attract a lot of comment from staff, who interrupted him and one another vociferously. It was noticeable that most of the comment was negative and that one of the senior teachers was a leading contributor. It took a long time to complete each item and the meeting dragged. Some staff ostentatiously looked at their watches. A major change affecting staff was introduced about half-way through the meeting. It seemed to take the staff by surprise, and there was a very hostile reaction. One of the deputies reacted to this by trying to deflect the criticisms, but his strong defence of the proposed change caused a number of staff to mutter to one another about railroading the change. From 5.00 staff steadily began to leave and at 5.10 the head declared the meeting closed. No decision had been made about the change under discussion, and it was not at all clear what the next step would be.

For action

This staff meeting illustrates most of the points made in the extract from Torrington and Weightman's research, and it was clearly unsuccessful:

❑ What were the mistakes made by the head and his senior management team in handling this meeting? What went wrong?
❑ What harm could result from it?
❑ How could it have been avoided?
❑ What could be done to retrieve the situation?
❑ What advice would you give this headteacher and why?

A checklist for effective chairing

Come prepared

Brief yourself thoroughly on all the agenda items. Know your arguments and be prepared for unexpected questions. Have the procedures at your fingertips and the relevant papers or information available.

Organize the agenda so that it will help you

Put the most important item at number two or three. Publish the agenda and circulate any supporting papers well in advance of the meeting. Sound out opinion so that you can anticipate the climate of the meeting. Brief the team so that they support you and know what their roles are to be.

Create a positive atmosphere from the start

Start the meeting off on the right foot by creating a relaxed, yet businesslike atmosphere. Be welcoming, talk to some staff, provide tea and give people the time to have tea and biscuits, but be punctual – arrive on time yourself, and make sure that the meeting starts on time.

Be businesslike

❑ Keep to the agenda. Never rehash the last meeting or repeat information that staff already have.
❑ Keep your eye firmly on the time and move the meeting on where necessary.
❑ Make sure that decisions are reached and that everyone is sure what the next step is.
❑ Have the decisions or minutes recorded and published, ie displayed in the staffroom so that staff can check what was decided and absent staff can find out what happened.

Being businesslike will help you establish control.

Aim for goodwill – use your interpersonal skills

❑ Use body language positively – smile, make eye contact, etc.
❑ Encourage participation, but do not allow monologues or arguments.
❑ Listen carefully to each contribution and show appreciation of useful suggestions.
❑ Do not be dismissive of individual views; it creates resentment and loses you good will.

Think on your feet

❑ Be flexible – a key skill is to be able to think on your feet.
❑ Keep an open mind – be prepared to adopt a good idea.
❑ React immediately – it is important to grasp when to be firm, when a joke would help the atmosphere, when to be kind, etc.
❑ Be sensitive to the mood of the meeting so that it does not become them versus us. Work towards consensus if possible.

❏ Keep cool, calm and collected at all times, so that you stay on top of the situation.

Senior management meetings

The senior management meeting is an example of the small group meeting where people of a similar level of responsibility come together to resolve issues and co-ordinate action. It is a meeting that is usually chaired by the head and, at first glance, this seems a much easier task than managing the much larger and more diffuse whole staff meeting, yet senior management meetings are often poorly managed or underutilized. It might even be fair to claim that they do not achieve their purpose because, in many schools, the head or the SMT has not worked out what the purpose is.

CASE STUDY 11.4 FOR REFLECTION

These are two views of a senior management meeting:

I dread senior management meetings. They never seem to be about anything and they ramble on for ever. The guillotine does not apply to senior management meetings. The senior teachers attend voluntarily, and every week I watch them surreptitiously look at the clock as the meeting drags on.

Deputy head

I think the meetings fulfil a very important function. They help to bind the team together, so I have a meeting even if there is no definite business to conduct. Sometimes I use it just to give them tea and biscuits and have a chat. That way they can't pretend that they do not know what is going on in the school.

Headteacher

The quotations above illustrate two very different perceptions of the same senior management meeting. The head sees it as a team-building exercise in which she raises senior staff awareness of current issues. The deputy sees the meetings as lacking both purpose and content. Something has clearly gone wrong. The head is not only failing to achieve her aim, she seems to be having an adverse effect on senior staff good will.

How could she improve the management of her senior management meetings so that she gets more out of them?

This headteacher appears to hold a lengthy after-school meeting every week. The frequency of senior management meetings varies from school to school. Some schools hold them daily, some twice-weekly, but most senior management meetings seem to occur weekly, while a very small number of schools only meet monthly but include 'all senior staff' (NFER survey, 1987). Perhaps this headteacher should give some thought to whether she could achieve her aim by varying the length or the frequency of the meetings. It is a sensible axiom not to hold a meeting when there is nothing to discuss, otherwise it deteriorates into 'tea and tattle'. A short briefing session for the senior staff once or twice a week, either before school or at lunchtime, could fulfil the purpose of bringing the team together and keeping them informed, and then the senior management meeting could be devoted to more strategic issues. There is also a lot of good will to be earned by occasionally saying to your hard-pressed team, 'There is no major business this week, so I shall not be holding a meeting.'

Clearly, if her deputy thinks there is no real content to the meetings, this head should review what she puts on the agenda.

The head's own comments indicate that she may have been guilty of 'agenda filling'. If hitherto there has been no formal agenda, it might be helpful in these circumstances to introduce one. This would elevate the meeting above the level of 'tea and tattle'. She should also give some thought to who decides the items for the agenda. Are they miscellaneous? Has she thought about how much time she should allocate to each item? Do the team members get the opportunity to suggest items for the agenda and if they do, how frequently in practice do they submit items and what effect does this have on the level of trivia on the agenda?

If a meeting is to be devoted to the exchange of information, this should be made clear at the outset, but most of the time the meetings should be used to discuss issues or to decide strategy. Sometimes it is helpful to create a single-item agenda, when there is a major issue to discuss. Other sessions could have two or three issues at the most, so that they can be explored adequately.

A major criticism of senior management meetings is that often they are no more than briefing sessions, in which the head gives the senior team information. 'Sometimes she just talks to us for the whole time. She thinks that she is consulting us, but really she is just telling us' (deputy's comment). This probably means that the consultation is not real. The head might be using the meeting as a sounding board, but not as a policy-making body, and she will take all the necessary decisions herself later on. This can be a very frustrating experience for the senior management team. If the head really saw the function of the senior team meeting merely as an awareness-raising session, she obviously had very low expectations of her senior staff as managers, and it is not surprising if they 'pretend that they do not know what is going on in the school'. A good senior management team meeting draws on the collective experience and judgement of its members in order to take collective decisions about how the school is to be run.

If the head really wants to build a good senior management team, she will need to involve the members in running the meeting. Not only do heads frequently fail to consult the team about items for the agenda, they also tend to monopolize the meeting. The comment above about 'talking to us the whole time' sums it up. Team members are not given the opportunity to take responsibility for particular items.

Another problem can be failure to reach any decisions. 'We talk endlessly, but nothing is ever decided.' This difficulty arises from ineffective chairing. The problem may have arisen because the head has allowed the meeting to get bogged down in detail, and failed to move it forward when necessary, or she may be bad at seeing an appropriate moment to put an issue to the vote. The role of the chairperson is to control and structure the meeting. It demands skill, but this can be learnt. Inset on chairing skills for running meetings is widely available to help with this problem. A short-term solution could be to minute the meeting, as this will have the effect of making the team members more conscious of the need for decisions — especially if you use action minutes, where only the decisions are recorded together with the name of the person who will be taking responsibility.

Because this particular meeting had lacked shape, formalizing its structure, eg with an agenda and minutes, is likely to strengthen it. Other meetings suffer from the opposite problem, that the use of formal procedures is making the session too rigid, with the result that the issues are not really addressed. In this situation the head would have to think about developing strategies to make the meeting more flexible.

Evaluating the senior management meeting might help the head to find out if changes are needed. Different aspects of the meeting could be monitored over a period of time. Monitoring four meetings would provide plenty of data as to what issues are discussed and how much time is spent on each item. This will indicate how much of the time is spent on trivia. Similarly monitoring will show who contributes most, ie the length and order of contributions, and will show whether the head is totally dominating the sessions. Monitoring the way in which the decisions are taken could also be revealing.

Communicating the decisions taken at senior management meetings is also a sensitive issue. There is often intense curiosity about what happens in these meetings. Should the minutes of this meeting be available to the staff? How should the meeting be reported back to staff? The answer to this question is to do whatever is most appropriate for your particular school while bearing in mind that to be implemented, important decisions have to be communicated. Usually items from the senior management meeting are included in the briefing sessions held regularly to update the staff with what is going on in the school.

Some ways to use a senior management meeting are:

❏ It can take an overview – helicoptering.
❏ It can act as a planning and policy group.
❏ It can co-ordinate and provide direction, eg about how to implement policies.

CASE STUDY 11.5 FOR ACTION

In theory using action minutes should concentrate the mind, but we occupy a large part of every senior management meeting going through the follow-up. When it came to my turn to write the action minutes I kept them very brief, but it didn't solve the problem, because the head went round the table getting each member of the team to say what he or she did last week. I wanted to scream!

An exasperated deputy comments on the SMT meeting

For action

What does this case study indicate about the head's use of the SMT meeting? What advice would you give this new head and why?

REPRESENTING THE SCHOOL

As a senior manager you have to represent the school at a variety of meetings and functions. Many of the meetings are held to address specific issues, but you also have to attend quite a lot of regular meetings, eg area heads meetings or consortium meetings. They fill up your diary and take you out of school all too frequently, but they do serve a number of useful purposes.

What are your objectives in attending these meetings?

❑   exchange of views with colleagues – area meetings provide a good opportunity to talk to colleagues informally;
❑   finding out what is going on in other schools or the LEA;
❑   putting forward the point of view of your institution;
❑   bidding for 'goodies', ie putting your school's case for available moneys, projects or anything going free;
❑   influencing others – other heads, LEA officers, advisers, etc;
❑   to be seen to be involved – part of the group or consortium;
❑   making an impression – reminding the meeting that you and your school should be noticed.

Meetings have become so frequent and time-consuming that it is essential to get as much out of them as possible, so how do you do this effectively? Sometimes you will be in the chair and can manage the meeting directly, but most of the time you will be one of the participants trying to manage the meeting indirectly.

Achieving your objectives at a meeting – some ideas

Do your homework before the meeting

Read the agenda and the preliminary papers, so that you can use the information to advantage in the meeting. It will certainly make people think that you are on the ball, especially if the papers arrived late. It is amazing how many people don't seem to have made the effort to read the documents and then they ask for data that has already been given.

Listen actively

Beware of:
❑   wool-gathering when the going gets tedious;

❏ thinking about what you want to say rather than listening to the speaker – you may miss something important;
❏ reinterpreting or filtering information, ie only hearing the points that you agree with or interpreting information according to your own priorities.

Be assertive, not aggressive

❏ Don't dominate every session or deliver monologues.
❏ Don't interrupt the chairperson or the speaker.
❏ Persevere politely – make sure that you do get your turn or make your point.
❏ Be clear and concise in what you say.
❏ Be sensitive to other people's feelings.
❏ Be constructive – it is more likely to bring you results than being negative.
❏ Be prepared to think on your feet and seize opportunities.
❏ Remember that if you help the meeting to achieve its objectives, it will probably help you to achieve what you want.

The following checklist is really a list of don'ts. Occasionally you may actually want to block a meeting and may need to use some of these techniques. Be very careful when, where and how often you use these techniques. If you adopt this approach too regularly, it is likely to rebound on you and make you extremely unpopular with your colleagues!

How to destroy meetings

❏ Arrive late, interrupt the progress of the meeting, eg by demanding a recap on proceedings so far, and then leave early.
❏ Always put the negative view – 'That will never work'. Negative body language can also be effective.
❏ Interrupt – regularly break in on other people or talk over them.
❏ Throw in a red herring – raise irrelevant issues that waste time and divert attention.
❏ Run a sub-meeting by talking with your neighbour(s) about some topic of importance to you.
❏ Attack – make personal attacks on other members. This wastes time as well as creating a negative climate. Sarcasm is an important weapon because it is both hurtful and destructive.
❏ Be destructive – about everybody else's ideas.
❏ Block – either by being totally negative or by wasting time, eg by

repeating information already given or by getting things wrong so that they have to be explained again.
❏   Talk a lot while saying little.

MANAGING MEETINGS THAT YOU DON'T ATTEND

As a headteacher you are responsible for some meetings that you don't attend at all, but which are run by the school's middle managers. Managing meetings from a distance requires both skill and sensitivity. The case study that follows illustrates the problem and suggests some approaches.

CASE STUDY 11.6 FOR ACTION

The department meeting

Margaret, the new head of Hillcliffe School, took over her post at the beginning of the summer term. She was surprised to find that she didn't receive agendas or a record of departmental or year meetings as a matter of course. She perceived them as essential information, which gave her an insight into what departments were doing and how they were managed. She issued a memo requesting that, in future, departments and year teams should submit agendas and minutes of their meetings. Most departments complied, although their documents raised all kinds of questions in Margaret's mind about the quality of the drafting and precisely whom they saw as the audience for their communications.

One department, however, continued to submit nothing. A few days before the department meeting in the second half of the summer term, Margaret sent for Henry, the head of department, an apparently enthusiastic and committed teacher in his 30s. She told him that she expected him to obey her instructions about the agenda and minutes. Henry said he would do so, but that he considered the priority to be classroom teaching and not bits of paper.

Margaret waited to see what would happen. She received a one-item agenda, which said: 'This department meeting will be about: modifications to the scheme of work.' After the meeting minutes certainly arrived –

about five lines, explaining briefly that the department would be offering some new courses in the following year and requesting substantial funding. However, a lot more information about the major row that had occurred at the department meeting was trickling through on the informal staff grapevine.

Henry had presented his development plan to the department. He had talked about the child-centred, active learning approach to teaching the subject and deplored the department's current didactic methods and anti-quated courses. He stated that the department had to revamp its scheme of work totally. He announced plans for several new courses to be intro-duced the following September, which would necessitate changes in teach-ing style and a much greater emphasis on the use of computers. In order to prepare for this, he was proposing to hold a series of twilight sessions, which would run weekly stretching over the next two terms. He felt that the responsibility for the development work should be shared, so that no one person took on too great a load, and so he was delegating the respon-sibility for each year group to a different member of the department. They could work in pairs if they chose, but then they would have to develop the curriculum for two year groups between them.

The department was largely middle-aged and somewhat set in its ways; moreover, several of its members had responsibilities outside the depart-ment, eg as year heads. Summer term was well advanced and the remaining two weeks were full with activities. Henry's announcement was completely unexpected and the response extremely negative. Henry, apparently taken aback by the hostile response to his scheme for departmental improve-ment and angered by the lack of appreciation of his plans, made some adverse comments on the willingness of certain members of his depart-ment to carry out their responsibilities, referring to 'dinosaurs' and 'spent volcanoes'. The discussion quickly became personal and acrimonious. Two of the department walked out of the meeting, one of them in tears. Eventually Henry wound up the meeting by telling his team to 'sleep on it' and that they would feel much better about the scheme in the morning.

In the morning, however, a deputation from the department went to see the headteacher. Henry's meeting had clearly failed.

For action

What was Margaret's responsibility and what action should she take?

Why had the meeting failed?

It had failed for two reasons: 1) the nature of the changes Henry wished to make – the members of the department found the proposal extremely threatening; and 2) the manner in which Henry introduced the changes to the department – suddenly and without prior warning, top down, combined with severe public criticism of everyone else's current practice.

What was the effect of this failure?

The result was a crisis in the department, hostility to Henry's proposals and anger about what Henry had done and his manner towards and treatment of his team.

What was Margaret's role in this crisis?

Margaret's responsibility as head was to ensure that the department functioned effectively, so that the pupils could be offered the best teaching possible. A major row in the department could not be allowed to continue because it impeded the smooth running of the department, and interfered with how the curriculum was delivered to the pupils. Moreover, the acrimony was unpleasant for everybody else and would affect general morale.

What alternatives did Margaret have?

1. She could override him – tell him bluntly that since he had consulted neither senior management nor his department, she would not allow him to go ahead with the plan.
2. She could defuse the situation for him, mollify the department and explain to them and convince them of the benefits of the scheme. She would have to suggest that in his enthusiasm Henry had sounded much more critical than he had meant to be, try to persuade them not to take it so personally and encourage them to consider his ideas on their merits.
3. She could bring Henry and his department together in her presence and thrash out the issues until the situation was resolved.

Using the first alternative would totally destroy Henry's credibility with the department and make it very difficult for him to control the department or make changes in the future.

The second alternative would do Henry's job for him. If Margaret adopted this strategy this time, she could find herself in the same position over and over again.

The third alternative was probably the best long-term solution, but for it to work, Margaret would need to talk things through with Henry, otherwise she could find herself presiding over a re-run of the row.

Henry had made a mess of running his department meeting, and his whole approach to managing an important curriculum change illustrated his lack of management expertise. He had committed a great many management sins:

- ❑ He had failed to consult either the head or any of the department.
- ❑ His method of communication was disastrous.
- ❑ He was negative about other people – apparently not valuing anything that they were doing.
- ❑ He failed to motivate or enthuse the department towards change.
- ❑ His administration contributed towards his failure because his record keeping did not inspire confidence.
- ❑ He hadn't secured funding for his project – he seemed unaware of the need to make budgeting arrangements over a period of time.
- ❑ His approach to difficulties was confrontational.
- ❑ He did not seem to understand the importance of good will.

Although Henry was an obvious candidate for a head of department or middle management training course, he was unlikely to benefit from this type of training unless he also changed his whole attitude to management, because the incident illustrated that Henry did not value management skills or think that he needed them. The impression given was that he saw himself as carrying out a mission, which he expected everyone else in the department to value as he did. He was hurt as well as angry that his scheme for improvement was not appreciated and inclined to be resentful about the opposition he encountered. To be able to develop, he needs to understand he has a problem. This is a difficult situation to manage because Henry's enthusiasm and vision for the department are important strengths and you want to help him improve his ability to manage personnel without making him feel he is being blocked by the team or the school.

Margaret was going to need to use her role as a developer as well as her conflict management skills to address the problem of Henry's attitude to management, and his complete lack of interpersonal and communication skills. She would probably have to start by trying to make him appreciate that whatever the potential of his programme of curriculum change, it had little chance of success if his department remained hostile to both it and him, and that his own approach had contributed to their refusal to co-operate. Helping him to understand his own strengths and weaknesses and how to learn from his mistakes could make him a much better manager. It would, however, take more than one session for Henry to stop blaming others for the disaster and to begin to move forward.

It was thus only after some sessions with Henry that a rerun of the meeting could be attempted. Whether Margaret, as head, should be present or not, depended on what progress had been made and how sensitive the situation was, but her presence would probably reassure the department and act as a restraint. A full and calm discussion of the plan would reveal how much of it was actually viable for the coming September, or whether a compromise, which would have the advantage of allowing both sides to seem to have gained something, would be to introduce the changes over a longer period of time.

This case study, although centring on a department meeting, could be used as training material for other purposes, eg for sessions with middle managers on management of change or to help you focus on your role as a developer of staff who hold management positions.

CASE STUDY 11.7 FOR ACTION

Cascading

Following an incident involving a mismanaged department meeting, Margaret, the new headteacher of Hillcliffe School, decided to evaluate the effectiveness of the school's meeting system. She decided to target her senior management briefing sessions held daily before school, and the follow-up sessions held with the year heads twice a week. She explained to the staff what she wanted to do and asked for two volunteers to monitor the meetings for a month. The head of PE and a teacher in the modern languages department expressed interest and attended the meetings over the four-week cycle.

They found that the senior management meetings were effective and lively sessions. They were held in the head's room round a table. The head gave a short résumé of events and activities for the immediate future and highlighted things further ahead that she thought would need attention. She followed this by going round the table so that the deputies and senior teachers could also raise items. Individual contributions were kept short, because the whole meeting took only 15 minutes, but this seemed to focus the discussion and lead to suggestions for action, which were frequently adopted. The deputy in charge of daily administration made a brief note of the decisions and this record was photocopied and distributed to everyone.

The follow-up sessions with the year heads were held in a classroom and chaired by the deputy in charge of daily administration, who sat facing the year heads. The evaluators observed that often people arrived late, and sometimes one or more of the year heads missed the meeting altogether. The deputy used the minutes from the senior staff meeting as a basis for the briefing session, but he did not invite contributions. There was rarely any comment or discussion and no record of the meeting was kept. The year heads seemed mainly concerned to hurry off to deal with other business. When questioned by the evaluators about their perception of the meeting, one of them said it was a waste of time and it would be more useful simply to circulate the minutes of the senior staff meeting to all concerned.

For action/discussion

❏ Why were the senior staff meetings so much more effective than the year head briefing sessions?
❏ Evaluation should be followed by action – what action should this new head take to remedy the problems found?
❏ What advice would you give this new head and why?

12

MANAGING THE ASSOCIATE STAFF

It is easy to forget, when you refer to the staff of a school, that you are talking not only about the teaching staff, but also about those who are not teachers, who make up something like a third of the total staff. School secretaries, technicians and caretakers have served in schools for many years and have established roles and patterns of work. The creation of other posts has been much more recent. The expansion in the area of non-teaching staff seems to have been spurred by a number of different factors. Some of the new posts were specifically designed to service new needs; others have evolved or developed from existing posts as a post holder had a good idea which led to the expansion of his or her role. The main catalyst for growth was perhaps the Education Reform Act of 1988 and the introduction of LMS, because the legislation provided new needs and created the flexibility to attend to them. Although most of the resulting expansion has been within the well-established boundaries determined by LEA rules and procedures, the new powers and available resources meant that an opportunity could be seized and acted upon, sometimes as a result of very careful analysis of needs, at others as the result of opportunistic thinking by a hard-pressed headteacher, and as a result there has been considerable innovation in the kind of posts created.

The support staff in a large secondary school include site managers, caretakers, clerical and office staff, librarians and library assistants, financial officers, welfare assistants, technicians, classroom or curriculum support staff, dinner supervisors and contract staff, eg grounds maintenance workers, food franchise workers and builders. Most schools also have a lot of volunteer helpers, who are not members of staff but who come in on a regular basis. All these people need managing and developing, and as the headteacher you are responsible for their performance and job satisfaction.

CASE STUDIES

This chapter explores, through a number of sequential case studies, the problems and issues that may arise in managing the non-teaching staff. If you want to use them for group sessions on different aspects of managing the associate staff, you may find it useful to have read them all first, as some of the initial ones raise and discuss ideas or issues that are assumed in later problems. Nevertheless, most of the scenarios can be used individually if required.

CASE STUDY 12.1 FOR ACTION/REFLECTION

'Why was Mrs Adams at the staff meeting again this week?' Ian Clarke asked a colleague at the end of the weekly staff meeting. 'I particularly noticed her last week and meant to ask "Why?". What is a member of the ancillary staff doing attending our meeting? I don't remember being consulted about whether she should be allowed to come. What do you think the head is up to? Is she quietly infiltrating Mrs Adams, hoping that we won't notice? Will this prove to be the thin end of the wedge? It's meant to be a staff meeting isn't it? Does she get to vote when we do? It worries me because confidential issues about pupils may arise and we won't be able to talk freely.'

The person whose presence at the weekly staff meeting this teacher so clearly resented is the school's bursar, Sarah Adams.

For action

❑ Why does this teacher resent the bursar's presence at the staff meeting?
❑ What issues are raised by the case study?
❑ This school is in the process of seeking Investors in People certification. What stage do you think it is at?
❑ How well has the headteacher handled or managed the situation?
❑ What advice would you give the headteacher and why?

For reflection

In this case study, Brenda Gatlin, the headteacher of Bestwick Park High School, has asked the bursar, Sarah Adams, to attend the weekly staff meetings. This decision by the new head to include a member of the non-teaching staff in a meeting hitherto attended only by teachers raises a number of issues, as detailed in the following sections.

What was her motive?

The role of bursar varies from school to school. Bursars may be administrators, carrying out fairly clerical tasks with little or no power to influence decisions, or they may be highly paid and influential members of the senior management team (SMT), responsible for making the school's finances work, or they may operate at a level somewhere between these two extremes. However much real power they have, bursars have become pivotal figures and central to the daily running of the school. Getting Sarah Adams to attend the weekly staff meeting could fulfil two purposes. Firstly, Mrs Gatlin may see it as good for the bursar to learn more about what goes on in the staffroom, and consider the sessions to be developmental for Mrs Adams, whose knowledge of education is limited. It could help her to understand better what the school is about and how the staff feel about things, and could help to integrate her into the staff. Secondly the presence of the bursar could lead to the teachers having to rethink who attends staff meetings and could serve as a first step towards creating one staff rather than two separate entities – teaching and non-teaching staff – and thus move the school's Investors in People initiative forward.

How well was the situation managed?

Was it a good idea simply to introduce a member of the support staff, even if that person is the most senior, into the teachers' meeting without prior consultation, or even informing the staff? Ian Clarke was clearly angry about the bursar's presence, but there is no indication whether his reaction was typical of other staff, or whether his suspicions about the head are based on her previous track record or have arisen because he feels threatened by this change. There are signs, however, that the bursar's presence could easily develop into a confrontation between the head and some of the staff, in which case the head may have misjudged her tactics. It might have been wiser to have at least explained why she had asked the bursar to attend, even if she wasn't prepared to seek the staff's consent. The element of surprise contributed to the distrust Ian Clarke felt. Did the head adopt this approach because:

❏ she genuinely regarded the matter as uncontroversial?
❏ she was totally insensitive to how the teachers might feel?
❏ she feared resistance and wanted to pre-empt it?

The incident raises questions about her dominant management style and her relationship with the staff, and it may be useful to think about what approach you might take in these circumstances. If you want to make a change to the personnel included in staff meetings, would you:

❏ act without giving the staff prior warning?
❏ inform and then act?
❏ consult, but use your own judgement?
❏ consult and only act if the teachers agree?

Should support staff be present during confidential discussions of pupils?

This is the most problematic of the issues raised in this case study. Staff meetings are often used to bring to the attention of teachers issues involving individual pupils. Often there has been a deterioration in the pupil's work, perhaps because of family problems, and the teachers need to know that there is a problem, to discuss how to monitor it and what approach they should take. Most teachers would not want support staff present during these discussions, as they would regard it as important to share this kind of information only with those who needed to know. Yet some support staff should be included among those who need to know, because they interact with the pupils concerned and need advice about how to react or deal with potentially difficult pupils. Providing relevant information could prevent an unnecessary clash between a technician or a dinner supervisor and a pupil with problems. The teaching staff might argue that sufficient information could be conveyed by the support staff's line managers without their having to be present at the meeting. Perhaps the solution to this is to classify the meetings (though this obviously reduces flexibility), but issues about pupils could be raised at particular meetings or at the end of meetings. When confidential matters are dealt with, those for whom the particular information is not essential could leave.

Should the staff meeting be purely a teachers' meeting?

Bestwick Park High School needs to clarify whether or not the staff meeting is purely a teachers' meeting. If it is a teachers' meeting, then support staff may not attend, but if, in its move to become an Investors in People school, Bestwick Park wants to create one staff rather than two separate entities, then all staff should attend the staff meeting, even though to make this possible some logistical issues might need to be resolved. It is a sensitive issue, and one that should be faced and discussed openly in order to reach a decision that reflects the views and culture of the particular school. If the headteacher of Bestwick Park wants to change the prevailing culture in order to create a partnership between the two sets of staff, then she should reflect on how it would be best to approach this, as, judging from the case study above, the staff might not be open to change without some awareness raising of the issues involved and the benefits that might accrue.

One of the main problems in managing two sets of staff is the almost total lack of respect each group seems to have for the other group's professional expertise. The case study that follows explores what can happen when a well-qualified and efficient bursar's administration of financial matters brings her into regular contact with the teaching staff.

CASE STUDY 12.2 FOR ACTION

The bursar, Sarah Adams, voices some complaints about the teaching staff over coffee to one of the office staff.

I might have guessed that one of them would hand in photograph money today. I told them quite clearly that I wanted it all in by the end of last week so that I could have everything clear for the end of term. I totalled up all the money that been given in and the photographer came into school and collected it on Friday afternoon, but they didn't listen to me and now all this money comes in today. Where has he been keeping it all this time, I wonder? It's a lot of money and it could easily have been stolen. Now I shall have to ask the photographer to come back and collect the additional money. It's duplicating work that I have already done and I don't know whether the photographer can manage to come before the end of term. He'll think we're utterly incompetent.

The teacher complains about the bursar.

She simply didn't or wouldn't understand that the children only brought in the money this week, although I had been asking for it every day for ages. You know what my form is like, and anyway she said at the staff meeting that she wanted it all in together and not in dribs and drabs, but when I handed it in she shouted at me and virtually accused me of being late on purpose and storing away huge amounts of money in a cupboard or something! She was quite unnecessarily nasty about it. It was quite galling; she gave me a lecture about not keeping to the deadline, talking to me the whole time as if I were a particularly stupid child. Who does she think she is anyway?

The bursar comments on another teacher.

I tried to get Mr Draper to understand that he couldn't place an order for that set of books because his department has already overspent on its allocation. He seemed to think that the head could simply find him some more money. Where does he think she will get it from? There's no pot of gold out there. Some of those teachers don't seem to live in the real world and have no understanding whatsoever of what it means to work within a budget. Absent-minded professors are all very well, but I have to balance the books.

Sarah Adams is an efficient and conscientious member of staff. With her in charge of the bursar's office, you do not have to worry that orders will be placed incorrectly or anyone will be allowed to spend over the limit. The reconciliation of the monthly statements is meticulous, goods are carefully checked in and reach the right department, bills and parcels really meant for the primary school across the road are noticed and dispatched to the correct address, staff are bullied into seeing that their account books are in order and petty cash is always in credit. She makes sense of the detailed financial information, keeps up with the constant changes of code used by the LMS system and is quick to pick up on mistakes made by the teachers or the LEA.

Unfortunately Sarah's relationship with the teaching staff is nothing like as good as her administration of finances. She expects the teachers to understand budgeting and why it is so important to get their orders right, because this is part of their job and she sees their mistakes as inefficiency. Her experience so far has not led her to rate teachers very highly because a lot of them are much less efficient than she is (especially about money matters), they dislike deadlines and they never read her memos. She often feels exasperated at their behaviour, and she can be quite curt and aggressive when they get things wrong. She always sorts it out for them later, though, because she likes things to be straight, and she is upset when the teachers do not seem to appreciate her efforts after all the extra work they have caused her.

The teachers, who tend to think that administration is far less important than their classroom teaching, feel that such tasks should be kept to a minimum (and preferably done by somebody else). They find her behaviour exasperating, and dislike the way she talks down to them.

For action

- ❑ What are the issues raised by this case study?
- ❑ What staff development should be provided for the bursar?
- ❑ What strategies should the headteacher adopt in order to resolve this problem?

In dealing with financial matters Sarah is a gem; in dealing with staff she is a disaster. The headteacher must address this problem before it worsens.

Analysing the problem

Sarah's problem arises partly from her lack of knowledge and understanding of the education system and partly from her own inflexible personality. She doesn't have the interpersonal skills needed to make the staff want to co-operate with her; she hectors them, which makes them feel both guilty and inefficient, and they respond by belittling her efforts. The problem is compounded by the fact that what is very important to Sarah is low-priority for the teaching staff. It is not surprising that they are not sorry they have caused her extra work or are not grateful for what she has done for them.

Confronting the problem

If the issue is not addressed it will become increasingly difficult for Sarah to do her job effectively, so Mrs Gatlin has to talk to her about the problem, ideally at her annual appraisal. The feedback from staff could legitimately be sought, especially if communication was one of the areas being appraised. Mrs Gatlin would need to ensure that Sarah received plenty of praise for the parts of her job that she did well, before she embarked on the more difficult stage of the appraisal, and then she must ensure that it is not too negative for Sarah to handle. The headteacher will need to use all the sensitivity of which she is capable in order to get Sarah to accept how she is perceived by the staff. Sarah will be hurt and initially defensive, saying that it is all because of careless staff. She will have to be persuaded that this is not the whole truth. If the headteacher fails at this stage, no progress can be made. (The skills needed to handle conflict or difficult staff are discussed in Chapter 8.)

Suggested strategies

Mrs Gatlin will have to reassure Sarah by offering her some support in the ongoing battle with the teachers. She could reinforce the importance of administration at a staff meeting and have a chat to the heads of faculty, to make it clear that she needs their co-operation in improving relations with the bursar's office. If the staff knew that the problem was recognized and being addressed, they could be persuaded that it was in their interests to co-operate.

Mrs Gatlin had already decided that one way of helping Sarah appreciate what the teachers do was to have her attend the weekly staff meeting. We have seen the furore this caused and that she should have consulted the staff first.

It could be useful to arrange for Sarah to have some sessions with heads of faculty so that they could give her a clearer idea of their administrative needs. In turn, it might help them to appreciate her problems and concerns. The teachers themselves could also usefully learn from the bursar about her role and begin to receive more training about how the finances of the school are run. Establishing a dialogue of this kind could benefit both sides of the battle.

It could be very beneficial for Sarah to watch some lessons, because it would give her some idea of the craft of teaching. Sending Sarah on a course dealing with interpersonal skills for administrative staff could also help her overcome her difficulties – at the very least it would show whether she was developable.

The headteacher would have to monitor progress. Ancillary staff appraisal is annual, so she can set fairly short-term targets.

Managing a two-tier system

The case studies so far have dealt with the question of the status of the non-teaching staff. It is not merely that you manage two sets of staff, but that you are managing a two-tier system. Within the organization the non-teaching staff are all too frequently the second-class citizens. The names given to this section of the staff reinforce this impression: non-teaching staff, ancillary staff, support staff. The teachers have the status of starring roles, the non-teaching staff of supporting cast. Two research studies (Mortimore *et al*) highlighted this problem: 'To name such a group of people according to what they did *not* do, rather than what they *did* contribute to the school was not only demeaning but unjust.' In the second survey the non-teaching staff are retitled associate staff.

Pay reinforces the problem: it tends to be very low. Support staff appraisal has always been directly linked to pay, so to earn a rise they have to give satisfaction and this can lead to exploitation. All too frequently, for example, good technicians work unpaid overtime to complete all the work requested by teachers, sometimes way beyond what they are paid for. They are doing more than the job, yet there is no scope for promotion and no extra money to pay them more for all the work they do. The line between giving people their heads and exploiting them is very narrow, and an honest school should at least face the problem and discuss the issue with its technicians.

The academic qualifications of the non-teaching staff will vary. Women technicians, for example, are often graduates and considerably overqualified for the job they are doing. This is for a number of reasons: sometimes they are using the post as a means of re-entry to the labour force, sometimes because of family commitments they have sought a less demanding position or they have opted for a part-time job because it enables them to be home before their children. Where this is the case and the well-qualified technician finds herself treated with little respect or consideration by some of the teachers, there can be problems.

CASE STUDY 12.3 FOR ACTION

Anne, the physics technician, has arrived in the headteacher's office, threatening resignation. Although she sounds belligerent, she has clearly been crying. The head knows she is a competent and responsible technician, and usually a willing worker, capable of using her initiative in a crisis. Anne tells the headteacher that the problem is the head of physics and his treatment of her. He orders her about all the time, never thanks her and complains at every opportunity. When things go wrong, he mentions that she is a graduate and so should be able to cope better. He talks down to her, and makes her seem a fool in front of the pupils. Although she likes to plan well in advance, he gives her so little notice that she can't always manage to do the task in time, and then he blames her and implies that she is not working hard enough. Sometimes his lack of planning causes problems if she is preparing something for the other physics teacher and can't just stop doing that job when he wants an experiment set up. This makes him angry and he shouts at her. She had taken this job, rather than look for something in industry, because she only wanted a part-time post until the children were older. But now almost every day, just before it's time for her to go home, the teacher comes to her with another big job to do. She has been late home every day for the past fortnight, and has had enough.

For action

- ❏ What are the issues involved in this case study?
- ❏ Should the headteacher accept Anne's resignation?
- ❏ What advice would you give this headteacher and why?
- ❏ Can being involved in Investors in People help the headteacher resolve this case?

The head of physics in this case study has been treating the technician with so little consideration that it almost amounts to harassment. He has publicly questioned her competence, he has made unreasonable demands, he has kept her beyond her working hours, he has tried to bypass the booking system, and he is regularly rude, sarcastic and shouts at her.

As a manager he seems to be singularly unsuccessful at creating a good working relationship. We do not know how regularly he loses technicians or how he treats his teaching colleagues, but his overall behaviour suggests that he is selfish, high-handed and inconsiderate. Nor does he seem to value any of the work Anne does. If we take this scenario a little further, and picture what might happen if Anne resigns, this head of department could be left without a technician until a replacement is found and, if his previous behaviour is anything to go by, he is likely to grumble about this and be critical of how long it takes 'them' to find a replacement and the quality of what he gets. If this is a fair picture of what has happened, he cannot be allowed to continue in this way and the problem must be confronted.

If the headteacher wants to keep a trained and responsible technician, Anne will have to be convinced that her work is valued and generally be treated better. Inviting her to attend physics department meetings could make her feel more a member of the team, but her time constraint would make it difficult for her to participate in after-school sessions. The headteacher should involve the head of science, as the head of physics' line manager, to resolve the immediate problem and devise a longer-term strategy to improve their working relations. Management training for the head of physics seems an obvious move but, for it to be successful, he has to understand why he needs it (see also Chapter 8).

Sometimes, however, the very experience and competence of a technician can create problems, as Case Study 12.4 indicates.

CASE STUDY 12.4 FOR ACTION

The head of science has come to seek your advice. The problem centres on the chemistry technician, Mrs Dodds. She is both knowledgeable and experienced, a graduate who is working as a technician to keep her hand in while her family are still too young for her to seek a full-time career. She has been with the department for a number of years. The head of science regards Mrs Dodds as an asset to the department, because she is an extremely efficient member of the team. She values her judgement so highly that she frequently consults the technician about the best way to handle a topic. This year the department has taken on an NQT, a conscientious and hard-working teacher, whom she feels will eventually develop into a valuable member of the department, but who is currently experiencing some teething problems. She is rather shy and hesitant and Mrs Dodds's competence and confidence are making the NQT extremely nervous. This is beginning to affect her relationship with the classes she teaches and, even more unfortunately, it is inspiring Mrs Dodds's contempt, and she is now treating the NQT in a rather high-handed way. There is almost role reversal, with Mrs Dodds giving the NQT orders rather than vice versa, and the NQT is becoming too dependent upon the technician.

For action

- ❑ What are the issues raised in this case study?
- ❑ You are the headteacher. What is your role in the situation?
- ❑ What advice would you give the head of science and why?

CASE STUDY 12.5 FOR ACTION

A deputation of angry technicians has arrived in your office with this week's edition of the local paper. They point to an advertisement the school has placed for an assistant systems manager for information technology. They want to know why an IT technician is to be called a systems manager, while they are called technicians. They ask if they are being downgraded. The biology technician is particularly incensed. She says that if she had realized that more hours were available, she would have offered to work them. The technicians want to know why they weren't offered the post first, and why they have to find out what is going on in the school by reading about it in the newspaper.

For action

- ❑ What are the management issues raised in this case study?
- ❑ You are the headteacher – how should you respond to this deputation?
- ❑ What advice would you give this headteacher and why?

Whereas some of the problems that concern technicians have arisen because they are overqualified for their job, the problems connected with the school office tend to be different in their nature. The case studies that follow illustrate the kind of problem that may occur.

CASE STUDY 12.6 FOR ACTION

They think they know best!

Mike Wade, the deputy head in charge of staff development, is grumbling to his colleague, Yvonne Perkins.

I put some forms into the office to be duplicated as part of our Investors in People initiative. I wanted a form to go to every department or section of the staff. I estimated this required about 40 forms and told the secretary so quite clearly. When I returned to collect the forms, I found that the pile was much smaller than I expected and so I counted it. There were only 19 forms, so I queried it with the secretary, only to be told self-righteously that they had counted up and as there were only 19 subject departments, they had done the right number. I was horrified, as the whole point was to target every section, not just the subject departments. I was so angry that I made an issue of it. 'Is the office on the list of subject departments?' I demanded. 'No', they said. 'Well, then you have not done a copy for your own department. Now please duplicate the additional 21 forms as required and next time please check with me before you change the instructions!' The problem is that because they process a lot of information, they glean a superficial overview of things and they pass judgement on what the teaching staff do, when a lot of the time they have very limited understanding of what is really going on.

For action/discussion

❏ What issues are raised by this case study?
❏ The deputy has raised the matter with the headteacher. What action should she take and why?
❏ What does this case study indicate about the success of Bestwick Park's Investors in People initiative so far?

In Case Study 12.6 the deputy head has identified one of the problems that may arise if the office is not well managed. The previous head, James Smythe, had not concerned himself with the activities of the school office and as a result it had got into bad habits. Case Study 12.7 explores this situation.

CASE STUDY 12.7 FOR ACTION

The office at Bestwick Park High School was a very friendly place. Visitors who came into the school were made welcome, teachers would stop for a chat when passing through to collect things and the pupils queued at the office window for attention. It seemed a hub of activity. What Brenda Gatlin found, however, after she had been in the school for long enough to see things for what they really were, was that productivity in the office was very low This occurred partly because the telephone never stopped ringing and the secretary seemed to do little but answer the telephone, making her output in terms of secretarial work extremely low. The office was very disorganized. Brenda would go through the week's priorities with the secretary on Monday morning, but unless she chivvied constantly, no progress seemed to be made and the priorities did not get through to the other office staff. Important letters were neglected or mislaid, deadlines seemed to be an unknown concept and very little work seemed to get done, yet the secretary and two part-time assistants always seemed to be working. Their work appeared well presented, but you had to check it carefully because the incidence of errors was high, especially in respect of dates or names, and you could not be sure that letters had been sent to their intended destination or indeed that they had been sent at all. On a number of occasions Brenda had found herself faced with a different set of parents from those she had been told to expect, presented with the wrong set of pupil notes or, even more embarrassingly, double-booked. 'Sorry, we forgot' or 'Whoops, we've got it wrong again!' became an increasing irritating feature of life with the office. Indeed her deputy, who was thoroughly fed up with this state of affairs, claimed that if you weren't told that it was the office, you'd think it was the school social club.

For action

❏ What were the main problems and why were they occurring so regularly?

❏   What strategies would you suggest for improving the performance of the office staff?

❏   What advice would you give this headteacher and why?

The school office holds a central position in ensuring the efficient running of the school, but the office at Bestwick Park had become a liability instead of an asset. The headteacher must confront the problem because the office clearly could not continue to perform so ineffectively. She would have to raise the matter initially through a meeting either with her secretary or with the whole office staff. She should record the meeting and subsequent actions in case the matter should become contentious. One way of approaching such a sensitive issue is to explain to the office staff that a new regime and changing demands necessitate a change in work practices and that they need to review as a team how they meet the new demands.

Strategies for improving performance

❏   Make the office staff log all their activities for a week. This could help to bring it home to them how much or little they do or achieve.

❏   Date-stamp letters, etc as they arrive, so that you can monitor how long it takes to process or deal with them.

❏   Limit personal telephone calls to one per person per day.

❏   Buy an answerphone for use when the office is under pressure.

❏   If punctuality is an issue, get the office personnel to clock in and out.

❏   Set weekly or daily targets. This will necessitate prioritizing work, and time for unexpected but urgent tasks must be included. This will also involve allocating work to particular members of the office staff, with a time allocation for each major task.

❏   Look at how the office is arranged. Are the staff working too closely together? Can the secretary, who answers the phone, be relocated so that she causes minimal disturbance.

❏   Have a job appraisal interview with each member of the office staff, which could also be an opportunity for some observation of how they work. Monitoring individual performance will help you analyse where the main problems are and through appraisal you can give each member of staff personal targets. It also allows you to review development needs and arrange training to improve skills or general performance. The fact that non-teaching staff appraisal is linked to pay will give it bite.

❏   Review the management structure of the office. Would the secretary respond to being given responsibility for managing her team, or is she so far into bad habits that this could not work? An alternative strategy could be to make the bursar, who is extremely efficient, responsible for supervising the office.

❑ Unrelenting supervision is clearly the key to this problem and a weekly review of progress is essential. Make a fuss about mistakes whenever they occur. This will convey the message that such a high a level of errors is simply unacceptable. Make it quite clear to the office who is boss and what standard is expected.

❑ Praise improvement when it occurs. This could help build loyalty.

CASE STUDY 12.8 FOR ACTION

As part of her efforts to improve the office, the headteacher brought in management consultants. One of the things they uncovered was that the various clerical staff had different titles and status, for example head's secretary, secretary and clerical assistant. Although their hours and pay varied considerably, their job descriptions indicated that they were performing identical tasks. This made some of the office staff very angry and for the second time in a few weeks the head found herself faced with a deputation of furious support staff.

For action

What are the management issues raised by this case study? What advice would you give this headteacher and why?

The comments made by the management consultants about the various posts held by the clerical staff made the senior management team think more clearly about the nomenclature and workload of other posts held by associate staff and by volunteers.

278

CASE STUDY 12.9 FOR ACTION

The school had always had a part-time librarian. She was not a teacher or even a qualified librarian, but an enthusiast who loved the library, worked well beyond the hours stated in her contract and regularly took work home. Now under the new head 's direction the library was becoming a study and resources area. New technology was being introduced and, to provide the librarian with some much-needed help, the head had appealed in the parents' newsletter for volunteers to help run the library and provide assistance for the pupils throughout the school week. There was a good response, with the result that there was someone working in the school library at all times during the school day. The librarian found, however, that she had a department of staff to manage in an area where she was actually an amateur. Her lack of experience as a manager worried her, and she was also concerned that this group of staff were unpaid volunteers – how can you manage volunteers? There was also the issue that she was called 'the librarian' and paid a salary, her assistants were called 'library helpers' and not paid, yet they all seemed to do much the same work.

For action

❏ What are the issues raised by this case study?
❏ What are the advantages to the school of the change to the system?
❏ What problems does it bring?
❏ What advice would you give the headteacher in dealing with the problems?

The management consultants also reviewed the role of the bursar in the school. The bursar's job description is given below as Case Study 12.10.

CASE STUDY 12.10 FOR ACTION/REFLECTION

Job description – bursar

General responsibilities

❏ to operate and control the financial system of the school – responsible to the headteacher;

❑ to liaise with the treasurer's department, central purchasing and other financial departments;
❑ to ensure that the school complies with financial regulations.

Specific responsibilities

❑ to calculate, check and record money due to or from the school;
❑ to collect and pay out money;
❑ to maintain accounting records and hold them securely;
❑ to ensure that the school is registered under the Data Protection Act;
❑ to operate an ordering system for all goods and services using an official order form, which is securely retained;
❑ to check goods and plan cash flow;
❑ to process invoicing;
❑ to be responsible for the safe;
❑ to keep a record of income;
❑ to reconcile all income with the sums deposited;
❑ to operate the chequebook system;
❑ to obtain monthly bank statements and to reconcile these with accounting records and investigate discrepancies;
❑ to operate the petty cash system;
❑ to ensure that there is a safe and efficient system for the custody and control of the school's voluntary fund.

For action

❑ What does the bursar's job description tell you about the perception of the role in Bestwick Park High School?
❑ In what ways could the school use a graduate bursar more effectively?
❑ Draw up a job specification for the head's secretary to ensure that you get value for money.

CASE STUDY 12.11 FOR ACTION

The bursar had been appointed by the previous headteacher and her role and job description derived from then. The management consultants suggested that Mrs Gatlin should review the bursar's role and use such a highly efficient and proactive worker more effectively. A part-time assistant bursar already existed. The consultants suggested her hours could be extended to take on more of the routine tasks in the bursar's workload, while Sarah Adams undertook more of the financial management that was taking up a lot of the head's time. As part of her new role, Sarah began to attend senior management team meetings. Although the head had explained to the SMT why she had asked Sarah to attend, to her surprise there was a very negative reaction from the senior team. When she asked her deputy why the SMT was so hostile, she was told that there were descriptions in every edition of the *Times Educational Supplement* about how schools found it more cost-effective to employ a bursar than a second deputy head. They knew that Fred was due to retire in the summer and a few would have liked to apply for his job. However, the message the teachers were receiving was that there might not be a job to apply for, as the headteacher was thinking of not replacing Fred and putting Sarah into the SMT instead of having a second deputy.

For action/discussion

❑   What are the management issues raised in this case study?
❑   What mistakes has the headteacher made in handling the matter?
❑   What advice would you give to the headteacher and why?
❑   Managing change is always a test of a headteacher's skill. How would you introduce and manage the kind of exercise suggested above?

Case Study 12.11 raises a fundamental issue for you as a manager. Cost-effective use of support or associate staff could save a school time and money, and Mrs Gatlin may well want to continue to use the consultants or create a task group to review whether some of the tasks currently undertaken by the SMT would be better done by an administrative officer. It could be argued that 'senior managers (on relatively high salaries) should be freed from much of the financial and administrative minutiae so as to be able to devote more of their time to their leadership role' (Mortimore and Mortimore with Thomas, 1994).

Similarly, in a climate of constantly increasing demands upon teachers' time and inadequate budgets, schools may have to take a hard look at which of the tasks teachers currently carry out don't need to be done by teachers and think about what the effects would be of increasing administrative or technician time, both on the number of teachers employed and on contact time. Whatever decisions are taken, this exercise could be very threatening for the different groups of staff and would need sensitive handling.

> Schools are staffed mostly and managed exclusively by teachers. There is a tendency for teacher-led management to choose to have smaller classes (and more teachers) than other more innovative ways of organizing the school. Teachers are bound to remain as core staff because their role is so fundamental to the work of a school. But what the delegated powers of LMS have allowed and what the case studies have shown is that it is possible to consider anew who should carry out all those tasks not directly related to pedagogy, but currently use up teachers' time.
>
> Mortimore and Mortimore with Thomas, 1994

Case Study 12.11 highlighted the issue of associate staff as managers and how threatening this development could be to the school's senior management team. Unlike the bursar, the caretaker is rarely invited to SMT meetings as yet, but his or her role is a pivotal one, as good caretaking is crucial to the appearance of the school. The caretaker interacts with a lot of visitors and contract staff, maintenance workers, builders, electricians, etc and is the school's representative on site whenever everyone else has gone home. His or her manner can affect the image of the school held by the public, as the case study below illustrates.

CASE STUDY 12.12 FOR ACTION

When the local playgroup rang up and asked if it could book the premises for several weeks in the summer holiday with the option of using it again at Easter, Brenda Gatlin was delighted because it would bring in much-needed income and at the same time would give some assistance to the local community by providing facilities. Jim Spicer, the caretaker, was however far from pleased with the turn events had taken. He was extremely hard-working and liked the school to look spick and span at all times. He used the holidays to get the school into good order and the thought of a multitude of small children creating havoc all round the premises appalled him. But Brenda insisted and, although Jim grumbled non-stop for the rest of term, he seemed to have accepted that he had to make the best of things. The playgroup duly came, but rang up after the holiday to say that they would not be taking up their option on further bookings, as the facilities didn't quite fit their needs. Brenda suspected that Jim had been so disobliging and put so many difficulties in their way that the playgroup had decided to look for another venue.

For action

❑ What are the issues raised in this case study?
❑ The caretaker's attitude to his job had cost the school dearly in terms of both cash and good will. How do you get the caretaker to understand and apply the mission statement spelt out in your development plan?
❑ What advice would you give the headteacher and why?

SKILLS AND TECHNIQUES IN MANAGING ASSOCIATE STAFF

The case studies described in this chapter highlighted some of the problems and issues that may arise in managing the associate staff and include discussion of their roles, job descriptions, status and pay, and their relationship with the teachers.

Employing associate staff presents you with both a challenge and an opportunity as a manager. It is an opportunity because it allows you to be innovative in how you use and deploy staff and gives worthwhile employment to some people who previously had very limited career choice. It could facilitate learning because it brings additional skills and expertise into the school and, if used efficiently, should free teachers from tasks other than teaching and allow them to spend more time on their professional role. It is a challenge for you as a manager to use the opportunity effectively and because you have to work towards creating one staff out of two disparate groups.

What kind of skills and techniques do you need in order to manage these problems successfully? Almost all the case studies concerned aspects of *managing people* and to deal with most of the problems discussed you would certainly need to draw on your interpersonal and conflict-management skills (see Chapters 5 and 8).

A lot of this chapter, however, has been about *managing change and development*. If you want to introduce innovative ideas in respect of staffing, you do not want to encounter wholesale resistance to your plans because they are incompletely understood or communicated and people feel threatened by them. I have written fully about this topic elsewhere (Nathan, 1991, especially Chapter 3) and suggest that if you need detailed guidance, you should peruse a work of this kind. A quick checklist can be a very useful means of focusing our thoughts.

Factors affecting successful change in schools

❑ Change requires support and pressure.
❑ Each change has two components – content and process.
❑ Headteachers have the most important role in managing change.
❑ Change needs to be communicated fully to those involved.
❑ Staff need to be convinced of the need for change.
❑ Individuals need to take ownership of change.
❑ Effective change needs clear plans and procedures.
❑ Moving towards small concrete goals works better than setting vast targets, no matter how desirable.
❑ Each stage needs to be assimilated for the next to succeed.
❑ Past experience of successful or unsuccessful change influences attitudes and expectations.
❑ Change works best in an organization that has been trained to accept change!

A lot of this chapter has been about creating the attitudes in which change can take place successfully, for example how formally or informally the school was organized, whether it was customary for members of the associate staff to attend staff or senior management meetings and how difficult it would be to change people's feelings about their presence. With this in mind, it could be useful for you to spend some time with your middle and senior managers in reviewing your organizational structures, because clarity helps motivate and support staff and in some of the more innovative posts the boundaries have not been clearly drawn. It could also be a worthwhile exercise to look again at any organizational analysis you have done (eg staff questionnaires for Investors in People) and think about the organizational style or ethos that these surveys revealed. All too frequently one hears headteachers say 'It wasn't until I did the gap analysis for Investors in People that I realized I was answering a lot of the questions with "Yes, except for the support staff!"'

Providing appropriate training and staff development for those involved is also an important factor in managing change. In the past, restrictions on how you spent the school's standards budget made it difficult to include associate staff in the staff development programme. Now more flexibility exists and the Inset co-ordinator's plans should take account of their needs. Remember that many of the associate staff are part-timers and the Inset sessions may not fit their working schedule in much the same way as departmental meetings were not always convenient. The advice here is always to *offer* the opportunity and to stress the value of training. Part-time teachers often attend in-service days in proportion to the amount of time they work (and according to their level of interest in or involvement in a particular initiative) and this could serve as a guide for associate staff.

The appraisal programme for associate staff is also an extremely useful vehicle for managing staff development because it enables you to discuss an individual's development needs in relation to both whole school development and their personal career development and to home in on where the individual fits into the scheme of things. In a primary school the head-teacher is most likely to conduct these appraisals personally, but in a secondary school the appraiser is more likely to be the line manager. It is important therefore that associate staff appraisal does not just go by on the nod but does play a central role in their staff development. To ensure this, some training may need to be provided for the appraisers. In Case Study 12.9 the librarian suddenly found herself a manager with responsibility for her team of helpers – she might need some management training if she is to carry out her new role effectively.

13

DEALING WITH STRESS

Case Study 13.1, which introduces this chapter, is expanded and referred back to throughout the first section of the chapter.

CASE STUDY 13.1 FOR REFLECTION

Wendy had always enjoyed doing the timetable. This was why she had been appointed as deputy head some 15 years ago. Originally a scientist, her interest in the mechanics of timetabling and ability to juggle option blocks had brought her early promotion. At that time the role of a deputy was limited and she spent her non-teaching time sitting in her office tinkering with her timetable blocks. Wendy's lack of interpersonal skills or interest in current educational issues had not constituted a problem while Mr Simpson remained the headteacher, but after he took early retirement the situation changed. Caroline, the new head, who wanted to revitalize the school to meet the demands of the more competitive environment that had resulted from recent legislation, expected Wendy to take responsibility for a whole portfolio of issues, which Wendy simply did not understand. She protested that she felt ill equipped to give a lead to hard-pressed colleagues, and the exasperated headteacher responded by sending her deputy on a number of courses aimed at improving her knowledge and understanding of the initiatives that she was now expected to lead. Wendy did not enjoy the courses. It took her a long time to grasp the ideas, as she got bogged down in the details, and basically she couldn't see the point of most of the changes that the new head seemed so keen to introduce. They seemed to Wendy to be a distraction that interfered with time that should be spent teaching. She felt battered by all the new information and she began to have severe headaches in the evenings. Her visible lack of enthusiasm made it difficult for her to enthuse others. The head's obvious irritation with her deputy made matter worse, because Caroline found it difficult to disguise her feelings either when she spoke to Wendy or in staff meetings when Wendy made some comment that the head felt betrayed her ignorance or lack of commitment.

Wendy felt very pressurized by all the new demands being made on her and increasingly depressed by her inability to please Caroline. The more sharply Caroline spoke to her, the more slowly Wendy seemed to function. Her headaches increased, and then she got flu badly and couldn't shake it off and for the first time in years had to take several days off work. When she returned to school, she found that Caroline had turned her attention to the timetable and suggested that Wendy should rethink how she approached the whole question of timetabling. The school had a computerized administration system, but Wendy's timetable was still done manually, as Wendy did not know how to use the options or the timetabling program and was suspicious of both. Caroline also suspected that a different timetable model could provide considerably more flexibility than the present system and that for Wendy to continue tinkering with it was becoming counterproductive. She told her deputy all this in no uncertain terms and suggested that it might be a good idea if the senior teacher responsible for administration helped her learn to use the computer program. This session with the headteacher reduced Wendy to tears. She had developed her model the first year that she did the timetable, and she loved it and did not wish to change it. It was her one refuge to which she could retreat to get away from people and pressure. She felt stabbed in the back, but she feared that if she protested, Caroline might remove the timetable from her job description altogether. She tried to accommodate Caroline's demands, but she didn't seem to have any spark and the other initiatives were taking up so much of her time that it was difficult for her to concentrate on the timetabling. She was so tired nowadays that when she got home it was difficult for her to do any productive work in the evenings, yet she was finding it difficult to sleep and the headaches were now so bad that in the end she went to see the doctor. He gave her a thorough examination and told her that she was suffering from severe stress.

WHAT IS STRESS?

Over the past few years there has been a recognition that some teachers are experiencing high levels of stress. Wendy, in the case study described above, is experiencing some of the physical symptoms of stress:

❏   severe headaches;
❏   illnesses, eg flu;
❏   inability to shake off minor illnesses;
❏   tearfulness;
❏   tiredness combined with inability to sleep.

If the stress continues it could lead to high blood pressure, ulcers or heart disease.

Stress is associated with fear, anxiety, tension and conflict. It is the body's reaction or response to a threatening situation.

Kyriacou and Sutcliffe have defined teacher stress as 'a response of negative effect (such as anger or depression) by the teacher resulting from aspects of the teacher's job' (1978).

Stress is an extreme form of pressure. Pressure can be good for us. It gets the adrenalin going and helps us draw on reserves of energy so that we can respond positively to a challenge. The degree of pressure that an individual can take varies enormously. Some people thrive on pressure and claim that it prevents them from becoming stale in a job. Stress occurs when someone cannot cope with the pressure being exerted upon him or her and it causes tension. The individual reacts physically and psychologically, with a resulting effect upon the person's behaviour. In the case study above, as well as her physical symptoms, Wendy also suffered from anxiety and depression, which in turn affected her ability to work. In other cases it can make a person behave irrationally or out of character. It not only affects an individual's work by making him or her less effective, it also makes it difficult for other people to work with him or her, because people suffering from stress may be irritable, aggressive or withdrawn.

WHAT CAUSES TEACHER STRESS?

What kinds of situations produce stress at work? As the recognition of teacher stress developed, it was accompanied by research into the causes of stress. Charles Handy in his classic work *Understanding Organisations* (1976) suggested that work-related stress is caused by three organizational situations:

1. having an innovative function that comes into conflict with other aspects of the organization;
2. responsibility for the work of others leading to problems of conflicting objectives and role conflict;
3. having a boundary role where one can become the focus of intergroup conflict.

Similarly, GE Wheeler (1971) identifies sources of stress for people in educational management positions thus:

❏ the feeling that you have too little authority to carry out responsibilities assigned to you;
❏ being unclear what the scope and responsibilities of your job are;
❏ feeling that you have too heavy a workload, one that you cannot possibly finish during an ordinary working day;
❏ thinking that you are not able to satisfy the conflicting demands of the various people over you;
❏ feeling that you are not totally qualified to handle the job;
❏ feeling that you are unable to influence your immediate superior's decisions and actions that affect you;
❏ feeling that you have to do things in the job that are against your better judgement.

Wendy, the deputy head in the case study, certainly experienced several of the causes of stress on GE Wheeler's list. She had no faith in the changes that she had to implement, and she felt unqualified to handle the job. Some of the changes that she had to introduce were unpopular and involved her in conflict. She felt that she had to run fast to stand still and that she could not cope with her workload. She felt that all the new demands prevented her from getting on with her real job, ie the timetable, and she feared that the head would give the timetable to someone else to do. What hurt most was that she felt humiliated when the head contradicted her or publicly put her down at staff meetings. (You may want to compare the symptoms shown by the deputy head in this case study with those exhibited by the deputy in Case Study 3.1.)

Managing other people is demanding and potentially stressful. Wendy did not find the change in her role challenging; rather she found it extremely threatening. It was frustrating for her not to be able to concentrate on her timetable. She had little faith either in her own ability to handle the new situation or in what she was doing and her head's derogatory attitude to her constituted another threat in an already difficult situation. No wonder she began to suffer from stress!

HOW DO YOU MANAGE TEACHER STRESS?

It is difficult to assess the extent of stress in teaching, though research over the past 20 years certainly indicates its presence. Helping teachers to avoid or reduce the stress that they are experiencing is an important part of your management task, but it is one that requires considerable sensitivity.

Managing stress involves:

❑ recognizing where stress is occurring;
❑ analysing the causes;
❑ generating practical solutions that will help to reduce the problem for both the individual and the organization.

Recognizing and analysing the problem constitutes the first step towards dealing with it. Wendy's condition went unrecognized until her own physical symptoms forced her to consult a doctor – no one had apparently noticed or cared. It is all too easy, particularly in a large school, not to notice a deterioration in an individual's performance or change in his or her behaviour until it is highlighted by a major incident, such as a confrontation with another member of staff or with a pupil. This also occurs because a lot of stress is concealed, as teachers tend to be reluctant to admit that they are experiencing stress because they associate it with weakness and failure. There should be someone in the senior management team who is in a position to monitor staff stress on a regular basis. Probably the best-placed person is the member of the team responsible for daily administration, because if you are dealing with cover or internal communications, you are constantly dealing with people and likely to notice changes in behaviour or increased absence.

How you deal with the situation will depend on what has caused the stress and the needs of the individual. If the pressure on Wendy wasn't lessened, her condition would worsen. She clearly needed help in coping with the new and conflicting demands that were being made of her. A first step towards helping Wendy would be for her to share the problem. This would help her confront it and also lessen her isolation. Usually this would be a job for the headteacher or a deputy with good interpersonal and counselling skills, but this situation would be difficult for the head or another member of the senior management team to handle because of Wendy's seniority and because Caroline's own unsympathetic behaviour had contributed to her deputy's stress. This case would probably need to be managed by someone who was less involved and who would be able to depersonalize the issues.

Using the school's link adviser proved the best route forward, because she had a good relationship with both Wendy and Caroline. In other circumstances a union fieldworker might provide the support Wendy clearly needed, but it might be difficult to find someone who could deal with both parties and, as most of the fieldworkers are headteachers, Wendy might feel that she did not want to discuss her problems with a headteacher.

The adviser had sessions with each of them separately before she brought them together. The adviser's generally sympathetic attitude made Wendy feel valued, and her detachment combined with her ability to bring the problem into perspective by breaking it down into its component parts did a lot towards making Wendy think realistically about the issues. They faced and discussed the issue of early retirement, but Wendy realized that she did not want to leave teaching yet. This meant that they had to find solutions to the problems. Improving her performance was the key to improving both her self-image and her relationship with the head, so what was the best approach to this and could she do it? What she could offer the school was her proven ability to timetable. If some of the other pressures were removed, at least for the time being, she might be able to demonstrate her ability to satisfy the head's timetabling demands. To negotiate this, she would have to show her willingness to use modern methods of timetabling.

The adviser's discussions with the head centred on the issue that in the interest of the school Caroline needed to think about how she could get the best out of her deputy. She stressed that improving Wendy's confidence was a priority because it would lead to an improvement in her performance and that, to bring this about, Caroline had to stop criticizing her deputy and generally improve their personal relationship. She advised Caroline to remove a lot of the new responsibilities for the time being, to give Wendy the opportunity to refresh her timetabling skills, but said that as Wendy recovered, the responsibilities should build up again, although gradually, and that this time round, they should be selected in consultation with Wendy and matched to her interests and abilities where possible.

At the doctor's suggestion, Wendy also joined a local sports club. He said that, as she didn't seem to have any hobbies, attending the club would provide a clear break with work on a couple of evenings a week and some physical recreation would be generally good for her. This had the additional effect that she had to organize her time more efficiently so that she could keep her sports club evenings clear of work, and after a while she found that the headaches had virtually gone and she was actually doing more work in less time. Although she still found her leadership role difficult, she began to enjoy using the computer to solve timetabling problems.

The case study highlighted a number of strategies you can use to help people reduce stress. They include:

❑ admitting or recognizing the existence of a stress situation;
❑ sharing the problem;
❑ depersonalizing the problem;
❑ breaking a complex problem down into its component parts in order to make it more manageable;

❏ setting achievable targets;
❏ improving personal time management;
❏ relaxation, including physical recreation.

ORGANIZATIONAL STRESS

Identifying pressure points in an organization

Organizational stress is also a problem for senior managers in education today, and it is worth considering how you can reduce the overall stress level within your school by identifying what the pressure points are. The case study below describes how Bestwick Park High School approached this issue.

CASE STUDY 13.2 FOR REFLECTION

Managing organizational stress

Brenda Gatlin, the headteacher of Bestwick Park High School, first raised the issue at a senior management meeting. She had noticed, she said, that there seemed to be more than the usual number of altercations between individual members of staff recently and that people seemed much more tired than was usually the case at this stage of the year. She asked Mrs Perkins, who managed the school's daily administration, what the current rate of absence was and whether it seemed heavier than usual, or whether anyone else had noticed anything unusual. Yvonne Perkins answered that the absence rate did appear to be higher than normal for this term. She knew that the supply bill would be higher this term than for several years and this had been concerning her. There seemed to be a lot of gastric flu around, which was affecting the staff, and a number of people had had to take several days off recently and seemed far from well even when they returned.

Mrs Gatlin suggested that they should try to identify what it was that was making the staff more tired, fractious and susceptible to illnesses than usual. 'We may not be able to do much about externally imposed demands, but we can see whether our own structures are working or whether there are ways in which we can improve working conditions so that people can cope better with all the new initiatives we are having to introduce.'

They discussed the best way to approach the task, and decided to deal with it in two stages. First, it would be discussed at the next long staff meeting. This would allow the head to explain to staff that she was concerned and give the staff an opportunity to discuss the matter and put forward their views and suggestions. The second stage was to undertake a staff questionnaire to find out where the pressure points were occurring, by checking what staff were finding most irksome or difficult to manage. Mrs Gatlin asked Mike Wade, the deputy head with responsibility for staff development, to design the questionnaire. As it was important to move quickly if they were to relieve the organizational stress, Mike prepared a draft questionnaire as a working document around which to centre the discussion. After the meeting, Mike would redraft it to accommodate any changes.

They decided to use a questionnaire because they felt that in this case the advantages outweighed the disadvantages. The advantages of using a stress questionnaire are:

❑ It is a quick way to collect a lot of information.
❑ It gets you started fast.
❑ It involves the whole teaching and associate staff.
❑ It is easy to analyse.
❑ It could highlight both staff and individual concerns.

The disadvantages of using a stress questionnaire are:

❑ It is very impersonal.
❑ People might not be completely honest.
❑ It is not a very accurate measure.

At the staff meeting, the staff were initially surprised that the head wanted to devote time to such an issue, but pleased at her clear concern for their well-being. They largely accepted the questionnaire in the form that Mike had drafted it, as they felt that it was already quite comprehensive, only adding a section at the end where they could write in positive ideas and suggestions, because they said the questionnaire was itself negative in its approach. The Bestwick Park stress questionnaire in its final form is reproduced below.

Bestwick Park High School organizational stress questionnaire

Please use the first box to tick for a stress factor.

Please use the second box to write H – high, M – medium or L – low, if you have ticked the first box.

1 Pupils

Size of class

Discipline factors – disruptive pupils

Other (please specify)

2 Organizational factors

Too many meetings

Too much paper work

Unclear/inadequate information/instructions

Too much paper to read

Cover too high because of absence or Inset

Disruption to lessons because of overfrequent interruptions to timetable

Other (please specify)

3 Workload

High level of continuous assessment

High level of coursework moderation

Preparation for curriculum development

Initiative overload

Too many activities and committees

Other (please specify)

4 Pastoral care responsibilities

Insufficient time for tutoring

Too much administration

Conflict between pastoral and subject role

Inadequate counselling skills

Other (please specify)

5 Time

Too much preparation/marking has to be done at home – erosion of free time

Difficulties of accommodating all the conflicting demands

Personal time management – not enough time to relax or socialize

Other (please specify)

6 Working conditions

No work bay in staff workroom

Lack of shelves/space makes it difficult to leave books/equipment

Nowhere to work quietly

Condition of the staffroom

Other (please specify)

7 Opportunities

Opportunities limited by present management structure

Lack of opportunity for career development

Derisive nature of the allowance/incentive system is affecting relationships

Other (please specify)

8 Support

Lack of support from SMT

Lack of support from parents

Lack of support from governors

Lack of support from LEA

Other (please specify)

9 External pressures

Family

Expansion of government control of education

Status of teaching

Hostile media

Other (please specify)

10 Positive suggestions for relieving pressure or improving working conditions

Results of the exercise

There seemed to be very little dissatisfaction with the way the school was being run. A few people commented on the lack of facilities, especially working space, which had long been a problem in the school, but the main problem revealed by the questionnaire was that there was a general feeling of pressure or overload from all the current initiatives. This was eroding free time both in school and at home and was making people feel tired and reluctant to volunteer for other activities.

Whereas the head could not remove pressures from centrally directed initiatives, she could increase the support that she was providing for development. She told the SMT to review the Inset programme, both in terms of the time allocation and the type of provision, and she allocated a member of the senior team to each major initiative to act as a support and facilitator.

Quite a lot of people commented on the management of time, and there were some requests for help here, so the school offered some sessions on time management as twilight Inset.

There was also a suggestion from a number of staff that at least once in every half-term there should be an optional short social after school for an hour, with refreshments, where staff could come, relax and talk. This suggestion was referred to the staff committee and adopted. A group of volunteers also worked out where some more shelves could be put into the staffroom and an appeal in the newsletter brought an offer of some badly needed filing cabinets for staff use.

The overall effect was an improvement in morale. The staff could see that the concerns they had identified had all been addressed and that the stress exercise had brought some positive results, which improved their working conditions. The absence rate improved, though it was difficult to decide if this was simply because by now it was the summer term, and the number of rows among the staff certainly decreased. Reviewing the exercise after half a term, Mrs Gatlin could claim that it had not revealed major stress, but it had indicated areas of pressure that had needed to be addressed. The exercise had been valuable both in terms of what it achieved and in developing a positive relationship with the staff.

The questionnaire used by Bestwick Park is intended to serve as an exemplar, but it could easily be modified to suit the needs of a particular school. If you don't want to design your own questionnaire, commercial questionnaires are easily available and could be used to help identify pressure points in a school.

CASE STUDY 13.3 FOR ACTION

The inspection was over at last. It was the third one that the school had experienced in recent years. The feedback indicated that the school had come through with a very good report, yet as the head you become increasingly aware that there is an unanticipated effect. The pace of activity in the school seems to be much slower than before the inspection. Morale, which should have been lifted by the promise of a good report, is actually lower than before the inspection, and overall the staff seem very much affected by the experience of inspection and slow to recover from it. In discussion with your colleagues, they refer to something called post-Ofsted syndrome, and tell you that this is what is affecting your staff.

For action

What issues are raised by this case study? What advice would you give this headteacher and on what grounds?

MANAGING YOUR OWN STRESS

Managing other people is a demanding and potentially stressful occupation and this is certainly true of teaching, where many people in senior management are affected from time to time in varying degrees.

Potential stressors include:

❑ time pressure and deadlines;
❑ satisfying conflicting demands;
❑ inadequate colleagues or subordinates;
❑ insufficient power or influence;
❑ introducing unwanted or unpopular changes;
❑ isolation – no one to talk to;
❑ uncertainty about impending decisions outside your control;
❑ long working hours;

❑ volume of work;
❑ managing conflict;
❑ leadership of teams;
❑ lack of support;
❑ unpopular decisions.

CASE STUDY 13.4 FOR REFLECTION

During the time I was managing the merger of the two schools, I found myself getting irritable in a way that I never used to. Every time that I thought about how much work there was still to do before the end of term, I found myself getting into a panic. We were doing a lot of interviewing for the new posts. It took up a lot of time, which interfered with other work and it was a strain because we could not reappoint all the existing staff and inevitably some were disappointed and very upset. I felt so exhausted that when I got home I was unable either to work or to join in things. My wife and kids said that I was like a bear with a sore head a lot of the time. Then I started waking up during the night and thinking of all there was to do. I suppose all the problems and pressures must have got to me. Once the merger had actually happened, it was nothing like as difficult as I had anticipated, and I felt much better.

Conversation at a headteachers' conference

The head in this example clearly experienced considerable anxiety about the impending merger between his and a neighbouring school. There was a lot of extra work to do before the merger took place and some difficult appointments to resolve. He also anticipated all kinds of problems after the merger, which did not in fact materialize. The volume of work combined with the responsibility for a very sensitive situation put him under considerable pressure, with the result that for a time he experienced stress, which affected his behaviour. For this head it was a temporary matter. When the merger was completed and some difficult personnel issues were resolved more amicably than might have been expected, the stress factor was reduced, but this case study typifies the kind of potentially stressful situations for which you, as a senior manager, may have to take responsibility. Leading teachers who are under pressure puts you under pressure. Thus in addition to managing other people's stress, you have to manage your own and this is far from easy. What is important is that you learn to recognize your own stress symptoms so that you can develop strategies to alleviate the stress when it occurs.

Key strategies to reduce stress

> A head or senior manager must not only perform management tasks competently and be skilled in different aspects of the role, but must also be able to organize so that personal time and energies are used to advantage. Being well organized is a matter of knowing oneself and managing time, self and environment and having the best self-discipline to maintain routines. One needs to know how to get the best out of oneself.
>
> Dean, 1985

This quotation sums things up well. To avoid stress you have to be a good manager of yourself, so the first set of strategies are 10 general precepts for successful managers. They are relevant in this context because, if you can follow them, they will help you avoid stress:

1. Don't keep things to yourself – this builds up anxieties.
2. Share your problems – this prevents management isolation.
3. Accept what can't be changed.
4. Prioritize.
5. Break down problems into 'bite-sized chunks' with achievable targets.
6. Don't handle paper more than once.
7. Say 'No' to unreasonable demands.
8. Try to be an effective manager of your own time.
9. Delegate wisely.
10. Try to keep things in perspective.

The following set of strategies is targeted specifically at dealing with stress:

❑ Learn to admit stress – it is not a mark of failure.
❑ Compartmentalize – don't let your worries about one issue interfere with how you manage other issues.
❑ Try not to take your work home with you – this does not mean that you should never work at home, but rather that you should try not to think about it over supper or at times when you are supposed to be relaxing!
❑ Clear definite spaces of time so that you can relax. It also refreshes you and helps the thought processes.

❑ Stop working some time before you go to bed so that you can unwind.

❑ Regular exercise is regarded as good for you because it releases pent-up energy and relieves tension, eg go swimming.

❑ A non-competitive hobby, especially something creative, eg painting, cookery or gardening, is also regarded as therapeutic. Making things seems to be a good way of relaxing.

❑ Healthy eating and regular meals help you to combat stress.

❑ Do not resort to palliatives or artificial stimulants – in fact regard any increase in smoking, eating or drinking, including endless coffee drinking, as a sign of distress, and act upon it.

❑ Specific relaxing exercises or yoga helps some people.

Charles Handy (1976) talks of creating 'stability zones', which he describes as places for rebuilding energy reserves. Holidays and week-ends are important energy reserves, and so are home and family. The idea of 'stability zones' sums up rather well what seems to be the best recipe for avoiding stress. What it comes down to is that a good manager has to develop the ability to work intensely and effectively while on the job, but be able to shut down work and turn off from it for significant patches of time so that he or she can relax, relieve the tension and return refreshed. If the hours start to escalate because that is the only way to keep on top of the job, that is the moment to review how you manage time. Sometimes the best way to deal with a problem is to lay it on one side for a time and do something else. If you let the job get to you, you stop being an effective manager, which is why avoiding stress is basically about keeping things in proportion and sensible self-management.

CASE STUDY 13.5 FOR ACTION

Susan liked computers

Susan, who worked in a middle school deemed secondary, liked computers and found that she was good at helping other people use them. She enjoyed the sessions she ran with her mathematics groups, in which she taught them to use computers to solve mathematical problems. The school seized on her enthusiasm, made her the computer manager and gave her a small allowance. Initially Susan was pleased as the school began to build up a network and soon there was a computer room in place. Then Susan found that her timetable was affected, as some of her mathematics teaching had to be replaced by classes where she taught computer skills, and then by technology as she became an integral part of the technology team. A computer club was formed and there were pupils in the computer room every lunch hour and after school as well. The staff were keen to develop their computer skills, and Susan found herself leading twilight Inset sessions for them. She rarely had time to visit the staffroom, because she was so much in demand to facilitate computing. She didn't mind this as she liked helping pupils, though she felt a lot more tired these days and was irritated by the number of meetings that, as the school's computer manager, she was having to attend. There was a constant stream of staff and pupils, each with his or her separate problem that appeared to need instant attention. The school had a whole variety of new equipment and all these machines seemed to work in different ways and regularly needed servicing. The school acquired a part-time technician and this should have freed up some time for Susan, but she found that she had to manage the technician's work and that, although very willing, she needed training from scratch. There were numerous different word-processing and graphics packages, again all with different procedures and techniques. The development was going so fast that it was impossible to keep up with the pace of change. The queue for help was endless, and the queries increasingly complex. All her free time was spent sorting out other people's problems. She had no time left to think about her own work. What really worried her was that she felt it was a case of 'the blind leading the blind'. She had got into this mess because she liked using a computer, but she had never pretended to be an expert. She felt less and less able to cope and only her extreme conscientiousness and innate 'niceness' kept her going, because many of her clients lacked any consideration.

Finally, one day when the music teacher was going on about some problem that demanded Susan's immediate attention, Susan lost control. It was 2.40 in the afternoon, and her only free period. Her marking wasn't finished because she had had to attend a computer evening at a neighbouring school the previous night and she still hadn't found time for lunch. Susan flicked the off switch on Moira's machine. 'That's it', she said. 'I've finished with computers. You're on your own now, dear. I've quit.' As the music teacher began to protest that a very important composition had been lost, Susan burst into tears.

For action

You are the headteacher. It is 3.00 the same afternoon and Susan has been brought to you by another member of staff. She is still crying hysterically. What do you do about her?

REFERENCES

Adair, J (1973) *Action Centred Leadership*, McGraw-Hill, Maidenhead

Back, Ken and Back, Kate with T Bates (1982) *Assertiveness at Work*, McGraw-Hill, Maidenhead

BBC, Governors' training project, *Working Partnerships*

Belbin, RM (1981) *Management Teams: Why they succeed or fail*, Heinemann, London

Bennis, WG (1985) Leadership in the 21st century, *Journal of Organisational Change*, **2** (1)

Bolam, R (1986) The first two years of the NDC: A progress report, *School Organisation*, **6** (1), pp 1–16

Bramson, RM (1981) *Coping With Difficult People*, Bantam Doubleday Dell, New York

Bridges, E (1992) *The Incompetent Teacher*, rev edn, The Stanford Series on Education and Public Policy, Falmer Press, London

Davies, B and Ellison, L (1999) *Strategic Direction and Development of the School*, Routledge, London

Davies, B *et al* (1991) *Education Management for the 1990s*, Longman, Harlow

Dean, J (1985) *Managing The Secondary School*, Croom Helm, Beckenham

DfEE (1995) *Governing Bodies and Effective Schools*, London

DfEE (1999) *NPQH Guide for Applicants*, London

Drucker, PF (1970) *The Effective Executive*, Pan, London

Drummond, H (1990) *Managing Difficult Staff: Effective procedures and the law*, Kogan Page, London

Everard, B (1986) *Developing Management in Schools*, Basil Blackwell, Oxford

Everard, B and Morris, G (1996) *Effective School Management*, 3rd edn, Paul Chapman Publishing, London

Handy, C (1976) *Understanding Organisations*, Penguin, London

Handy, C and Aiken, R (1986) *Understanding Schools As Organisations*, Penguin, London

Hersey, P and Blanchard, K (1982) *Management of Organisational Behaviour: Utilising human resources*, Prentice Hall, Englewood Cliffs, New Jersey

Herzberg, F (1974) *Work and the Nature of Man*, Granada Publishing Ltd, London

Hunt, JD (1986) Motivating people at work, in *Managing People at Work: A manager's guide to behaviour in organisations*, ed Hunt, JW, McGraw-Hill, Maidenhead

Hunt, JW (1986) *Managing People at Work: A manager's guide to behaviour in organisations*, rev edn, McGraw-Hill, Maidenhead

Kemp, R and Nathan, M (1989) *Middle Management in Schools: A survival guide*, Stanley Thornes, Cheltenham

Kyriacou, C and Sutcliffe, J (1978) A model of teacher stress, *Educational Studies*, **4** (1)

Maslow, AH (1954) *Motivation and Personality*, Harper and Row, New York

Mortimore, P and Mortimore, J with H Thomas (1994) *Managing Associate Staff*, Management in Education Series, Paul Chapman Publishing, London

Mortimore, P *et al* Non teaching staff in primary and secondary schools, and Innovative staffing policies in City Technology Colleges, DfEE/ESRC

Murgatroyd, S (1986) Management teams and the promotion of staff well-being, *School Organisation*, **6** (1)

Nathan, M (1991) *Senior Management in Schools: A survival guide*, Basil Blackwell, Oxford

Nias, J (1980) Headteacher styles and job satisfaction in primary schools, in *Approaches to School Management*, ed T Bush *et al*, Harper & Row, London

Peters, TJ and Waterman, RH (1982) *In Search of Excellence*, Harper and Row, New York

Secondary Heads' Association (SHA) (1989) *If It Moves. . .*, Survey of deputy heads, Secondary Heads' Association Press, Leicester

Stewart, V and Stewart, A (1983) *Managing the Poor Performer*, Gower Press, London

Sutton, J (1985) *School Management in Practice*, Longman, Harlow

Todd, R and Dennison, W (1978) The changing role of the deputy headteacher, *Educational Review*

Torrington, D and Weightman, J (1985) *The Business of Management*, Prentice Hall, Hemel Hempstead

Torrington, D and Weightman, J (1989a) *Management and Organisation in Secondary Schools: A training handbook*, Basil Blackwell, Oxford

Torrington, D and Weightman, J (1989b) *The Reality of School Management*, Basil Blackwell, Oxford

Trethowan, D (1985) *Teamwork in Schools*, pamphlet, Industrial Society, London

TTA (1998) *National Standards for Headteachers*

Weindling, D and Earley, P (1987) *Secondary Headship: The first years*, NFER/Nelson, Windsor

Wheeler, G (1971) Organisation stress, in *College Management Readings and Cases*, ed DD Simmons, The FE Staff College, Bristol

White, P (1983) Foreword, *Delegation*, pamphlet, Industrial Society, London

White, P (1984) Foreword, *The Leadership of Schools*, pamphlet, Industrial Society, London

FURTHER READING

Audit Commission (1986) *Towards Better Management of Secondary Education*, HMSO, London

Balchin, R (1993) *Governors and Heads In Grant-Maintained Schools*, Longman, Harlow

Belbin, RM (1997) *Teamroles at Work*, reprint, Butterworth Heinemann, London

Blake, R and Moulton, J (1978) *The New Managerial Grid*, Gulf Publishing Co, Houston, Texas

Bush, T *et al* (1999) *Educational Management: Redefining theory, policy and practice*, Paul Chapman Publishing, London

Crease, M and Earley, P (1999) *Improving Schools and Governing Bodies: Making a difference*, Routledge, London

Donnelly, J (1992) *The School Management Handbook*, Kogan Page, London

Drucker, PF (1968) *The Practice Of Management*, Pan, London

Drucker, PF (1989) *Managing for Results*, Heinemann, London

Duffy, M (1999) *Staff Health and School Effectiveness*, Network Educational Press, Stafford

Elliott Kemp, J and Williams, GL (1980) *The Dion Handbook*, Sheffield City Polytechnic, Sheffield

Fiddler, B and Cooper, R (1992) *Staff Appraisal in Schools and Colleges*, Longman, Harlow

Firth, D, ed (1985) *School Management In Practice*, Longman, Harlow

Glatter, R *et al* (1988) *Understanding School Management*, Open University Press, Buckingham

Gold, A and Evans, J (1999) *Reflecting on School Management*, Falmer Press, London

Grace, G (1995) *School Leadership: Beyond educational management*, Falmer Press, London

Handy, C (1989) *The Age of Unreason*, Hutchinson, London

Handy, C (1994) *The Empty Raincoat*, Hutchinson, London

Handy, C (1997) *The Hungry Spirit*, Hutchinson, London

Holmes, G (1997) *Essential School Leadership*, Kogan Page, London

Hoyle, E and Macmahon, A, ed (1986) *The Management of Schools*, Kogan Page, London

Hughes, M (1973) *Secondary School Administration: A management approach*, 2nd edn, Pergamon Press, Oxford

Hume, C (1991) *Grievance and Discipline in Schools*, Longman Agit Books, Harlow

Hume, C (1993) *Effective Staff Selection in Schools*, Longman Agit Books, Harlow

Jacques, D (1991) *Learning in Groups*, Kogan Page, London

Jenkins, HO (1991) *Getting It Right*, Basil Blackwell, Oxford

Jones, A (1987) *Leadership for Tomorrow's Schools*, Basil Blackwell, Oxford

Leithwood, K, Jantzi, D and Steinbach, R (1999) *Changing Leadership for Changing Times*, Open University Press, Buckingham

Macbeath, J and Myers, K (1999) *Effective Leaders*, Prentice Hall, Hemel Hempstead

McGregor, DV (1960) *The Human Side of Enterprise*, McGraw-Hill, New York

Morley, L and Rassool, N (1999) *Effectiveness: Fracturing the discourse*, Falmer Press, London

Nicolson, R (1989) *School Management: The role of the secondary headteacher*, Kogan Page, London

Peters, TJ (1987) *Thriving on Chaos*, Harper and Row, New York

Rogers, K (1963) *Managers' Personality and Performance*, Tavistock Publications, London

Rutter, P *et al* (1979) *15,000 Hours*, Open Books, London

Stevens, DB (1991) *Under New Management*, SHA/Longman, Harlow

Tannenbaum, R and Schmidt, WH (1956) How to choose a leadership style, *Harvard Business Review*, March/April

Trethowan, D (1985) *Target Setting*, pamphlet, Industrial Society, London

Trethowan, D (1991) *Managing with Appraisal*, Management in Education Series, Paul Chapman Publishing, London

Walsh, M (1999) *Building a Successful School*, Kogan Page, London

Warwick, D (1982) *Effective Meetings*, pamphlet, Industrial Society, London

Westburnham, J (1991) Human resource management in schools, in *Education Management for the 1990s*, ed B Davies *et al*, Longman, Harlow

INDEX

References in italics indicate figures or tables

Visit Kogan Page on-line

Comprehensive information on
Kogan Page titles

Features include

- complete catalogue listings,
  including book reviews and
  descriptions

- on-line discounts on a variety
  of titles

- special monthly promotions

- information and discounts on
  NEW titles and BESTSELLING titles

- a secure shopping basket facility
  for on-line ordering

- infoZones, with links and
  information on specific areas of
  interest

PLUS everything you need to know
about KOGAN PAGE

http://www.kogan-page.co.uk